PARLIAMENT: A SURVEY

PARLIAMENT
A Survey

LORD CAMPION   L. S. AMERY
D. W. BROGAN   J. J. CRAIK HENDERSON
SIR ARTHUR SALTER   H. E. DALE
IVOR THOMAS   F. W. LASCELLES
E. C. S. WADE   SIR CECIL CARR
A. L. GOODHART   G. M. YOUNG

*

London
GEORGE ALLEN & UNWIN LTD
RUSKIN HOUSE · MUSEUM STREET

PRINTED IN GREAT BRITAIN
in 11pt. Baskerville type
BY WILLIAM BRENDON AND SON, LTD.
THE MAYFLOWER PRESS (LATE OF PLYMOUTH)
AT BUSHEY MILL LANE
WATFORD, HERTS.

PREFACE

A NUMBER of parliamentarians, lawyers, historians and civil servants were invited by the Department of Extra-Mural Studies, University of London, in the summer and autumn of 1947 to join a Group to study Parliamentary Government in Britain. It was suggested that the objects should be as follows:

(1) To promote discussion among a group of experts.

(2) To formulate material as a basis of a possible course of lectures to follow the meetings of the Group.

(3) To publish the results of the Study, if desired and practicable.

The following accepted invitations to join either at the beginning or at a later stage: Mr. L. S. Amery, Sir Henry Badeley (the late Lord Badeley), Professor D. W. Brogan, Mr. Ernest Brown, Sir Henry Bunbury, Sir Gilbert Campion (now Lord Campion), Sir Cecil Carr, Mr. R. C. Fitzgerald, Professor A. L. Goodhart, Mr. J. J. Craik Henderson, Commander Stephen King-Hall, Professor J. H. Morgan, Mr. J. P. Plamenatz, Sir Arthur Salter, Lord Soulbury, Mr. Ivor Thomas, Professor E. C. S. Wade, Mr. C. H. Wilson, Mr. G. M. Young. Mr. F. W. Lascelles, and Clerk Assistant House of Lords, joined the Group as one of the speakers in the series of lectures subsequently arranged.

I was appointed Chairman of the Group. The Secretaries were Mr. A. M. Parker, of the Department of Extra-Mural Studies, and Mr. R. C. FitzGerald, Reader in English Law in the University of London; and the thanks of the Group and myself in particular are due to them for their untiring assistance.

The first meeting of the Group was held in October 1947. The Group held twenty meetings in all.

The Group would also like to express its gratitude to Lord Hurcomb, Sir Stephen Tallents, Sir John Wardlaw-Milne and

Captain C. R. P. Diver for attending meetings on one or more occasions and for advice and information.

Mr. D. W. S. Lidderdale supplied certain information on the French Parliamentary system.

A series of ten weekly evening lectures was given between 18th January and 22nd March, 1950; these form the basis of this volume. We are glad to have obtained a contribution from Mr. H. E. Dale on the civil service, which was not included in the series of lectures.

The Group owes its existence to the University of London and I am sure all members would like me to express the thanks of us all for the constant encouragement and support we received from successive Vice-Chancellors, the Principal and all others with whom we were associated. After reading this book it will be for the readers to decide whether anything has been produced that was worth while, but I know all members who attended the meetings regularly (and nearly all who could did) felt that their own knowledge and understanding had been increased and extended. The meetings were very pleasant occasions.

I am only sorry that in this volume no contributions are included from some of our best members. If this book is well received perhaps a further volume may appear.

Finally on behalf of the Group we must thank one of our members for undertaking the arduous duty of Editor. Lord Campion is a busy man, but it is always the busiest men who can still undertake the difficult task.

J. J. CRAIK HENDERSON

CONTENTS

CHAPTER I

PARLIAMENT AND DEMOCRACY

By Gilbert Campion

How is the British parliamentary system working in the uneasy world of today? Is this ancient institution, which has preserved its continuity so long without ceasing to adapt itself to political and social change, still responding successfully to a new and formidable challenge? The series of studies in this volume seek to provide the materials for an answer to this question by depicting particular aspects of the system in an objective spirit, without conscious political bias, and with a common reverence for parliamentary traditions. The subjects selected for examination are: the Cabinet, the civil service, political party organization, considered in their relation to Parliament; the functions and procedure of the House of Commons and the problem of a Second Chamber; constitutional problems connected with the courts of law, subordinate law-making authorities and nationalized industries. The working of parliamentary machinery is illustrated by examples drawn from the French and American systems. Views about the dangers and difficulties of the present phase and as to the future of British parliamentary government form the subject of separate essays. The whole series is preceded by an analysis of the nature of parliamentary government.

The days of unquestioning faith in the parliamentary system as a recipe for good government, characteristic of the second half of the nineteenth century (which led to the setting up of more or less faithful copies of the English model by most of the Continental nations) have long since gone and do not seem likely to return. The critics now have it all their own way. They are never tired of pointing to the distortions which the traditional parliamentary system has undergone in this country—the increasing ascendancy of the Executive over Parliament; the submergence of the House of Commons beneath the mass of business which falls upon it as a result of the continually widening scope of state activity; the growing stringency of Party discipline and the exaltation of the Party machine; and the lowering of the status of representatives as a result of the doctrines of popular sovereignty and the 'mandate'. Among some nations these tendencies have led to deadlocks amounting almost to the paralysis of the representative system; among others opponents have passed from criticism to action and destroyed parliamentary institutions by straining the rights of majorities to the point where the party system passes over into single-party rule.

It is a natural explanation of the heavy weather which the parliamentary system is making abroad to say that in these nations the traditional seamanship which we have painfully learnt through centuries of experience is lacking; as are also many of the basic conditions for the health of Parliament— genuine local self-government, habits of co-operation in voluntary institutions, general acceptance of the rule of law and the spirit of toleration. But this does not account for the fact that in most of these countries the parliamentary system, when newly established, worked for a time quite reasonably well— at any rate, a great deal better than it works today. How is it, too, that in the country of its origin Parliament is running into new and unforeseen difficulties? These difficulties and perplexities are examined, and their causes traced, in the chapters that follow—either as a whole or by concentration on single problems—and certain remedies are suggested. In this chapter I have tried to trace historically the reactions between the traditional and the popular elements in the parliamentary system during the last seventy or eighty years during which democracy has been the accepted goal. This seems to me the general background against which the problems raised by the other contributors might be considered. I need not duplicate what Mr. Amery has to say about the essential nature of parliamentary government. I propose merely to inquire how the House of Commons worked in pre-democratic days up to about 1870 and what specific changes have been introduced by democracy. Only the broader aspects will be dealt with here; in a subsequent chapter I will examine the complementary changes in the procedure and functions of the House of Commons.

The irresistible march towards democracy, which has changed the whole climate of national life and affected all pre-existing institutions, has also created institutions of its own, political, social and economic. No part of this many-sided process would be irrelevant to a full-length study of the development of Parliament. But I shall have to take many things for granted and concentrate on *political* changes. In the progress to democracy, no group or party has had a monopoly; particular landmarks have been the work, now of this party, now of that; and each stage has found more or less general acceptance before the march has been resumed towards the next. Macaulay's comparison of the two parties of his time to the fore and hind legs of a running stag is as true today. The direction, though not perhaps the *tempo*, of the advance is accepted by all parties alike.

Parliamentary democracy—the more important word in the combination is 'Parliamentary'—has more in common with parliamentary aristocracy than either has with 'pure' aristocracy or 'pure' democracy. What parliamentary aristocracy and parliamentary democracy have in common is the very essence of their institutions of government, machinery designed for the purpose of agreement rather than compulsion. It is by such machinery that political progress and political continuity are reconciled, as is shown by the fact that Parliament has kept more than it has lost of its original character throughout the transition from seventeenth and eighteenth century aristocracy to twentieth century democracy. Without Parliament, eighteenth century aristocracy might have stiffened into a system like that of the contemporary French régime, with its *corvées, lettres de cachet,* and a privileged nobility immune from taxation and without political responsibility. Without Parliament, modern democracy might have followed the familiar revolutionary path, beginning with the establishment of social equality, direct popular government and the divine right of the majority; and passing through a stage of intolerable confusion to the oldest form of reaction, a personal dictatorship exercised in the name of the people. The chart of the course of 'pure' democracy, plotted first by Socrates, was followed in a manner highly flattering to Socrates by the French and Bolshevik Revolutions. 'The ultra-democratic is the undoing of Democracy.'

Parliamentary government has been defined as 'government by talk' or, more precisely, 'control-of-government by talk'. The primary purpose of parliamentary talk is internal—for members to convince one another or the Government, or for the Government to convince the members. But there is a secondary purpose, increasingly important, to convince and instruct the people. How is one to judge whether the parliamentary system is attaining its purpose? The question *why* it is succeeding or failing would involve an inquiry into current political, economic and social conditions. But there is a shorter answer to the question *how* Parliament is working. I suggest the following tests. How far is parliamentary discussion (1) open, (2) free, (3) representative, and (4) comprehensive. 'Open' and 'representative' explain themselves. 'Free', as commonly used, has two meanings: first, 'not suffering interference from outside', and, secondly, 'not excluding any person from the rights of discussion'. 'Free' thus means both 'effective' and 'tolerant'. By 'comprehensive' I mean that there is no substantial block of business which is withheld from Parliament by the Government or which Parliament has not the capacity or time to deal with, itself. For Parliament to be running sweetly on all four engines would, of course, be the ideal, though one unlikely to be realized. I propose to look at two pre-democratic periods to see how the system was working, judged by the above tests, and then to consider how it works under democracy.

It is a commonplace that the eighteenth century House of Commons was neither representative nor free from outside interference. Nor had it much use for open debate. But it had proved its effectiveness in times of crisis; it regarded nothing within the sphere of government (as it then existed) as outside

its purview; and, on the whole, it maintained in its own debates
the tradition of toleration which it had inherited from the days
when it was the focus of opposition to the royal government.
It abolished the political disqualifications of Roman Catholics
and Nonconformists. No doubt, the potential effectiveness of
debate in the House of Commons was the cause of the only too
successful efforts to capture representation and of the methods
practised by Walpole and the Duke of Newcastle to 'tame' sitting
members. It was, indeed, a paradox that, while the House of
Commons was the centre of gravity of the political world, a
majority of its members were dependent for election on patronage of which the Crown and the peerage were the chief dis-
pensers. Under the curious code which governed relations between members and patrons, it was an obligation of honour to
offer resignation when a member's action displeased his patron;
the convenience for this purpose of the practice of granting the
Chiltern Hundreds, instituted about 1750, was obvious. Perhaps
it was because so many members had so little to represent in the
way of constituents that they claimed with P.... to represent
the nation at large. Yet it cannot be said that, for the greater
part of the century, the Unreformed House did not represent
public opinion, since anything deserving that name was limited
to the opinions of the gentry and the educated sections of the
middle class. As to the way in which it exercised the function of
representation, the House claimed to be its own judge; it
prohibited the publication of debates lest this should be an
admission of its accountability to the electors. This prohibition
has not been enforced (except as a method of securing a secret
session during the two world wars) since the struggle with the
printers in 1771 ended with the moral victory of their champions,
Lord Mayor Brass Crosby and Alderman Oliver (who were
committed by the House but treated as heroes by the public).
It has not been enforced, but has not been explicitly withdrawn. The declining news value of House of Commons
debates has often been deplored. In the eighteenth century the

---

[1]It was calculated in 1793 that 307 members (out of a total of 558) represented
154 individuals. Petition of the Society of the Friends of the People, c. Porritt, *The
Unreformed House of Commons*.

House discouraged the eager attentions of the reporters; in the nineteenth, it enjoyed steady publicity; in the twentieth, only its wilder moments are popular 'news'.

The eighteenth century parliamentary system was vulnerable to criticism at almost every point. But it worked—it gave England an empire and Englishmen a greater measure of liberty than any other country in Europe. Even patronage had its good side; it was sometimes used with imagination to bring in men of talent who could not have found seats for themselves—even under democracy. Continental professors then and later sought for the logical principle of its success. Montesquieu went astray with his 'separation of powers', as Mr. Amery points out. Perhaps Gneist a hundred years later came nearer the secret in finding 'an organic connexion between State and Society', or, in other words, that the political arrangements were suited to the social conditions.

The most important achievement of the Reform Act of 1832 was the abolition of patronage and the trade in seats and, secondly, the grant of representation to the new manufacturing towns by redistribution. The creation of a uniform borough franchise to include the ten pound householder, did not add very greatly to the electorate and incidentally disfranchised a substantial number of working class voters in the 'scot and lot' boroughs, such as Westminster and Preston.

The short period of thirty or forty years, lasting until the results of the next extension of the franchise, in 1867, became apparent, deserves its title of the 'Golden Age of Parliament'. It was an age of reason in politics, of individualism and *laisser-faire*. Power was reasonably balanced between the executive and the legislature; the problems of the period were chiefly political—of a nature within the competence of the average member of the House of Commons.

The House freely exercised its power to make and unmake governments. Peel in 1846, Russell and Derby in 1852, Aberdeen in 1855, Palmerston in 1858, Derby in 1859 and Russell again in 1866 were all put out of office by defeat in the House; and in the cases where the defeated Prime Minister dissolved Parliament, the decision of the House of Commons was endorsed by the verdict of the electors. In 1858 the House turned against the Palmerston Government, although it had won a large majority at the polls only the year before. Whether they were due to reason and argument or to the intrigues of individuals and groups, there was no doubt that the *results* of debate were effective.

The party system in the House was fluid enough to permit a large degree of independence to the rank and file. Party ties were loosened, it is true, by what may seem accidental causes—the irreconcilable split in the Tory Party between Peelites and Protectionists and the personal friction between the leaders of the two wings of the Liberals. The existence of a third party between 1846 and 1859 was an added complication, especially as the two main parties were often separated by marginal majorities. 'Penal' dissolution was rare, and generally unfortunate in its results. Ministers were willing to accept the collaboration of private members in the shaping of their measures; they not infrequently consented to be overruled in matters of policy. Even Palmerston whose Premiership heralded the era of party consolidation, accepted on an average twelve defeats a session with, possibly, Christian but, certainly, no other kind of resignation. Such pliability became incompatible with ministerial dignity in the succeeding period; between 1886 and 1905 Government defeats averaged one a session, and in 1895 a 'snap' division in Committee of Supply afforded Rosebery a respectable excuse for resignation.

Debate really counted for something. It was carried on chiefly by the 'big guns' on both sides, while the bulk of members were content to sit as a jury and listen to the evidence and arguments. There was always the possibility that a speech might turn votes; the result of a division was not a foregone conclusion. Perhaps the analogy of a jury suggests too much open-mindedness. Sectional interest might be as immune to persuasion as strong party feeling. The Tory country gentlemen, described as 'the finest brute votes in Europe', seem to have had some of the characteristics of what is now called 'lobby fodder'.

Party machinery was being rapidly established in the

constituencies, but a 'fit and proper person to be a candidate', i.e. a big landowner in his county or a large employer in one of the industrial towns, could feel that he owed his return more to his own position than to the local party organization. Bagehot, writing in 1865, was perhaps too cynical about the relationship of member and constituents. 'Aristocracy was a power in the constituencies . . . a real earl, though Irish, was coveted by half the electing bodies'. But, other things being equal, wealth was the test of eligibility. Bagehot quoted the *Saturday Review* as saying that 'at the door of the House of Commons there was a differential duty of at least £2000 a year'. Members combined a decent show of consideration with a comfortable independence of the views of their constituents— Bagehot's 'deferential lower middle class'; no notions of a popular 'mandate' or electoral delegation were invoked to interfere with a member's discretion between elections. The country 'looked up to' the House of Commons, was satisfied with the kind of representation the governing classes gave it, and liked it the better for being ornamental.

The range of governmental activity was confined to the traditional subjects—foreign affairs, defence, the maintenance of order and the administration of justice—subjects which were within the competence of the average member and were well suited to the House's methods of business. There was as yet little state interference with trade or industry or social conditions. *Laisser-faire* meant cheap government as well as straightforward estimates; expenditure climbed from fifty million in the 1830s to seventy million in 1860, but did not reach a hundred million till the turn of the century. There was little need for fiscal ingenuity; Gladstone was able to reduce the income tax from sixpence to fourpence in 1865 and did not despair of getting rid of it altogether. Although the output of legislation was considerable, judged by the stout volumes of the statute book, its subject matter was simple and did not call for much specialized knowledge. The bulk of legislation is deceptive; until 1867 the annual volumes of the statute book contained local acts which took up little of the time of the House; also in the absence of official draughtsmen the style was unnecessarily long-winded. In spite of the absence of modern restrictions on debate, the House had ample time to get through its business without sitting more than six months in the year.

The rules under which the House worked are described in a later chapter. But it is worth recalling here, in tribute to the spirit of toleration characteristic of this period, that it succeeded in finally establishing the Speaker in the position of an impartial umpire, whose primary duty is to secure fair play for the minority. This conception of the Chair had been accepted in theory a hundred years earlier, but had made slow headway against the pull of party influences. In the Speakership of Shaw Lefevre (1839–57) it was so firmly established that it has ceased to be questioned. The conventions by which the impartiality of the Chair is fortified and many older rules and conventions which embody the parliamentary spirit were handed on by this period; and it is of incalculable advantage to parliamentary democracy that it has had the good sense to maintain them as the common heritage of all parties and classes.

In this period the parliamentary method of control-of-government had actually worked better on the whole than it had before or has since. Debate was educative—great debates, giving all sides of important questions were fully reported in the daily Press, because there was a public which read them. Debate was effective—it could turn votes in the House of Commons and bring down governments. Some Members were independent of party and many, who *were* party men, sat pretty loose to party control. Business was not so specialized that the average member could only grasp a quarter of it, nor so congested that there was no time to discuss it fully. The early- and mid-Victorian system was a happy stage in parliamentary government. Most of the political abuses had been swept away in the early years of Reform; government, which continued to be that of the upper classes, had never been more reasonable, moderate and high-minded. Political arrangements were admirably suited to social conditions—if you did not look beyond the narrow circle of electors. But those who studied the first principles of government—and there were unusually many such among politicians—could not be satisfied with a

B

synthesis of opinions and interests which left out about ninety per cent of the nation. And the practical-minded, who mostly claimed in that period to be progressive, realized that the ten pound householder could not be the last word in representation and that the practical question about reform was, 'How far—and how fast?' It was in the House of Commons, rather than in the country, that the demand for further extension of the franchise was most vocal.

The advance of electoral reform continued to proceed on two fronts—the lowering of the franchise qualification and the redistribution of seats according to population.

The principal concession of the Reform Act of 1867 was the household franchise in urban constituencies, which gave the vote to the town working classes. This left the urban franchise noticeably more popular than the county franchise—a grievance which was remedied, without undue haste, by the Act of 1884. In 1918 women (over thirty years of age) were at last admitted, and ten years later the differential age limit was removed. Finally, in 1948 university representation, together with the other remnants of plural voting, was suppressed; and a single uniform franchise was established dependent simply on registration. The total effect of these reforms of eighty years has been the raising of the electorate—excluding Ireland—from 1,130,000 (about 10 per cent of the adult male population) in 1864 to nearly 33,700,000 (practically the whole adult population) in 1949—women considerably outnumbering men.

The effects of redistribution have been almost as far-reaching. The Act of 1885 extended the principle of single-member constituencies; it carved up the counties and big cities into electoral districts, leaving only the city of London, the universities and some twenty medium-sized towns two-member constituencies. In the Act of 1948 representation was based in principle on a quota of 55,000 voters, and permanent commissions were set up to adjust boundaries in accordance with shifts in population. Although certa'n concessions have been made to Scotland and Wales, the resulting electoral map may be regarded as a monument to Democracy's long pursuit of equality and uniformity.

All parties have contributed to the democratization of the electorate. For the Reform Act of 1867 the Conservatives, and for the Acts of 1884 and 1885 the Liberals, were responsible. The Act of 1918 was the agreed product of a War Coalition; the principles of the Act of 1948 were worked out by a conference presided over by the Speaker, though their application by the Labour Government was modified in certain particulars, such as the abolition of university constituencies, against the wishes of the Opposition. The decisive step of 1867—the admission of a large element of the working classes, which led inevitably to universal suffrage—was taken by a minority Tory Government and went beyond what either party thought prudent. The Liberals, as the party of reform, could not openly resist it. For the Conservatives, generally, it was a 'leap in the dark'. But Disraeli, who was a better political weather-prophet for being something of a weather-maker, was on the whole proved right, so far as his party's prospects were concerned. He lost the next election, but won in 1874. Between the coming into effect of the Reform Act of 1868 and the Liberal landslide in 1905 the Conservatives were in power for twenty-three years out of thirty-seven, whereas they had been in a majority for only five years out of the previous thirty-five.

That the democratization of the House of Commons—its personnel and its parties—lagged so far behind the democratization of the electorate is understandable, though the length of the lag might be surprising in any other country. A 'differential duty' long kept the door of the House shut to the majority, and it was not until 1911 that the State somewhat reduced the inequality by a moderate subvention. During the whole nineteenth century the House remained, so far as the two major parties were concerned, the preserve of the governing classes. To the traditionally minded leaders, who survived into the next century, there was no incompatibility between an aristocratic House and a democratic electorate. In their view 'nineteenth century parliamentarianism had worked successfully because the personnel of parliaments and cabinets was still . . . upper class, and the function of the lower orders was limited to giving the system a popular imprimatur by helping

to choose which of two aristocratic parties should hold office'.[1]
Although they were enfranchised so much earlier, it was only
in company with a quota of trade-unionists that a substantial
body of lower middle-class representatives first entered the
House in 1906.

After 1918 and for most of the period between the two wars
(when, except for two short Parliaments, the Conservatives
enjoyed a majority, often a very large majority, in the House of
Commons) the quality of membership tended to revert to the
pre-1906 type. Since the second war the personnel of the House
is more like a cross-section of the population, though with a
decided shift towards the upper strata. According to the
analysis of the social origins of candidates and Members contained in studies of the general elections of 1945 and 1950[2],
the public schools and universities were well represented in
both the major parties. In the House elected in 1950, Conservative Members included 223 public-school men and 185 University men, while the corresponding figures for Labour were
61 and 129. In the Labour Party the total of working-
class candidates may be put at 183, while in the Conservative
Party it was 7. In both the major parties the professions
contributed the highest proportion of candidates—Labour, 258;
Conservatives, 308. Among the Conservative candidates, 63
were directly descended from Members of Parliament and
78 were connected directly or by marriage with the Peerage
(and, of these 78, 54 were elected). Of Labour candidates,
19 were descendants of Members of Parliament and at least 4
were sons of Peers. If, as might be expected the Conservatives
have a large sprinkling of upper-class members, and Labour
a solid block of trade unionists and Co-operatives, yet it seems
that the professional classes constitute the largest element in
both parties.

The fears and hopes, prevalent in the last century, that
under democracy parties would be divided on class-lines and
the classes be swamped by a permanent and overwhelming

[1]Ensor, *England*, 1870–1914, p. 387.
[2]MacCallum and Readman, *The British General Election of* 1945, Nicholas,
The British General Election of 1950.

majority of the masses, have been belied—at any rate, so far. Both the major parties make their appeal to all sections of the community and have adherents in all. Even if there is a distinct shift towards the left as it descends the social pyramid, the line of division between the parties remains vertical rather than horizontal. That the Conservatives have strong support among what is euphoniously called 'the lower income brackets' is proved by the fact that they have held a parliamentary majority for twenty-four of the thirty-two years between 1918 and 1950. 'We are all Socialists now', including some millionaires and some sons of peers. The averagely intelligent observer may be excused for thinking that all that has happened is that the Labour Party has taken the place of the Liberals as the fore-legs of Macaulay's stag.

It is a fact of political experience that an advance in democracy is accompanied by an increase in the power and elaborateness of party machinery. This is not surprising since the handling of large numbers puts a premium on organization. With the first extension of the electorate in 18.. both ... Tories and Whigs had realised the value of setting up party organizations in the constituencies for registering their supporters and then, naturally, for canvassing. But it was not till after 1867 that these associations, originally self-constituted bodies, began to organize themselves on a representative basis with elected executive committees. The Birmingham Radical Caucus (which leapt into fame in 1868 by its skilful disposal of its voting strength) was the largest and most elaborately constituted party association; its organization, consisting of a large representative general committee, and a small council, was taken as a pattern by Liberals throughout the country. The Conservative type was not dissimilar; both systems, under a decent appearance of representative self-government, left control in the hands of a few managers.

The linking up of the constituency associations into centrally controlled nation-wide party organizations—the Liberal Federation and the Conservative Union—was a step of greater political importance. The Liberal Federation, initiated in 1877 under the presidency of Joseph Chamberlain, with the declared purpose of promoting 'the participation of all members in the direction (of the party)' conceived itself as a sort of 'outside Parliament' with the mission of pressing Radical policy on the Liberal leaders. The Conservative organization, founded in 1867—ten years before its Liberal counterpart—was a much quieter affair, designed principally to assist the local associations and clubs in spreading Conservative principles. In its annual Conferences it made no attempt to dictate policy, seldom passing resolutions except votes of confidence in its leaders.

For a short period towards the end of the nineteenth century each of the two great party organizations proved to be a thorn in the flesh of the parliamentary leaders. After Chamberlain's inclusion in the Liberal Ministry of 1880 the Liberal Federation ceased to be a menace, but its fertility in proposals for reform, culminating in the Newcastle Programme of 1891 (which contained matter, it was calculated, for the work of at least ten sessions) remained a standing nuisance. Even the Conservative Union 'went wild' for a few months in 1884 under the presidency of Lord Randolph Churchill and threatened to wrest the control of party policy from Lord Salisbury. In both cases the parliamentary leaders succeeded in recovering control and took steps by reconstituting their organizations to make the party machines innocuous. Writing in 1908, Lawrence Lowell could say that 'as organs for the popular control of the party', both the party organizations 'are shams, but with this difference that the Conservative organization is a transparent, and the Liberal an opaque sham'.

The constitution and functions of party organizations, as they exist at present, are described in a subsequent chapter by Mr. Ivor Thomas, and I will refer to them later. But the history of party machinery in its first phase during the generation after 1867 is not without permanent interest. It shows how the first impact of democratic ideas, even on the two traditionally minded parliamentary parties, was accompanied—however mildly—by a tendency which has since become familiar in democratic countries: the temptation to use party machinery, under the plea of making it more popular, as a political organ alongside Parliament and in rivalry with the parliamentary leaders. It was a premature attempt with little prospect of success, but it showed for the first time in this country an alternative way to the parliamentary for manipulating the inert mass of a party, which appealed to the more impatient type of party politician.

After 1867 the growth of party organization in the country was reflected by the tigh ening-up of party discipline in Parliament. It became more and more difficult for a candidate to win or hold a seat without the help of one of the local party machines. Returned to the House as a party member, both his constituency association and his party whips took care to see that he steadily supported the party line—in speech, if need be, but certainly in vote. Few members could disregard the threat of having the party whip withdrawn and being opposed by an 'official' candidate at the next election. During the last quarter of the nineteenth century there was a steady increase in the practice of 'putting on the whips' on every question of policy—both by the Government and by the O___ ___ a steady decrease in th___ ___ or members who failed to obey. Other factors contributed to the hardening of the line of division between the parties:—the prolonged and dramatic parliamentary duel between Disraeli and Gladstone; the series of highly controversial issues, such as Home Rule, Free Trade *versus* Protection, the Lloyd George Budget and the Liberal quarrel with the House of Lords. When the Labour Party took the place of the Liberals as the alternative Government, the disagreement between the parties came to include some of the fundamental principles which had previously been generally accepted. Neutral standing ground between Left and Right became harder to find, and 'crossing the floor of the House' (which had been comparatively easy for Palmerston, Stanley and Gladstone) almost equivalent to political suicide.

The British party system has grown up as a method of providing government rather than as a means of expressing shades of political opinion—a fact which is embodied in and reinforced by the maintenance of the 'majority' system of voting at elections. In the House of Commons there are only two division lobbies and almost always to cast a vote is to say 'Aye' or 'No' to the Government. This makes the survival of a third party, especially a party of the centre, very difficult. Despite substantial support in the country, the fact that the Liberal Party is not regarded as a potential government is a fatal handicap at elections; and in the House of Commons its internal cohesion is continually threatened on issues raised by the Government or the Opposition. Since the support of a party machine has become more and more indispensable to a candidate, the Independents are in an even worse case. The abnormal conditions of the war and its aftermath raised their number to over twenty; but at the general election of 1950, with the University seats gone, they were one and all eliminated.

During the democratic period the 'political' sovereignty of the people, which Dicey used as a clue to explain the mysteries of constitutional conventions, has become so vocal that it is more and more restricting the 'legal' sovereignty of Parliament. For instance, the choice of a Ministry—the 'elective function', which Bagehot thought the most important function of the House of Commons—has since 1868, with rare exceptions, been exercised not by the House but by the voters at a general election. As has been pointed out, before 1867 the House of Commons frequently effected a change of government in the course of a Parliament; a Ministry defeated at the polls thought it due to the constitutional position of the Commons to meet Parliament and receive its congé from the new House. But since Disraeli initiated the practice (which Gladstone criticized as doubtfully constitutional), every defeated Prime Minister, including Gladstone himself in 1874, has in normal circumstances accepted the verdict of the polls as final and resigned without meeting Parliament. In 1905 Balfour, with his parliamentary majority intact, found a plausible ground for resignation in the fact that a series of by-elections showed he had lost support in the country.

In one set of circumstances alone does the House of Commons still exercise the function of election, and that is when no party emerges from a general election with a clear majority. In 1890 Salisbury, and in 1924 Baldwin, retained office to meet the new

House and be beaten on the Address, because the intentions of a third party, whose support was necessary to give either of the main parties a majority, were not certainly known. From the practical point of view, there is much to be said for a government acting promptly on the nation's notice to quit and not thinking it necessary to 'caretake' in office until the House of Commons turns it out. The truth is that democracy has made Ministers the servants of the electors, not of the House; but perhaps Gladstone was right in regretting the failure to keep up appearances.

As far as the individual Member is concerned the fall in status has been even more depressing. Like a delegate to the electoral college for the election of an American President, he is returned primarily as a tied voter for a potential Premier. His own merits matter little compared with his label. On the other hand, the position of the party leaders, and particularly of the Premier, is enhanced. The bulk of the electors in a large modern constituency may know little of the personality of the candidates; but they do know by reputation the Prime Ministers and a few of the other leaders on both sides. A general election is staged for their benefit as a sporting struggle between two rival teams for the prize of office; and the Party managers and Party Press find it pays best to concentrate the spotlight on one or two 'national' figures.

The changes which accompanied the democratization of the electorate—the development of party machinery, the growing stringency of party discipline, the replacement of the House of Commons by the electors as the government-choosing agency— have all worked in the same direction, to increase the ascendancy of the Executive over Parliament. The Government has also been the chief beneficiary from the restriction of the legislative powers of the House of Lords. There has been a deterioration in the position of the House of Commons, as a body, and in the status of individual members. A few points may be mentioned to illustrate this conclusion.

Strong government balanced by strong popular control through a representative body is the underlying principle of the English system. The democratic party system has upset this balance. To their authority as servants of the King, wielding the powers of the prerogative, Ministers have added a second source of power, the power of Parliament itself. Through their command of a devoted party majority they have to a large extent in practice reversed the constitutional relation of the Executive to the House of Commons. As Ministers, they may be subject to the control of the House of Commons; as party leaders, they are in a position to control the controllers.

The sanction for the control of the House of Commons is its power to force the resignation of a Ministry by defeating it on a question of policy. This sanction was freely employed before 1867. In this century no Government with an independent party majority has resigned on account of a defeat in the House of Commons. Mr. Chamberlain resigned in 1940 because he realized he had lost the confidence of the House, although he retained a majority (reduced by two-thirds) in the critical division. But war conditions made this an abnormal case. Usually the reply of a Ministry to a defeat in the House is an appeal to the country. The modern party system has made the threat of dissolution a convincing answer to the threat of defeat. A member of a party has always had to balance his dislike of a particular measure against his general support of his Government's programme, reinforced by his dislike of the programme of the opposing party. Now, in addition, there is the fear of the imputation of disloyalty, of the resentment of his constituency association and of the risk which a general election (and his part in bringing it about) may involve to his own career. To a growing number, too, the potential loss of the parliamentary salary must be a weighty argument.

It is not merely in rising superior to the negative controls of the House of Commons that the ascendancy of the Government is apparent. The exclusive possession of the initiative in finance had long given the Government the chief rôle in legislation. Now it has acquired a practical monopoly. The widening of the sphere of governmental activity has vastly increased the complexity of legislation as well as its volume. Each of the many branches of social and economic development can only be mastered by specialists. Legislation on any such subject can only be prepared by the competent department, drafted by a government draftsman and expounded by the responsible Minister. Thorough criticism of such measures is beyond the power of the average Member; it is generally conducted by one or two front-bench members of the Opposition, with experience of the department concerned, supported by a small group who happen to have business experience or professional training which can be turned to account.[1] The amount of such legislation and the insufficient time for its digestion and examination add to its distracting effect. The same difficulty confronts the House in its efforts to control the administration and expenditure resulting from such measures. In an age of specialization the House suffers from all the disadvantages of amateurs pitted against professionals.

Since the first world war the position of the Government has been strengthened by improvements in Cabinet machinery —the establishment of a secretariat, the systematic division of work between Cabinet committees, methods of consultation with outside interests likely to be affected before action. Some departments are provided with advisory committees for the latter purpose. Such consultation, which helps to shape a bill before it is introduced, enables a Government to forestall parliamentary criticism and to take the wind out of the sails of the Opposition. Critics may hold that there is room for improvement in Cabinet organization—they may say in particular that Ministers are too much engrossed with departmental matters to be able to look ahead on general policy— and specific reforms are suggested by Sir Arthur Salter later in this book. But, as the Haldane Report pointed out, any improvement in Cabinet machinery will further increase the ascendancy of the Government over Parliament.

If the Cabinet owes its present predominance in Parliament very largely to party organization, signs are not wanting in democratic countries that the party machine may not always be content with a subordinate role. The Conservative and Liberal Parties have, as already noted, had experience of unsuccessful attempts made by the party machine to capture

[1]Or rather it is they alone who have something to contribute.

control of party policy from the parliamentary leaders. Since Labour was a party before it was a parliamentary party, its machine has never been so indisputably in the hands of the parliamentary leaders as has been the case with the two older parties, which had been formed through long periods of office and opposition in Parliament before they began to organize party machines outside Parliament. A comparison of the constitutions of the various parties (see Chapter VIII) shows that Labour Party policy is controlled by the representative annual Party Conference to a greater extent than is the case with the Conservative and Liberal Parties. Also the periodical party meeting, which is common to all parties, has more control over the individual Labour Member in respect of his parliamentary activities, since he is bound by the standing orders of his party not to speak or vote in a sense contrary to the decisions of such a meeting.

When the Labour Party is in office, however, democratic control of the parliamentary leaders is relaxed; the conventions of the Cabinet and its relations to Parliament are too well established for that to work. Since 1945, the party standing orders have been suspended. All the factors which increase the stature of Ministers over ordinary mortals have had their natural effect. It seems that Cabinet Ministers can generally convince the majority at party meetings; and the discontented minority are free, within the ordinary limits of party discipline, to express their disagreement in the House of Commons.

To see the full development of the democratic chain of party control, one must look abroad—to France or (where there is closer kinship with the British parliamentary system) to Australia or New Zealand. In the latter countries Labour methods (which are disavowed, but to some extent imitated, by other parties) have turned Labour Members of Parliament into delegates of the Party machine and Ministers into spokesmen of the Caucus. The Prime Minister and the whole Cabinet are elected by Caucus—unless the Prime Minister is exceptionally strong, the portfolios of his colleagues are distributed by caucus voting; control of policy has naturally gone with power of appointment to office.

Nothing could be more destructive of the true purpose of parliamentary debate than the Caucus system. In the first place, it has all the rigidity of remote control in a situation which requires flexible tactics; the leader in charge of a measure is so tightly confined by instructions given by his party meeting that he has no room for manœuvre or compromise. The committee stage of a bill in the Australian House of Representatives is often reduced to a tedious formality, which few members of the majority take the trouble to sit through, because it is known that every amendment moved by the Opposition will be voted down without consideration of its merits. Secondly, parliamentary debate is based on the belief that the exchange of argument between opponents is calculated to promote a sense of proportion and willingness to compromise, which favours moderate views. In Caucus, on the other hand, discussion takes place in private, where all the views heard are those of a single party, and extreme party policy (as is usual when members of each of two rival parties debate separately) gets a better hearing than moderate views. The system strikes at the validity, for Parliament, of the majority principle: for nobody knows by now large a majority a Caucus decision is supported or whether, if its size were known, it would not prove to be a minority in Parliament.

The growth of party organization and discipline, which has so greatly strengthened the hands of the modern Ministry, has contributed something by way of compensation towards the maintenance of the parliamentary system. It has consolidated the forces and enhanced the importance of the Opposition in the House of Commons. The need of a check on executive power is deeply ingrained in the parliamentary tradition. In the seventeenth century opposition had been the function of Parliament, as a body. When the selection of Ministers from the largest party in the House of Commons made it clear that consistent criticism could not be expected from the majority of the House, this function passed to the minority. 'His Majesty's Opposition'[1] acquired a recognized official status as an indis-

[1]The name was given by John Cam Hobhouse in 1826. Porritt *Unreformed House of Commons*, I, 510.

pensable element in the constitution. There may be several parties in opposition, but *the* Opposition means the second main party, temporarily in a minority, with leaders experienced in office, who are ready, when the need arises, to form an alternative government. This affords a guarantee that its criticism will be directed by a consistent policy and conducted with responsibility—not in a spirit calculated to ruin the game for the sake of the prize.

The 'Official Opposition' is a standing proof of the British genius for inventing political machinery. It has been adopted in all the Dominion Parliaments; the lack of it is the chief weakness of most of the Continental systems. It derives, of course, from the two-Party system; but in its developed form it represents a happy fusion of the parliamentary spirit of toleration with the democratic tendency to exalt party organization. The system involves the discouragement of individual initiative almost as much on the Opposition back benches as on those of the Government Party, for party organization seems more adapted to frontal attack in mass formation than to individual sniping. While admitting the loss to parliamentary life resulting from the sacrifice of the independent private Member, it cannot be denied that under modern conditions the concerted action of the Opposition is the best means of controlling a Government—by criticizing defects in administration loudly enough for the public to take notice. This is not a particularly pleasant, if salutary, experience for Ministers; and it is only natural that they should be tempted to think both that the Opposition abuse their opportunities and that their opportunities are unnecessarily ample. The facilities which the Opposition enjoy for initiating criticism on subjects of their own selection are dependent on technical forms and parliamentary conventions which it would be out of place to explain here. (They are dealt with in Chapter VII.) But the share of the time of the House which the Government (who nominally control the disposal of time and are always short of time for their own business) put at the disposal of a body whose *raison d'être* is to show up the mistakes of Ministers and eventually to turn them out of office—this share of time, which during the last fifty years has not fallen below a quarter of the effective days of the session, is worth more interest than it usually receives. The least that can be said is that, since it is only through the Opposition that some measure of parliamentary control survives, the uninterrupted respect for the rights of the Opposition which contemporary Governments have shown should be accepted as *prima facie* evidence of the soundness of their parliamentary faith.

It cannot be denied that the power of the party whip has been harmful for parliamentary debate. If speeches cannot turn votes, they tend to be directed over the heads of Members to the gallery, whence they may be reported outside. Such control as the House still exercises over the Government is often said to be indirect—through appeal to public opinion. Two democratic nations, New Zealand and then Australia, where parliamentary debate is even more party-bound than it is here, have taken the logical step, on this hypothesis, of broadcasting the debates of their Chambers. The implications of such a departure from parliamentary conventions are far-reaching. Taken in conjunction with the new techniques of measuring mass-reactions and movements of opinion, it is as if the representatives of the nation had handed their mandates back to the people and contented themselves with registering decisions instead of working them out for themselves.

The House of Commons has not arrived at the stage at which debate has lost all effectiveness. The majority may be more subservient in one Parliament than in another; the Opposition may be stronger or weaker. But no Government can afford never to adapt its actions to the public opinion of the House, never to recast or even withdraw bills which have had a hostile reception on second reading, never to accept amendments in committee, not to take anxious care that its administrative action shall be defensible. It may be alleged that such compliance is really due, on the one hand, to awareness of the Press and the 'Pollsters' or, on the other, to back-bench representations behind the scenes. But without parliamentary debate —or the possibility of it—such extra-Parliamentary forces would find no purchase. One striking example out of many that could be given was the hasty retreat of the Baldwin Government in 1935 on the question of the 'Hoare-Laval pact'. The truth seems to be, as usual, somewhere in the middle—namely, that while spectacular results, such as the fall of a Government are seldom to be expected from debate (but remember 1940), and while compromises may more often be 'huddled up' in party conclave or between leaders of different parties than worked out on the floor of the House, still British parliamentary democracy has not yet reached a stage at which debate is to be regarded (as some critics would have us believe) as mere deference to an outlived tradition and as having no longer any effectiveness in controlling the activities of government.

The purpose of this Chapter is to review briefly the principal features of the parliamentary system, in its present phase, and the stages by which they were reached. Suggestions for remedying some of the defects which I have mentioned will be found in later chapters. I have dwelt, perhaps at undue length, on the want of balance caused by the predominance of the Government over the House of Commons as a result of the growing stringency of party discipline, on the one hand, and, on the other, of the vast increase during the democratic period in the complexity and volume of parliamentary business. It seems that the first step towards the restoration of control by the House of Commons would be to relieve it of some part of the burden under which it labours. The problem of Devolution, regional or functional, needs to be re-examined. An industrial sub-Parliament, as recommended by Mr. Churchill in his Romanes lecture of 1930, seems more promising than the type of industrial co-Parliament, recommended by the Webbes in their book published a few years earlier. Any such reform would require a long time for study, probably by a Royal Commission, and also for the subsequent legislation. Meanwhile, a comparatively modest domestic reform, which the House of Commons could institute in its own machinery, might have some effect in relieving the strain of its present burden, and might also help to develop a common parliamentary spirit by accustoming members of different parties to work together outside the House.

Most legislative bodies have recognized the need to organize themselves, through making opportunities for their Members to acquire specialized experience, in such a way as to cope with the complexities of modern state business. The House of Commons itself in the seventeenth century relied for leadership on its select committees.[1] The United States, France, and all the Continental legislatures which have adopted French procedure as a model, employ the system of standing committees (*commissions permanentes*), each with a range of competence corresponding to an administrative department, or group of departments. Every member belongs to one of these bodies, and thus has the opportunity of familiarizing himself with at least one sphere of state activity. The functions of these committees cover not only the consideration of bills and motions introduced into the Chamber, but also certain rights of supervision over the administration of departments falling within their competence. A full account of this organization will be found below in the chapter on the French and American systems by Professor Brogan.

The adoption of such a system has often been recommended to the House of Commons, notably by Lord Haldane in the 'Machinery of Government' Report. But it has been consistently opposed by Ministers and their official advisers, and has not found much support among Members. The principal argument against the adoption of this system has been that it is inconsistent with Cabinet government, since it might set up competing organs of leadership, intermediate between Ministers and their responsibility to the House of Commons as a body, and would seriously interfere with their control of their departments. There is some force in this contention. Undoubtedly, as it works in France, the system of *commissions permanentes*, with its elaborate organization and continuity, is too strong for the ephemeral Ministries. The Parties find it useful as a rival organ; it has acquired powers of initiative in legislation and finance which

---

[1] This system was superseded partly by the emergence of the Cabinet as the source of leadership, and partly by the growing mastery which the rules of the House provided of the difficult art of orderly discussion by a large body—an art which the Continental countries have never mastered.

undermine ministerial responsibility[1]. Such powers are, admittedly, inconsistent with the Cabinet system, as we understand it. But it does not seem beyond the wit of man to devise a committee system which, while retaining the essentially subordinate and advisory character of committees, might make the House of Commons more generally capable of informed criticism.

On general grounds it may be suggested that some change in this direction would have useful results. Greater opportunity to familiarize themselves with particular branches of administration might help to reduce the sense of frustration, of which many private members, especially new members, complain; the practical knowledge they acquired might be of value to debate. There is perhaps another direction in which such a change would do no harm. Permanent committees, composed of members of various parties, tend somewhat towards compromise, to the cooling down of Party spirit; such a committee develops something of a corporate sense, and its Members become inclined to defend conclusions thrashed out in common against at any rate the more ignorant party objections that may be raised in the Chamber. Even the limited experience of the House of Commons with permanent specializing committees shows this. The Committee of Public Accounts and the Estimates Committee (which are permanent bodies, though their functions are not very specialized) have a strong corporate sense, and tend to consider questions on their merits rather than on party lines. The emergence of a non-party, or super-party, spirit in these committees is no doubt helped by the fact that their competence to deal with matters of policy is restricted. But even on a more comprehensive scale, a system of permanent committees might be expected to preserve these characteristics and thus to make some contribution towards loosening the grip of democratic Party Government.

The changes accompanying the advent of Democracy can

[1] The proceedings of the Assembly, 23rd to 27th February, 1951, on a bill for the reform of the electoral law, which had been agreed between the Parties in the Pleven Ministry but rejected by their representatives in the competent commission, are a good example of the confusion resulting from division of responsibility and competitive leadership.

be summarized by saying that parliamentary control, which means and can only mean control by discussion, has been seriously weakened. The House of Commons has lost influence with the electors; the space given to its debates in the Press is diminishing; their quality has suffered from the greater electoral value of slogans as compared with argument; the shiftings of majority opinion, which can be calculated with accuracy by recent techniques, are given disproportionate importance by representatives. The strength of the party machine and the discipline it has imposed on party members in Parliament has had a distorting effect on the relations between the House of Commons and the Government. Ministers are almost immune from defeat—the narrowest majority seems adequate for survival. Although parliamentary conventions are strong enough to protect the rights of the Opposition to have its views recorded and make its voice heard, the almost mystical belief in the rights of the majority makes that voice, except on matters of secondary importance, ineffective. The amount and complexity of business and the congestion of parliamentary time reduce the capacity of members to review departmental administration and have the effect of transferring to the departments substantial powers of legislation which thereby largely escape from parliamentary control.

The parliamentary system works best when party distinctions are well defined by differences of principle but leave room for some independence of judgment; when government is strong but not too strong to be controlled by the House of Commons; when Representatives accept the duty of leading public opinion and are not too anxiously concerned with temporary unpopularity; when majorities are not tyrannical and minorities have no cause to be resentful. These conditions came nearest to being satisfied during the period between the first and second Reform Acts, when social organization, being hierarchical, was admirably suited by political arrangements; when the representatives of a small minority of the nation supported and controlled an upper-class government drawn from a still smaller minority. Succeeding generations, actuated by a generous desire for extending freedom and equality, have re-based Parliament on the widest possible franchise; but find that in doing so they have lost some of the qualities on which the successful working of Parliament depended. Are we to say 'So much the worse for Democracy'? Or, alternatively, 'So much the worse for Parliament'? Or should we not continue to search earnestly for means to restore the lost balance?

CHAPTER II

THE NATURE OF BRITISH
PARLIAMENTARY GOVERNMENT

By L. S. Amery

If by a constitution is meant a written document or series of documents embodying in statutory or declaratory form the principles and structure of our Government, then there is, in that sense, no such thing as the British Constitution. What we mean by the constitution is not any deliberate attempt to control and confine our political growth on the basis of a preconceived intellectual plan, reflecting the political theories of a particular group of men or the prepossessions of a particular age, but a *living structure* continuously shaped in the course of history by the interaction of individual purposes and collective instincts with the requirements of ever varying circumstances.

Certain main elements of that structure, such as the Crown and its servants, the Houses of Parliament, the Judiciary and the National Church, have continuously played their part in it, but in widely varying relationship and significance. It includes some memorable documentary milestones like Magna Carta, the Declaration of Rights and the Statute of Westminster. But some of its most important features are no part of its formal and legal structure, and have little other sanction beyond use and precedent. The whole, like the law of the land, of which it is a part, is a blend of formal law, precedent and tradition. It can only be understood in the light of our national history and indeed, of the national character, which it has both expressed and moulded. It is the political aspect of our way of life.

Our national character, like the English language, is the result of the impact, adjustment and blending, under the new political and social conditions created by the Conquest, of two entirely different elements: a compromise and balance between two antithetical temperaments. The ever initiating, constructive, domineering Norman had to come to terms with the slower Saxon, yielding in much, but tenacious of his rights and usages. Much interpreting of each to the other was necessary before either the English language or the English mind found themselves. There was much parleying locally long before there were Parliaments. New demands were made and complied with: but always on terms.

The habit of compromise, of give and take after free discussion, of readiness to see something in the case of the other side, sank deep into the national character. Only once in our political history was there a complete breakdown in the national temper. That was when extreme theories of royal and parliamentary right, exacerbated by bitter religious controversy as well as by economic issues, led to civil war and dictatorship. The Restoration of 1660 was a true restoration, not so much of the pre-Rebellion constitution, as of the ancient good temper of the nation. Its most significant step was Charles II's Act of Indemnity and Oblivion commended to Parliament by Lord Chancellor Clarendon in words which no one who believes in the continuance of free government in this country should ever allow himself to forget:

"The King is a suitor to you, makes it his suit very heartily, that you join with him in restoring the whole nation, its primitive temper and integrity, to its old góod nature—good nature, a virtue so peculiar to you, so appropriated by God Almighty to this nation, that it can be translated into no other language, hardly practised by any other people. . . ."

Closely linked with this compromising and reasonable temper is the sense of responsibility which is, indeed, the most characteristic feature of our national political character. Our system of government is usually described as Parliamentary Responsible Government. It would be difficult to find a better description. But it must be remembered, first of all, that

Parliamentary Government means government, not by Parliament, but to use the old phrase, government 'by the King in Parliament'. Secondly, that the responsibility is not merely one towards the majority in Parliament. Ministers on taking office accept a first and dominant responsibility to the Crown, as representing the unity and continuity of the life of the nation and of the Empire, for defending the wider national and imperial interest. They each accept a corresponding individual responsibility towards the particular services over which they have been called to preside. As members of Parliament themselves they are responsible to Parliament as a whole and to the nation for the effective working of Parliament as the centre of our national life, for the maintenance of full and free discussion of every aspect of government policy, and for support of the Speaker in upholding the dignity and impartiality of debate. It is only subject to these wider responsibilities that, as Party leaders, they owe a responsibility to their own Party for promoting its particular views and forwarding its interests.

The word 'responsibility' has, however, two senses. It connotes not only accountability to some outside or final authority. It also connotes a state of mind, which weighs the consequences of action and then acts, irrespective, it may be, of the concurrence or approval of others. It is the strength of our constitutional system that it encourages and fosters responsibility in that higher sense. A British Government is not merely responsible to those who have appointed it or keep it in office in the sense in which an agent is responsible to his principal. It is an independent body which on taking office assumes the responsibility of leading and directing Parliament and the nation in accordance with its own judgment and convictions. Members of Parliament are no mere delegates of their constituents, but, as Burke pointed out, representatives of the nation, responsible, in the last resort, to their own conscience.

Nor is the responsibility of the Opposition in these various respects any less than that of the Government and of its supporters. On the Opposition rests the main responsibility for what was once the critical function of Parliament as a whole, while at the same time it directs its criticisms with a view to convincing public opinion of its own fitness for office. It is with the importance of this responsibility in mind that Lowell in his *Government of England* said that:

> "The expression 'His Majesty's Opposition' . . . embodies the greatest contribution of the nineteenth century to the art of government, that of a party out of power which is recognized as perfectly loyal to the institutions of the State and ready to come into office without a shock to the political traditions of the nation."

The same point was made by Lord Simon:

> "Our parliamentary system will work as long as the responsible people in different parties accept the view that it is better that the other side should win than that the constitution should be broken."

The combination of responsible leadership by Government with responsible criticism in Parliament is the essence of our Constitution. Our aim must be to preserve it through the inevitable changes which the needs and demands of each generation bring about in its outward structure and in the adjustment of its parts.

No less characteristic is the instinctive English love of concrete detail and suspicion of abstract principles and logical deductions. Our Norman conquerors and the clerics and lawyers that came in their train could add copiously to our vocabulary. But they never succeeded in implanting the tendency, universal in countries of Latin derived speech, of arguing from general principles to particular conclusions. Even in the domain of law the broad principles of the Roman Law were never able to displace the English belief that the merits of any particular case could only be judged in the light of decisions on similar cases which had commended themselves. In mediaeval philosophy it was an Englishman, William of Ockham, who was the keenest critic of the Platonic notion that abstractions were something more than a verbal convenience, while another Englishman, Francis Bacon, could challenge the whole accepted order of thinking by his inductive philosophy and by his warning against the danger arising from 'the spacious liberty of generalization'.

In the field of politics this has been no less characteristic. Except in the Civil War the appeal has never been to general principles, but for concrete demands and the remedying of specific grievances. Magna Carta is a jumble of such specific claims. If it embodied the principle of the reign of law it did so negatively by denouncing the arbitrary violation of it which marked King John's exercise of power. Our legislation, like our roads and old country houses, has been a continuous patch-work embodying the alterations required by immediate needs and rarely carried beyond them. We have, on the whole, bene-fited. The principle which may seem to justify a particular measure, may be entirely unsuited to general application. On the other hand the instinctive leaning on precedent, in one sense conservative, may also lend itself to rapid and indeed revolutionary change. Within a generation social measures like old age pensions and insurance, avowedly introduced on a small scale as a supplement to and encouragement of indi-vidual thrift, have blossomed into the quite different practice and conception of the Welfare State.

To appreciate the historic evolution of our system of Govern-ment it is essential to remember that, save for the one revo-lutionary period already referred to, there has never been a complete break in its continuity. It is still in a sense true, as Hearn states in his *Government of England*, that ours is 'the very constitution under which the Confessor ruled and which William swore to obey'. It has, at any rate, through all the changes in its working, retained certain main features and been inspired by certain vital principles which have remained con-stant, and which have continued to assert or reassert themselves according to circumstances. It is not so much flexible as elastic, tending to revert to form as the material or ideological influences which have deflected it in one direction or another have weakened or been superseded. It is to these main and vital features that I wish to draw attention, because they may not only help to explain some of the changes of recent years, but also afford some guidance as to the nature of the even greater changes which may follow the political and economic development of the years immediately ahead of us.

There are, as Dicey points out in *The Law of the Constitution*, two main features from which all our constitutional development has proceeded. The one is 'the Rule or Supremacy of Law' and the other 'the omnipotence or undisputed supremacy throughout the whole country of the central Government'. The former feature was one deep-seated not only in Saxon, but in all mediaeval thinking, until superseded elsewhere by the influence of Roman Law. The latter owes everything to the insight and masterful personality of William the Conqueror. With a clean slate to write upon he took care so to distribute the spoils of conquest among his followers as to prevent the building up of large territorial fiefs which might in course of time dispute the royal supremacy. In this way he laid the foundation of a strong centralized government which had no parallel in mediaeval Europe. In the long run, indeed, the clear gap thus created between the King and his subjects, great or small, tended to draw the latter together in resistance to arbitrary royal power and in defence of the recognized law and custom of the land. The barons and citizens who met together at Runnymede represent the obverse of William's policy when the royal power he created fell into tyrannous but weaker hands. At the same time William utilized the existing Saxon shire as a means of by-passing feudal authority through his sheriff, who, sitting in its court of freeholders as the King's representative and at the same time bringing the King's government in touch with local needs, foreshadowed the centralized parley between the Crown and the Commons or 'communities' of later days.

From William's day onwards the key to our constitutional evolution is to be found in the interaction between the Crown, i.e. the central governing, directing, and initiating element in the national life, and the nation in its various 'estates', i.e. classes and communities, as the guardian of its written and unwritten laws and customs. The ambitions or needs of the Crown continually demanded changes in the law which the nation was only prepared to accept after discussion or parley with its representatives and on terms. Out of that parley, progressively

more continuous and more intimate as needs increased, and
out of those terms grew our system, as we know it, of Government in and with Parliament, subject to the ever increasing
influence of public opinion and to periodic review by the
nation as a whole.

The story of that evolution is so familiar that I need only
touch on a few of its most salient features. The financial needs
of the Crown long furnished the main lever by which Parliament increased its power. At the same time, the provision of
actual money freed the Crown from dependence on feudal
services and reinforced its effectively centralized authority.
The same process of discussion and bargaining led to other
changes or restatements of the law—at first suggested to the
Crown by way of petitions, but from the fifteenth century
onwards embodied in detailed Bills. These, whether initiated
by or on behalf of the Crown or by Parliament itself, were then
in their final form submitted to the King for his personal
approval. No less important was the development by which the
occasional parliamentary disapproval of the executive action of
individual servants of the Crown, expressed in impeachment or
attainder, grew into that milder but constant day-by-day
questioning and criticism of Ministers with which we are
familiar. Out of that development, helped by the doctrine that
the King can do no wrong, sprang that division between the
personal and the official powers of the Crown which is one of the
most characteristic features of our Constitution. Of this I shall
have something to say presently.

But to continue the main thread of my story. The Restoration
of 1660 was, as I have already said, a true restoration of our
national approach to the problem of government. It accepted
both the Monarchy as the indispensable directing and initiating element in the national life, and Parliament as representing the no less indispensable element of national assent. It
also unhesitatingly dropped into limbo, for good and all, those
ideas of a formal written constitution which had figured so
prominently, and proved so ineffective, in the troubled years
over which we were resolved to wipe the slate. At the same
time, it was much more than a mere restoration. Taken together

with the Bill of Rights of 1689 and the Act of Settlement of 1700 it set the course of the development of our constitutional system for the future. The theory of Divine Right and Prerogative was superseded by that of Constitutional Monarchy and of the Prerogative as a defined branch of that Common Law, which was now definitely accepted as governing the whole constitution and not merely the mutual rights of subjects. The control of Parliament over the granting of revenue became complete. Meanwhile other elements of the future system of government began to emerge. Departmental Ministers were found more useful by the Crown than a large and amorphous Privy Council, no longer itself a potential rival to Parliament as a partner in the sphere of government, and the happy repeal of a clause in the Act of Settlement which forbad their sitting in the House of Commons paved the way to the eventual interlocking of Government and Parliament.

For most of the eighteenth century the fluctuating balance between the Crown and Parliament was maintained by personal management, first by the great Whig lords through their hold over the grossly over-represented boroughs and with non-conformist support, later by George III's placemen. This was the system glorified by Montesquieu, followed by Blackstone[1] as based on the clear separation and equipoise of the different powers in the State. Contrasting the English give and take between equal political forces and the independence of our judges—the natural and logical consequences of the reign of law—with the rigid centralization of all powers in the French monarchy, Montesquieu rightly emphasized the true secret of English freedom. But in doing so he tended to ignore the extent to which the separate powers were increasingly interlocking in Parliament itself. Where he went more seriously astray was in treating the division as one between the executive and legislative functions, abstractions bearing no relation to the reality of our political life. Parliament is not, and never has been, a legislature, in the sense of a body specially and primarily empowered to make laws. The function of legislation, while shared

---

[1]"Herein consists the true excellence of the English government that all the parts of it form a natural check upon each other."

between 'King, Lords and Commons in Parliament assembled', has always been predominantly exercised by Government which, indeed, has never allowed Parliament, as such, to take any initiative in one of its most important fields, that of finance. The main task of Parliament is still what it was when first summoned, not to legislate or govern, but to secure full discussion and ventilation of all matters, legislative or administrative, as the condition of giving its assent to Bills, whether introduced by the Government or by private Members, or its support to the executive action of Ministers. But Montesquieu's error was destined to exercise no small influence on the shaping of the American Constitution, and even to affect our own thinking about the function of Parliament, and still more that of other nations which have followed the outward forms of the British parliamentary system.

It was not, however, until discontent with royal corruption and resentment at the loss of the American colonies stirred men's minds to the need for constitutional improvement, that the informal business of the individual management of members of Parliament finally gave way to the conception of a government with some basis of political principle to support it. Burke's definition of Party as 'a body of men united for promoting by their joint endeavours the national interest upon some particular principle upon which they are all agreed', expressed a felt want. The existing Whig and Tory factions with their established clientele in the country furnished the natural working nucleus, and their old traditions, brought up to date by such critical issues as India and the French Revolution, provided a no less natural division of principle. The younger Pitt's Ministry of 1784 is generally regarded as marking the definite inauguration of our government by a Party Ministry able to guarantee a parliamentary majority for the business of the Crown, without recourse to the old methods of personal influence or corruption.

The Cabinet system itself had meanwhile been steadily developing. I need not go in detail into the well-known story, whether strictly correct or apocryphal, of the origins of the Cabinet as the outcome, in part, of Harley's informal Saturday dinners and, in part, of George I's reluctance to attend ministerial councils at which, as he knew no English and his Ministers no German, discussion had to be confined to such Latin as they could muster between them. The essential point is that the growth of the system of collective responsibility, based on previous private discussion, strengthened the hands of the Ministry, not only as against the monarch, but also as against Parliament. To single out an individual for dismissal or denunciation is far easier than to denounce or urge the dismissal of a team, especially if the only alternative is another and even less welcome team. All this naturally became more effective after 1784.

What is essential to keep in mind is that the new system of Responsible Parliamentary Government, while in one sense subordinating the policy of the Crown to Party exigencies, yet in another, meant an accession to the actual power of Government, as such, in exercising control over Parliament. It meant converting the leading poachers into the Crown's gamekeepers. It meant converting the majority in Parliament into placemen, within at least the penumbra of office and influence, while at the same time under constant threat of losing their places (and nowadays their members' salaries) if their lack of support to the Government should cause the latter to dissolve Parliament.

At the same time neither Ministers nor their supporters have, in their individual capacity, ceased to remain representatives of the nation or of their individual constituencies. Nor have they entirely abandoned to the Opposition the original critical and debating function of Parliament. Subject to the varying strength of party discipline, government supporters can still criticize this or that feature of the Government's legislation or administration in public—and even more freely behind the scenes to the Whips or at Party meetings in committee rooms. So, too, Ministers feel a kinship with other members, with whom they share the responsibilities and problems with which they have to deal in their constituencies. What is more, they hope, even if they lose office, to remain in Parliament and so continue to exercise their influence over affairs pending their return to power. They are parliamentarians first and for the greater part of their public life; Ministers of the Crown at intervals. It is as parliamentarians that they are first tested and judged, both for ability and for character, by their seniors and their fellows; that they win and then keep or lose their right to office. Above all, whether Ministers or back-benchers, in office or in opposition, they are all subject to the firm and impartial control of Mr. Speaker, as the embodiment of the traditions of Parliament and of the rights of its humblest Member. All these factors have combined to keep Parliament as the centre and focus of the nation's affairs, the conspicuous stage on which the great drama is acted, the great game of politics played. It is their interlocking and interchangeability which have maintained the unity and harmony of our political life, and it is in that sense that we rightly boast of our system as one of parliamentary government.

All the same, throughout the evolution of that system, the two main elements of our political life have remained distinct, though progressively harmonized and integrated. Our constitution is still, at bottom, based on a continuous parley or conference in Parliament between Crown, i.e. the Government, as the directing and energizing element, and the representatives of the nation whose assent and acquiescence are essential, and are only to be secured by full discussion. The whole life of British politics to quote Bagehot, 'is the action and reaction between the Ministry and the Parliament'. One might almost say today 'between the Ministry and the Opposition', for it is the latter upon which has devolved most of the original critical function of Parliament.

There was much else that needed reforming at the end of the eighteenth century besides parliamentary corruption. But the great issues raised by the French Revolution overshadowed such less urgent questions as the franchise, the redistribution of seats and economic policy, to which Pitt would have wished to devote himself. By the time they could be dealt with the national outlook, at any rate in the Whig (and afterwards Liberal) camp, had not escaped the influence of the abstract ideology of revolutionary France. The Reform Bill of 1832 did not, in its immediate effect, go outside the old constitutional basis of a parliamentary representation of communities as such. It swept away boroughs that had lost all national significance in order to enfranchise the new active centres of industrial life. But it did so avowedly on the assumption that it was dealing with parliamentary representation on a general principle. Even more revolutionary was the claim, implicit in the title of the Act, that it was 'to amend the representation of the people'. Once these two conceptions of 'the people', i.e. of individuals entitled as such to a share of political power, and of representation on the basis of some general principle, held the field, there could be no stopping at the property qualifications of 1832. The universal adult suffrage and numerical constituencies of today followed inevitably, each step affording a precedent for the next, from the new doctrines which influenced the Whig reform of 1832.

The new outlook was not confined to the problem of the franchise. It increasingly coloured the whole conception of government in that Liberal individualist school whose writers dominated political thinking in the last century and still largely dominate it today, and led to a fundamental misreading of the essential nature of our constitution. Writers like Bagehot, interpreting the parliamentary situation of their own time in the light of their general prepossessions, persuaded themselves that our constitution had, in fact, become what they thought it ought to be, namely, a system based on the delegation of authority by the electorate to a Parliament which, in its turn, delegated the day-by-day exercise of that power to a Cabinet which was, in substance, only a committee—to use Bagehot's phrase—of the parliamentary majority. That reinterpretation, though queried by eminent authorities like Seeley and Lowell, and contested fundamentally by so thoughtful a constitutionalist as Hearn, became the prevalent text-book theory, and still colours most current journalistic and political phraseology.[1]

[1]How little real importance the writers of that period assigned to the part played by the Crown, as embodied officially in the Cabinet, is indicated by the fact that not one of the eighteen chapters of Mill's *Representative Government* is devoted to the functions of the Cabinet. So stalwart a survivor of mid-Victorian Liberalism as my old chief Lord Courtney of Penwith, in his *Working Constitution*

There was, indeed, much in the external circumstances of the time to encourage that assumption. The mutual interlocking of Government and Parliament had by then been fully achieved. The laissez-faire theories of the age in economic matters, and the absence of any serious external menace since Trafalgar and Waterloo, had reduced the active work both of administration and of legislation to a minimum. A few broad issues of general policy could be spread over prolonged and eloquent debates. Parliamentary debate as such dominated the attention of the public and created the great parliamentary figures of that day. In the comparatively evenly balanced and less strictly disciplined Parliament of the time, with both Parties and the Electorate itself drawn from a limited social stratum, it was not unnatural to conclude that Parliament, which so frequently upset Government, was, in fact, the body which governed and did so in response to the positive wishes of an actively interested electorate.

What was not foreseen by the Liberal theorists of those days was that the progressive extension of the franchise, on the one hand, and the continuous increase in the volume of government work, on the other, would, by leading to stronger party organization in the country and to stricter Party discipline in Parliament, reinforce the inherent tendency in our system for government, as such, to reassert itself whenever the opportunity or the need might arise. As for the fears of Conservative critics, whatever dangers or disadvantages may, or may not, have resulted from the spread of democracy in this country, the weakening of government has not been one of them. The strength of the innate tendency of our governmental tradition has been sufficient to overcome the danger which Burke foresaw in democracy, as preached by the individualist school, when he wrote:

---

of the United Kingdom, writing as late as 1901, could still dismiss the Cabinet in five pages out of nearly 200 devoted to Parliament, and could speak of the 'absolutely unqualified supremacy of Parliament' as 'embodying the supreme will of the State to which every partial authority must yield'. In this respect the Socialist Party has inherited many of the theoretical misconceptions of its Liberal precursors, and the late Mr. Laski and Mr. Herbert Morrison have both referred to the Executive as a 'Committee of the Legislature'.

D

"No legislator has willingly placed the seat of active
power in the hands of the multitude; because then it admits
of no control, no regulation, no steady direction whatever.
The people are the natural control on authority; but to
exercise and to control together is contradictory and
impossible."

In that respect our constitution has throughout conformed
to that principle of balance between initiative and control
which Burke laid down. It has never been one in which the
active and originating element has been the voter, selecting a
delegate to express his views—to carry out his mandate—in
Parliament as well as, on his behalf, to select an administration conforming to those views and subject to that mandate.
The starting-point and mainspring of action has always been
the Government. It is the Government which, in the name of
the Crown, makes appointments and confers honours without
consulting Parliament. It is the Government, in the name of the
Crown, which summons Parliament. It is the Government
which settles the programme of parliamentary business and
directs and drives Parliament in order to secure that programme.
If Parliament fails to give sufficient support it is the Government, or an alternative Government, which, in the name of
the Crown, dissolves Parliament.

At a general election the voter is not in a position to choose
either the kind of representative or the kind of government he
would like if he had a free choice. There is a Government in
being which he can confirm or else reject in favour of an alternative team. The candidates before him—the only candidates
worth taking seriously—are either supporters of the team in
office or of its rivals for office. It is within those narrow limits
that his actual power is exercised. He may be influenced by
the personality of the candidates, still more by that of the
leaders of the parties, by a Government's record or by its
opponents' promises, by sheer Party loyalty or light-hearted
desire for a change. No doubt, too, he has had his continuous
share in the making of that public opinion which helps to shape
Parties and influence governments. But by the time it comes to

an actual decision his function is the limited and essentially passive one of accepting one of two alternatives put before him.

Our whole political life, in fact, turns round the issue of government. The two-party system is often referred to as if it were the happy result of an accidental historical development, or as the consequence of a natural division between two types of mind. Both statements contain a substantial element of truth. But the decisive and continuous influence has been the fact that a governing team with a majority in Parliament can normally only be displaced by another team capable of securing an alternative majority. Parties which are not in a position to make their own government may, like the Labour Party in the early years of the century, represent the intrusion of a new school of political thought, content to make its voice heard and its influence felt, pending the day when they can take office for themselves. Or, like the Liberal Party today, they may be survivals of a past political alignment, not yet despairing of resuscitation or at least of influence as a balancing factor. But they are essentially transition phenomena. The two-party system is the natural concomitant of a political tradition in which government, as such, is the first consideration, and in which the views and preferences of voters or of members of Parliament are continuously limited to the simple alternative of 'for' or 'against'. It is indeed, only under the conditions created by such a tradition that there can be any stability in a Government dependent from day to day on the support of a majority in Parliament.

It is precisely on that issue that the nineteenth century Liberal exponents of our constitutional system so grievously misled the outside world. They created the belief that it was possible successfully to combine the British form of constitution with the prevalent continental conception, derived from the French Revolution, of political power as a delegation from the individual citizen through the legislature to an executive dependent on that legislature. That conception naturally involves the widest freedom in the citizen's choice of Party regarded as the end in itself. In many countries it has led to the almost indefinite multiplication of Parties. Another consequence has been the adoption of systems of proportional representation based on Party lists, in order to secure for the individual voter or individual Party their fair share of the composition of the legislature. It equally implies the right of the legislature to the initiative in all respects, including finance, and the denial to the Government of the power of dissolution. All these logical deductions were, indeed, asserted as self-evident consequences of popular and parliamentary sovereignty by the great majority of those who were engaged in drafting the new French Constitution.

Such a system of government, not in and with Parliament, but by Parliament, is bound, by its very nature, to be weak and unstable, subject to the continual shifting and reshuffling of coalition ministries and to the influence of personal ambitions. Face to face with the growing need of the age for more governmental action and more definite leadership, it has almost everywhere broken down. The rise of dictatorships and of one-party governments has been the almost inevitable consequence of the ineffectiveness of constitutions which reproduced the outward form of the British Constitution without the spirit of strong and stable government which is of its essence.

Democratic government based, in principle, at least on delegation from below can, no doubt, be made to work. But in order to do so, the Government, however chosen, must enjoy a real measure of independence and for a reasonably long period. The United States affords one example. An even better example is Switzerland, where the executive is directly elected by the legislature and reflects its composition, but, once elected, remains independent for the lifetime of the legislature. What cannot work, as Mill[1] himself admitted, and as Cromwell decided somewhat more forcibly before him, is government by an elected assembly or subject to continual direction and inter-

[1]"Instead of the function of governing, for which it is radically unfit, the proper office of a representative assembly is to watch and control the Government. . . . To be at once the nation's Committee of Grievances and its Congress of Opinions. . . . Nothing but the restriction of the function of representative bodies within these rational limits, will enable the benefits of popular control to be enjoyed in conjunction with the no less important requisites (growing ever more important as human affairs increase in scale and complexity) of skilled legislation and administration." J. S. Mill, *Representative Government*.

ference by such an assembly. In any case that is not the kind of government under which we live ourselves. Our system is one of democracy, but of democracy by consent and not by delegation, of government of the people, for the people, with, but not by, the people.

In our own system there is, indeed, a real danger in the ever increasing efficiency and rigidity of the Party machines. The Party tends to be regarded as an end in itself. Those who control the machinery are only too apt to look upon themselves as the real framers and arbiters of policy and upon Ministers as mere nominees appointed to push that policy through the routine processes of Parliament with the minimum of time wasted on unnecessary discussion. The danger of thus by-passing and overriding Parliament arises, not so much from Party organization in itself, as from the same misconceptions as to the nature of our system of government and as to the meaning of majority rule which have wrecked the imitations of our Constitution in other countries. The first of these misconceptions is that our system of government is based on the initiative of the voter and on delegation from below. If that really were the case, then it would always be open to argue that the voter's Party organization embodies his definite and final conclusions, his 'mandate' on all subjects and is, in fact, entitled on his behalf to prescribe the policy of the Government which he has created. Once that argument is accepted the Party Executive becomes the master and not the servant of the Government. Parliament becomes a mere instrument for registering its decrees. The personal character and quality of members no longer matters—debates lose all real significance. Policy is shaped, not in the light of full and free discussion, nor even in that contact with realities and with that sense of national responsibility and continuity which influences a Cabinet, but by an irresponsible partisan caucus, thinking only in terms of Party aims or Party interests. The danger of irresponsible power is even greater when an outside body, like the Trade Union Congress, primarily existing for industrial purposes, attempts to use its influence in Party organization and finance in order to direct the general policy of a government.

The second and kindred misconception concerns the meaning of majority decision and majority rule. Decision by majority is not an absolute and unquestionable principle. Our constitution, to use Burke's phrase, 'is something more than a problem in arithmetic'. There is no divine right of a mere numerical majority, of $\frac{x}{2}$ plus 1, any more than of kings. Majority decision is a measure of convenience essential to the dispatch of business, 'the result', to quote Burke again, 'of a very particular and special convention, confirmed by long habits of obedience'. Thanks to that convention Government is carried on with the acquiescence of the minority. When it comes to legislation it is of the very essence of our conception of the reign of law that it should not be regarded as a mere emanation of the will of the Government, but as something accepted by the nation as a whole. The independence of the judiciary loses all meaning if any judicial decision unpleasing to the Party leaders can at once be reversed by fresh and even retrospective legislation, or if an almost unlimited and unquestionable power of supplementary legislation is delegated to Ministers and their subordinates by Parliament. That requisite of consent for changing the law, or at least of acceptance when changed, is the root from which sprang our whole parliamentary system with its representation of the various interests and elements in the national life and with its elaborate provisions for full discussion. The idea that a majority, just because it is a majority, is entitled to pass, without full discussion, what legislation it pleases, regardless of the extent of the changes involved or of the intensity of the opposition to them—the idea, in fact that majority edicts are the same things as laws—is wholly alien to the spirit of the constitution.

It is not unnatural, perhaps, that this doctrine of the unqualified right of a party majority, and the concomitant theory of ultimate control by a Party Executive, should in the past have exercised so strong a hold over the Socialist Party. Unlike the older historic Parties it originated outside Parliament, more concerned for many years with organization in the country and with dissemination of its principles than with the tasks of government which indeed, it has tended to conceive as primarily, if not exclusively, concerned with translating those principles into legislation. The Party Executive was in its case anterior to any Cabinet or 'Shadow Cabinet' and still maintains its separate existence and authority. In Australia, indeed, Labour Party Executives have insisted on settling in detail both appointments to, and distribution of, offices in the Cabinet and have even gone to the length of demanding from Ministers signed, but undated, resignations enabling them to be recalled at any moment.

Even here, as recently as 1933, Sir Stafford Cripps and his co-authors in *Problems of a Socialist Government* could advance the view that 'the Party' should appoint the Ministry subject to 'the right at any time to substitute fresh Ministers in the place of any it desires to recall'. Going even further, they proposed that an Emergency Powers Bill should be passed through all its stages on the first day of the session, to be followed by an Annual Planning and Finance Bill which would 'take the place of the King's Speech, the Budget, financial resolutions and the second reading debate on most of the important measures of the year. . . . It is idle once Parliament (*sic*) has decided upon a certain course of action, to discuss its wisdom again and again.' Freed from attendance at superfluous debates the Socialist Members of Parliament were to be liberated as Commissioners to see that 'the will of the Central Government is obeyed'. Mr. Attlee in setting forth the duties of the Commissioners frankly accepted the comparison with the Soviet Commissars. 'We have to take the strong points of the Russian system and apply them to this country.' This would indeed, in Sir Stafford's words, have meant 'a complete severance with all traditional theories of government'.

Happily, the passage of years, partnership in the conduct of a great war, and since then the full responsibility of office would seem to have toned down these vagaries. The late Prime Minister and his Cabinet came into office in accordance with ordinary constitutional practice. They pushed through their legislation expeditiously—some may think too expeditiously— but certainly on normal constitutional lines. There was no violent breach of continuity in the great departments of State.

Socialist Party Conferences have been marked by a domination of the debates by Ministers and a deference by delegates
very much in accord with the tone of similar gatherings of
the older parties. The traditions of our constitution, like those
of our parliamentary life, are, indeed, strong and pervasive, and
tend to imprint their mould on even the most revolutionary
elements. But it would be unwise to disregard the danger to
the constitution when widespread misconceptions of its character
and spirit combine with the eager desire to reconstruct our whole
social and economic life in the minimum of time through the
machinery of an overworked and congested House of Commons.

From this general sketch of the evolution of our parliamentary system let me turn to the position and function of the
main elements of what is still government 'by the King in
Parliament'. The essential point to keep in mind is that in this
evolution the Crown as an institution, in other words the
element of government and direction, has maintained and,
indeed, enormously increased the sum total of its power and
influence. The Monarchy itself, divorced from arbitrary
personal power, has become increasingly the symbol of the
unity and continuity of our national and Imperial life. But that
conception has not been without its profound psychological
influence on the position of the Crown in its official capacity,
both in the sense of responsibility which it infuses into Ministers
and in the instinctive tendency of the nation to acquiesce loyally
in their decisions, however open to criticism. That Ministers
are His Majesty's servants does mean something both to themselves and to the public, however well known it may be that
they, in fact, receive no orders from the Monarch in person,
and that his power of dissenting from their conclusions on public
affairs has shrunk by usage and sufferance to the narrowest of
spheres. It is, indeed, customary to speak of that power as if it
were limited in these days to a very occasional option in the
choice of a Prime Minister among more or less equally eligible
candidates. Of that I shall have something to say presently.

Meanwhile it is enough to say that in the present century
the Monarch has carefully refrained from any such measure of
intervention in matters of policy or display of political partner-

ship or of personal objection to appointments as Queen Victoria frequently exercised. But, within the limits of a strict impartiality, the King has more than once in recent years played a mediating part in a political crisis, as for instance in connection with the Parliament Act of 1911, over Home Rule in 1914, and again in the financial crisis of 1931. It is believed, too, that the King's right to encourage as well as to warn was not without its influence on the settlement of the Irish question in 1921.

In any case there is no absolute definition of the limits of that authority which can hold good for all time or for all circumstances. In the Dominions that authority, by usage somewhat wider than here, has in our time ceased to be exercised with reference to advice from a Secretary of State in London, and is exercised solely on the personal judgment and discretion of the Governor-General, or Governor, in his ultimate responsibility to the nation or State concerned. This was clearly established by Lord Byng's refusal in 1926 to consult me, as Dominions Secretary, when he decided to reject Mr. Mackenzie King's demand for a dissolution on the ground that the Leader of the Opposition in the Canadian House of Commons, Mr. Meighen, was able to carry on without one. In 1926 when an issue affecting the Governor's powers arose between Sir Dudley de Chair, then Governor of New South Wales, and the State Premier, Mr. Lang, the latter sent over his Attorney-General, Mr. McTiernan, in order to secure from me either assent to the principle that a Governor must always subscribe to his Minister's wishes or at least some definition of the limits of his rights to differ. With neither of these requests was I prepared to comply, basing myself on my statement in Parliament on 15th March 1926 that 'it would not be proper for the Secretary of State to issue instructions to the Governor with regard to the exercise of his constitutional duties'. Sir Philip Game, subsequently, in 1932, dismissed Mr. Lang, basing his action on the latter's illegal conduct in instructing State officials to prevent payments being made under Commonwealth legislation whose validity had been upheld by the High Court. The result of the subsequent election confirmed the Governor's decision.

A much discussed question has been that of the extent of the Crown's discretion in granting, refusing or insisting upon a dissolution. In 1916 Mr. Holman, Premier of New South Wales, proposed to retain office with the support of the Opposition after the defection of the majority of his own party. The Governor, Sir Gerald Strickland, wished to insist upon a dissolution, but was overruled by the Colonial Office on the ground that the utility of Parliament was still unexhausted. The same argument, in substance, was put forward in the strongest terms by Mr. Asquith in 1924:

"The Crown is not bound to take the advice of a particular ministry to put its subjects to the tumult and turmoil of a series of general elections so long as it can find other ministers who are prepared to give contrary advice. The doctrine that a Minister who cannot command a majority in the House of Commons . . . is invested with the right to demand a dissolution is as subversive of constitutional usage as it would be pernicious to the paramount interests of the nation at large."

Mr. Asquith, indeed, seems to have hoped, by putting the Socialist Party in office, to create a situation in which the Conservatives might be willing to support a Liberal Government when Mr. MacDonald got into difficulties. That situation did not arise, and there was no question of the King's refusing a dissolution to Mr. MacDonald when he was defeated in the House. In the case of Lord Byng's refusal to grant a dissolution to Mr. Mackenzie King in 1926, the slender majority on the strength of which Mr. Meighen accepted office proved unreliable, and the subsequent election would seem to have been an endorsement of Mr. Mackenzie King's claim. A more conclusive precedent was afforded in 1939 by Sir Patrick Duncan, as Governor-General of South Africa, when he refused General Hertzog's request for a dissolution on the ground that General Smuts was able to show that he had a workable majority prepared to support his policy over the war.

Still less capable of definition, of course, is the scope of the personal influence of one who not only enjoys the natural prestige of his position as sovereign, but may have the advantage of an even longer experience of the inside of government than his Ministers, and who is entitled to seek advice in every quarter, even if there is only one source of advice which he is formally bound to follow. It has, indeed, been suggested that the whole course of our constitutional evolution might have been modified if Queen Victoria had continued to enjoy for another generation the support of so able and far-seeing a private counsellor as the Prince Consort.

To return to the main thread of my argument. The essential thing to keep in mind, from the constitutional point of view, is that the monarch's personal power has never been abrogated or its precise limits defined. Circumstances might conceivably arise in which it might on some particular issue be reasserted with national approval. As to that it can only be said with Aristotle

$$\text{'εν τῇ αἰσθήσει ἡ κείσις}$$

The question can only be decided in the light of all the circumstances of the time, and the verdict of the nation alone will settle whether such an assertion of the royal authority will have been constitutional or not. To quote Sir David Keir's conclusion in his *Constitutional History of Modern Britain*, page 491:

> "The King's prerogative, however circumscribed by conventions, must always retain its historic character as a residue of discretionary authority to be employed for the public good. It is the last resource provided by the Constitution to guarantee its own working."

The Cabinet, to whose origins I have already referred, is the central directing instrument of government, in legislation as well as in administration. It is in Cabinet that administrative action is co-ordinated and that legislative proposals are sanctioned. It is the Cabinet which controls Parliament and governs the country. In no other country is there such a concentration of power and such a capacity for decisive action as that possessed by a British Cabinet, provided always that it enjoys the support of a majority in the House of Commons.

The essence of our Cabinet system is the collective responsibility of its members. All major decisions of policy are, or are supposed to be, those of the Cabinet as a whole. They are supported by speech and vote by all its Members, and, indeed, by all the Members of the Government in the wider sense of the word. The rejection or condemnation by Parliament of the action taken upon them affects the Cabinet, as a whole, and is followed, if the issue is one of sufficient importance, by its resignation. The secrecy of Cabinet proceedings, originally based on the Privy Counsellor's oath and antecedent to collective responsibility, is in any case the natural correlative of that collective responsibility. It would obviously be impossible for Ministers to make an effective defence in public of decisions with which it was known that they had disagreed in the course of Cabinet discussion. There is no other mystery about it.

The collective responsibility of Ministers in no way derogates from their individual responsibility. If the two conflict a Minister may always resign or be requested to resign. In 1917 Sir Austen Chamberlain, as Secretary of State for India, resigned after the report of a judicial inquiry into the conduct of the Mesopotamian campaign for which he was technically responsible. In 1922 Mr. Montagu had to resign for publishing, without consulting the Cabinet, a telegram from the Government of India pressing for a revision of the Sèvres Treaty with Turkey. In 1935 Sir Samuel Hoare (Lord Templewood) resigned when the Cabinet threw over the Hoare-Laval compromise over Abyssinia. In 1938 Mr. Eden resigned in order to dissociate himself from the policy of conciliating Mussolini which Mr. Chamberlain was pursuing. The point has derived added importance since the innovation of War Cabinets excluding the holders of many of the most important offices. The responsibility of Ministers of 'Cabinet rank' for the general policy of the Government may have been reduced, but their responsibility for decisions relating to their own department is not affected or superseded by any overriding responsibility on the part of the actual Cabinet.

The Cabinet normally consists of Members of the same Party, relying on the support of a disciplined majority in the

House of Commons. This is the natural concomitant of our system of organized, and in a sense forensic, debates in Parliament and in the country on behalf of or against one or other of two alternative governments. But in times of national emergency only a Coalition Ministry can concentrate the mind, as well as the individual ability, of Parliament on the common task. So long as the emergency dominates everything such coalitions remain effective. They speedily acquire a corporate sense of mutual loyalty and good will, and such divisions as occur tend to be much more the outcome of differences of temperament and individual outlook than of Party affiliation. They may even afford incidental opportunity for far-reaching agreed reforms such as the franchise reforms and Mr. Fisher's Education Act of the Lloyd George War Cabinet or Mr. Butler's recent Education Act and that whole recasting of our social security system, usually associated with the name of Lord Beveridge, which was framed and partly carried out under Mr. Churchill.

On the other hand, outside the immediate action required to deal with a supreme emergency, they lack the underlying unity of outlook and identity of instinctive reaction of a Party Cabinet and are even more prone to hand-to-mouth decisions based on no consistent policy. On issues where there is a fundamental divergence there is a tendency to evade discussion or, if postponement is impossible, to find weak compromises defended on grounds which shirk the real issue of policy.

Nothing could more effectively illustrate the unreality of the mid-Victorian theory of our constitution than a comparison of Bagehot's definition of the Cabinet as a committee of Parliament, or rather of the majority in Parliament, with the actual process by which Cabinets come into being and are, in fact, constituted. A committee usually implies definite appointment in detail by the parent body. Nothing of the sort takes place in the creation of a British Cabinet. The starting point is the selection by the Monarch of a Prime Minister. The Monarch's choice, like that of the voter, may in most cases be very limited. If the majority Party has a recognized leader, that is the obvious person to send for. Still there may be occasions when the Monarch's personal judgment can be exercised as between possible alternatives. The most recent case quoted by the text-books is that of Queen Victoria's selection of Lord Rosebery instead of Sir William Harcourt, whom the House of Commons would have preferred, or of Lord Spencer, whom Mr. Gladstone would have recommended, if asked, in 1894.

There are, however, later instances. King George V's decision in 1923 to send for Mr. Baldwin instead of Lord Curzon (Mr. Bonar Law declining to make any recommendation) is often referred to as having been the natural consequence of the latter's being in the House of Lords and so under modern conditions disqualified. As a matter of fact Lord Curzon's appointment was practically settled when two junior Members of the Cabinet, the late Lord Bridgeman and myself, intervened with Lord Stamfordham and urged reconsideration in favour of Mr. Baldwin, as likely to be more acceptable to his colleagues and to the rank and file of the Party. Lord Balfour, who was called up from the country, agreed and suggested Lord Curzon's peerage as a sound reason for passing him over. The final decision was, to the best of my belief, made mainly on the issue of the personal acceptability of the two candidates. If a constitutional precedent was created, it was largely as the *ex post facto* cover for a decision taken on other grounds. Again, when Mr. MacDonald resigned in 1931 it was the King's personal appeal to him and to the Opposition leaders that kept him in office as the head of a coalition, and that weighed with Mr. Baldwin in not pressing his natural claim to be invited to form a government.

Far wider is the field of choice open to a newly appointed Prime Minister. No doubt he has to consider the claims and views of leading Members of his Party in both Houses. But, subject to Parliament putting up with his selection of his colleagues and his arrangement of offices, he has a very free hand in shaping his government according to his own view of what is likely to work best and according to his personal preferences. It is for him to decide on the size of the Cabinet and what Ministers to include in it. He may consult a few leading colleagues or the Chief Whip or his personal cronies. In 1929

Mr. MacDonald settled his chief appointments in consultation with Messrs. Snowden, Clynes, Henderson and Thomas. What formal or informal consultations may have taken place in the formation of the late Cabinet is not within my knowledge. In the case of the present Cabinet Mr. Churchill summoned to his country house the individuals whom he thought most useful, and told them what he wanted them to do, and that was that. Hitherto, in this country, at any rate, the Prime Minister has never been under any sort of direct dictation either from Parliament or from a Party Executive outside in making up his government. He may go outside the Party ranks, or even outside Parliament, to choose someone whom he may think specially fitted for a particular post. Thus in 1903 Mr. Balfour offered the Colonial Office to Lord Milner, who was then still High Commissioner in South Africa and had never played any part in parliamentary life. In 1923 Mr. Baldwin offered the Chancellorship of the Exchequer to Mr. McKenna, a Liberal ex-Cabinet Minister, who declined on grounds of health, while Mr. MacDonald in 1924 made Lord Chelmsford, a non-party ex-Viceroy, First Lord of the Admiralty. Even more remarkable in its disregard of his Party's views was Mr. Baldwin's appointment in that same year of Mr. Churchill to the Exchequer. At that time, Mr. Churchill was almost the last person to whom Conservatives would have dreamt of entrusting that key position, not only because he had until only quite recently been a political opponent, but because he was known still to be vehemently opposed to the main constructive policy of the Party. But the appointment was made and the Conservative Party in Parliament, though never quite reconciled to it, grumbled and submitted.

Few dictators, indeed, enjoy such a measure of autocratic power as is enjoyed by a British Prime Minister while in process of making up his Cabinet. In France, or in any other continental country, which has imitated the outward form, but not the essentials, of our constitution, newly appointed Prime Ministers have had to go round hat in hand to appeal for co-operation from political rivals, each determined to make his own bargain as to the particular office he might wish to hold or as to the

filling of other offices, and by no means sure that he might not
do better for himself by holding back and waiting for the next
ministerial reshuffle. With us there has been no instance of a
Prime Minister failing to form a government owing to the
irreconcilable claims or views of Party colleagues since Russell's
failure to form a government in 1845 because Grey would not
serve with Palmerston. It was, indeed, widely bruited about in
1905 that Sir Henry Campbell-Bannerman could not form a
workable government in face of the anticipated refusal of the
Liberal Imperialist Leaders, Asquith, Grey and Haldane, to
serve under him. But when it came to the point the strength of
the Prime Minister's position easily asserted itself and they
joined unconditionally. In 1916 Mr. Asquith resigned in the
confident but, as the event proved, mistaken belief that, except
for Mr. Bonar Law and Sir Edward Carson, no Conservative
or Liberal of any standing would be willing to serve under
Mr. Lloyd George.

A British Prime Minister may, no doubt, while forming his
Cabinet, be besieged by insistent candidates for this or that
office, but rarely is such a candidate prepared to reject the
Prime Minister's final allocation. Refusal may mean exclusion
from office, not merely for that Parliament, but for good and all.
In 1924 Sir Robert Horne, who had been a successful President
of the Board of Trade and Chancellor of the Exchequer,
refused the Ministry of Labour which Mr. Baldwin offered him.
He was never considered for office again. It is only exceptionally
forceful or fortunate political rogue elephants that, once extruded
from the governing herd, can find their way back into it, as both
Mr. Churchill and the present writer discovered for a decade
after 1929.

This power of the Prime Minister to appoint, reshuffle, or
dismiss his colleagues continues throughout his term of office.
It is, no doubt, mainly influenced by considerations of administrative or parliamentary success or failure. But it is a purely
personal authority and makes the Prime Minister something
very much more than a *primus inter pares* in the Cabinet. His
exact position must always depend in large measure upon his
own personality and that of his colleagues in the Cabinet, as

well as upon parliamentary and Party influence outside. But he is, in effect, both captain and man at the helm, enjoying, as undisputed working head of the State, a power far greater than that of the American President—so long as he does not actually forfeit the allegiance of naturally deferential and loyal colleagues in the Cabinet or of his followers in Parliament.

The fact that Parliament does not appoint, but accepts a Prime Minister and a Cabinet, is even more strikingly evident in time of war or acute crisis. Mr. Asquith's coalition Cabinet of 1915 resulted immediately from Lord Fisher's resignation as First Sea Lord and from consequent negotiations with the Conservative leaders. It may, however, be said to have conformed to a general desire on the part of the House of Commons that he should strengthen his government by including the leaders of the Opposition. But the Lloyd George War Cabinet at the end of 1916 was not one that could have emerged from any method of ascertaining the wishes of Parliament beforehand. Few Liberals and still fewer Conservatives would have actually chosen Mr. Lloyd George as Prime Minister. Nor was there any demand, outside a very small circle, for a drastic change in the structure and working of the Cabinet as such. The whole affair was, in effect, a Palace Revolution brought about by a handful of men in the inner circle of the Asquith Government who were convinced that the war could not be won under the existing leadership and by the existing methods.

Still more notable, in that respect, was the formation of the MacDonald-Baldwin-Samuel Coalition of 1931. It is doubtful whether a Gallup poll taken in advance in favour of that particular solution would have secured even ten per cent support from either Socialists or Conservatives in Parliament. The bulk of the Socialist Party indeed broke away as soon as it was formed, and the Conservatives only acquiesced on the most explicit assurances given by Mr. Baldwin to a Party meeting that the emergency arrangement would be terminated the moment a balanced budget had been passed. By then, however, Ministers had begun to feel at home in their offices and to persuade themselves that the economic emergency still called for a 'National Government'. Unable to agree upon any policy to

E

meet the emergency, they appealed to the country for a 'doctor's mandate'. The public, impressed by the vigour of the effort to balance the budget, and persuaded by the consensus of political and non-political 'expert' authority of the imminent danger of inflation and soaring prices, gave by its vote a majority in Parliament of ten to one, not so much for the Coalition, as against the unhappy and bewildered rump of the Socialist Party. The subsequent necessity of having some sort of positive economic policy was met, for several months, by the fantastic expedient of certain Ministers dissociating themselves from the collective responsibility of the Cabinet and voting against its measures, and by their resignation after the Ottawa agreements.

The change of government in 1940 was, indeed, the direct result of a parliamentary demonstration of dissatisfaction with Mr. Neville Chamberlain's war leadership. How the succession was arranged has been told most dramatically by Mr. Churchill himself.[1] The matter was settled in a few minutes across the table between Mr. Neville Chamberlain, Lord Halifax and Mr. Churchill. No one can doubt that the advice then given by Mr. Chamberlain to the King to send for Mr. Churchill was the right one. All the same, if the matter had been left to a parliamentary vote, a majority vote both of Conservatives and of Socialists would have favoured Lord Halifax.

I have purposely dealt at some length on these particular instances in order to make it clear that, however essential it may be for a British Government, once formed, to be sufficiently acceptable to Parliament to secure support in the division lobbies, its formation is in no sense the result of a parliamentary initiative, and that its composition may bear little relation to the wishes and views of Parliament at the time. They are the result of an independent process beginning with the Monarch and carried on by the Prime Minister. It is still the Monarch who selects the individual who is likely to make the most effective Prime Minister, and that individual who acts on his own responsible judgment of the situation. The Cabinet which he has formed then unite to support him to the best of their ability in administration and in debate, while those useful

[1] *The Second World War*, Vol. I, pp. 523-4.

adjuncts to the Cabinet system, the Government Whips, fulfil their day-by-day duty of exhortation, encouragement, or discreet menace, in order to maintain the disciplined support of the back benches. Government and Parliament, however closely intertwined and harmonized, are still separate and independent entities, fulfilling the two distinct functions of leadership, direction, and command, on the one hand and of critical discussion and examination on the other. They start from separate historical origins, and each is perpetuated in accordance with its own methods and has its own continuity.

The continuity of government in our system is symbolized in the person of the Monarch. But it is also maintained in substance by the fact that the vast majority of the Servants of the Crown carry on their duties permanently. What we call a change of government, is in fact, only a change in that small, if important, element which is required to direct the general policy, while securing for it parliamentary and public support or at least acquiescence. A change of government, to quote Hearn, means that:

> "The vigour and uniform action of the Executive are maintained; but the direction of its forces is altered according to the wishes of the legislature . . . the vessel of state is entrusted to other hands and proceeds upon a different course. But it is essential to the success of the operation both that the crew should be skilled in their work and that they should render due obedience to their commander for the time being, whoever he may be."

The parallel, perhaps, suggests a much greater freedom than does in fact exist to change a ship's course—or, rather, the course of a fleet of a number of separate ships. Each of our great departments of State has its own tradition and policy, founded on long experience. Its crew has an accumulated knowledge of wind and weather, of reefs and shoals, by which a new captain is inevitably guided. It has its own private cargoes and destinations which a new captain soon tends to make his own, and to advocate with vigour and conviction at the captains' conference. It may have projects for which the last captain could not secure that conference's assent, and may return to the charge with better hope. In any case by far the greater part of the field of administration, and even of policy, is governed by factors which cannot be changed by Party theories or pre-possessions, or at any rate not to the extent which Ministers may have thought or said when in Opposition. The emphasis may be changed, new methods introduced. But much of whatever is done has to be a continuation of what was done before.

How far the actual working of our Cabinet system and the machinery of Government associated with it may be susceptible of improvement is a theme that is dealt with by Sir Arthur Salter. I have, in my *Thoughts on the Constitution*, given my reasons for advocating some development of the system of a small policy Cabinet inaugurated by Mr. Lloyd George in the First World War. I will only say here that the evergrowing volume of administrative and legislative business to be dealt with adds greatly to the danger of Party caucus dictatorship to which I have already referred. Some substantial easement could and should be afforded by once more making a reality of the House of Lords. On that issue, there is, I think, a growing consensus of opinion that reform should be based on the original principle of a House summoned in virtue of the personal distinction and experience of its Members, who should be individually independent of the control whether of political or of economic organizations and reasonably balanced in their general affiliation as between the main political Parties. To exercise any influence by its deliberations such a House should enjoy at least the powers assigned to the House of Lords by the Act of 1911.

Personally I have expressed my doubts whether even that easement would be sufficient to deal with the highly technical economic and social issues with which we are confronted. The basis of parliamentary representation before the Reform Act, and in practice for some time afterwards, was representation of communities with specific economic interests. It was, in other words, essentially functional or corporative. Today the reality of economic power has found recognition of a kind in the avowed dependence of a Socialist Government on the Trade Union Council. No Conservative Government now coming into office could ignore that body and at the same time give a corresponding predominance to the views of the Federation of British Industries or of the Associated Chambers of Commerce. Yet in the present critical conjuncture of our economic affairs the views of these latter bodies are at least as important as those of the former. The natural inference would be to bring both sets of bodies together in some such assembly as the House of Industry, an economic sub-parliament which Mr. Churchill suggested in his 1930 Romanes lecture and which has been more fully discussed in Mr. Christopher Hollis's recent book *Can Parliament Survive?*[1]

If the evolution of our constitutional system in this island by-passed all that happened between 1642 and 1660, its evolution in America, on the contrary, ignored nearly all that happened after the Restoration. The Cromwellian 'Instrument of Government' and other constitutional projects, which we here tacitly consigned to limbo, were, as the late Mr. Harold Stannard showed in his suggestive book *The Two Constitutions*, living influences in the shaping of American constitutional thinking. In any case the restoration of Royal authority in the American Colonies did little to affect the strong Puritan republican tradition in the colonial assemblies. The Royal governors and their officers, representing a distant, and at times, unsympathetic, more often uncomprehending, authority, never contrived that degree of effective management of the assemblies which made government possible at home. It was this inability of the British Government ever to secure any agreement on measures essential to the security of the Colonies which drove it to courses which, with a restless, self-assertive, and legalistic political community, ended by provoking revolution.

But the success of revolution left the problem unsolved. The new state governments, unable to manage their assemblies, were never able to carry out any policies agreed upon in the common interest. Given governments unable and assemblies

[1] See also *Thoughts on the Constitution*, pp. 64–9.

unwilling to 'deliver the goods', the only workable solution was a single government and a single assembly. Given also the assumption that ultimate political power and initiative rested on the individual citizen, and that government was by delegation from him, it was natural to base that single government directly upon him in respect of those functions which needed to be exercised in common. Federalism was, in fact, the logical conclusion from the necessity of securing united action from political bodies based on the division of powers, as preached by Montesquieu and practised in America.

Under the British system, as it developed after the Restoration, government learnt increasingly how to control Parliament and so to be in a position to 'deliver the goods' in respect of any policy on which it determined or of any agreements into which it entered. This applied no less to the Colonies, as the principle of responsible government was extended to them. Fortunately, too, when they federated into Dominions they—and India and Pakistan have since followed suit—only adopted the principle of distributed powers without abandoning the vital British principle of effective government from above sustained by consent. Consequently, when distance and the growing consciousness of full nationhood precluded anything in the nature of a rigid scheme of Imperial Federation, the way still lay open to effective co-operation by governments animated by common ideals, conscious of common traditions as well as of common interests, and in a position to carry their parliaments and peoples with them. That, at any rate, is the line on which we have advanced, tentatively and hesitatingly no doubt, towards the new conception of the Commonwealth, of a system of nations, fully independent, yet capable of acting as a real unit in essentials, something both spiritually and practically much more than a mere alliance. The development of that conception, both in itself and as an influence and example in promoting the formation of other nation groups, based on community of interests and outlook, may well prove the most important feature in the evolution of the world in the next generation.

So far at any rate as our own Commonwealth is concerned, the successful fulfilment of the hopeful experiment on which we have embarked depends, in no small measure on the effective maintenance of the British tradition of strong and stable government sustained by, but also controlling, Parliament. Unfortunately we have, I fear, been only too inclined in recent years, in our rightful desire to promote self-government, to encourage the conception that such self-government can be carried into early fulfilment everywhere by the mere bestowal of a wide franchise, of elections and of governments dependent on parliamentary majorities, instead of laying stress on the first essential of strong and stable government, and of then thinking out methods by which the secondary, though still essential, element of consent can be secured on lines adapted to more primitive and less homogeneous communities.

Our particular form of constitution relies, for its successful working, on the possibility that the minority of one election can become the majority of the next. Where the cleavage of racial or religious communities is too deep to allow of such a change in the control of power the minority may see no way out of permanent subjection except by secession, where geographical conditions permit of it. This has happened in the case of India where the Swiss type of constitution might conceivably have averted partition. Again, in the case of primitive communities, some form of indirect election through local administrations might secure the necessary steadying effect while still allowing some voice to the mass of the population.

It is only by keeping to the essential spirit of our constitution, rather than to its outward mechanism, that we can avoid setting others on the road to disaster.

CHAPTER III

COMPARISON WITH AMERICAN AND FRENCH PARLIAMENTARY SYSTEMS

By D. W. Brogan

WE all know that the English House of Commons is 'the Mother of Parliaments' and we all know, from human experience, how children can grow up and change so much that even their mothers cannot recognize them. The American Congress and the French National Assembly are both children of the House of Commons and, although their ancestry is visible they have changed a good deal and some of their most characteristic features are not discernible in the lineaments of their mother.

It is true that the American and French legislative systems owed a good deal, in their origin, to other legislative bodies than the English House of Commons. The American colonial assemblies had developed some indigenous habits of their own by 1787 and, in 1789 and later, French constitution mongers have paid some attention, mainly verbal, to the habits of the old States General. But, by and large, the makers of the American and French constitutional systems thought they were imitating the House of Commons and, where they consciously differed from it, they were deliberately improving on the model or restoring that model to its primitive simplicity, purity and efficiency—or so they thought. Here endeth the first lesson; institutions as well as books have their own fate, their own inner logic and in departing so much from the primitive prototype, the American and French systems have underlined an important and sometimes neglected political truth.

In that imitation of course, attention had to be paid from the beginning to visible differences in circumstances. At times in French constitutional history, there has been only one house and the name of the present 'lower' house, the 'National Assembly' recalls those days. At all times in the American system, there has been the federal complication. Congress has never, like the 'King in Parliament' been omnicompetent. Each of these differences has some importance. The preponderance of the directly elected chamber in the French system (it would now be improper to use the old term, 'Lower House') does not mark it off much from the present House of Commons under our new law and, consequently whenever I shall refer to the French Parliament, I shall mean the National Assembly not the Council of the Republic whose functions are limited by law and not yet adequately illustrated by custom.[1] On the other hand, the division of powers between the two Houses in the American system is a very important reality for which we have no equivalent. It is not easy to say what is the balance of power over a long period; even the generally true commonplace that the United States Senate is the only upper House that is more powerful than the lower, requires modification. But, in general, the organization of business is much the same in each House, the problems of federalism, the Party system, the division of powers between Congress and the President work much the same results in each House. So one can talk, and I shall talk, of 'Congress' meaning either House or both together and only insist on differentiating when there is a point to be made which is true of one and not of the other. It must be insisted, too, that, despite very important differences, the House of Commons, the Congress of the United States, and the French National Assembly are more like than unlike. They do their business by debate; they guarantee much the same kind of privileges to their Members; they conduct their business in the same general kind of way; they are all responsible to the voters who chose them freely and whose servants, in democratic theory, they are.

[1] All that it is safe to say, so far, is that the Council has been more important than was foreseen, that it has developed more *esprit de corps* than was anticipated (as witnessed by the assumption by its members of the title of 'Senator') and that it is more like the Senate of the Third Republic than some of the authors of the present constitution can really like or have expected.

They are all three institutions with the same professed object, the implementation of the will of the people in law, the checking, the 'control', in the French sense, of the Executive; they are all based on the idea that minorities have a right to exist, to be heard—and to become a majority by peaceful and legal means. They are not Party States in the late German or present Russian sense and they are not to be judged only by the technical efficiency of their output but by the spirit in which laws are made or amended. *The means are as important as the end.*

It might be as well to get out of the way a formal difference. The United States and France are republics; Great Britain is a monarchy. But as Bagehot argued eighty odd years ago, the essentials of the British system are compatible with Republican institutions and the French Executive system, in its relation to Parliament, is more like the British than that of its Republican sister. M. Vincent Auriol, that is to say, fulfils a function more like that of King George VI than that of Mr. Truman and the 'President of the Council' is a Prime Minister, not a President. Indeed, the President of the French Republic is not a President either—in the American sense, where it is not nonsense to assert that the real character of the Executive Government is more monarchical than it is in our formal monarchy. It is when we turn to the realities of the political systems of the different countries that we see the important resemblances and differences. There is, first of all, a difference that puts Britain and France on one side and the United States on the other. The House of Commons and the French Assembly have the duty of providing and supporting an executive committee, the Cabinet. That is their first duty, not legislation, though a given legislative programme may be the most obvious and dramatic way of supporting the Executive, the failure of its programme, the most devastating blow to the authority of the Executive in London or in Paris.

In Washington the situation is very different. The Congress has no duty equivalent to 'seeing that the King's government is carried on'. The President is elected to do that and elected independently and, seldom in modern times, is he chosen from the Congress or for congressional services or eminence.[1] This, with the results of the federal system, is the greatest difference between the English and American systems and must continuously be borne in mind. Congress is a mutilated Parliament, excluded from some of the most important functions of the House of Commons, in whose presence, if not under whose effective governance, the Executive carries on—and from whose membership the Executive is chosen.

To turn to the other side, both Britain and the United States are countries with highly developed Party systems, two-Party systems in normal times, countries in which the old maxim 'measures not men' has been amended to 'measures and men', to the identification of a policy with a known group, the Party, sometimes especially in America, to the exclusion of anything but formal agreement on principles or details of policy. At no time in French modern history has there been any equivalent of this Party discipline. True, the present constitution formally recognizes Parties, and the electoral law fosters the growth of big Parties, but there has been no effective imitation of the English or American Party system and even the old division into 'Right' and 'Left' has been complicated by the split on the Left caused by the growth of Communism, a non-parliamentary Party, and by the various divisions on the Right caused both by the decline of the old religious feuds (and consequent cohesion) and the ambiguous position of Parties like the Mouvement Républicain Populaire which we may translate, adequately enough, as 'Christian Democrats'. From the absence of an automatic majority much of French practice flows and, oddly enough, often ends up in devices like those imposed on Congress by its separation from the Executive.[2]

Since it is parliamentary government with which we are concerned, it is on the differences that affect the efficiency of the

[1]Only once since 1880, has a serving member of Congress been elected to the Presidency, Senator Harding in 1920 and there have been few cases of successful presidential candidates chosen from men with congressional claims.

[2]It is worth noting that all countries which have had British political training, for some time, fall naturally back on the two-party system, even on two-party systems with little intellectual consistency. This is true of Canada, South Africa, and Ireland as well as of Australia and New Zealand. Whether it will prove true of India, Pakistan, etc., remains to be seen.

legislative bodies that attention should be directed and the first and probably the most important of these is the difference in the committee systems, the resemblance of the systems in the United States and France and their common difference from that of the House of Commons. Briefly, in Paris and Washington all important business is sent before committees specializing in one field before it is acted on in the House. In Congress and the Assembly, this committee system arises inevitably from two features of the systems that mark them off from ours. In Congress, there is the permanent exclusion of the executive from the legislative body, in the French Assembly, there is the absence of a fixed majority lasting out the life of a legislature. In the first place, there is no cabinet united as a 'buckle' to use Bagehot's metaphor, with the legislative body. There cannot, therefore, be the automatic control of the business of the Houses of Congress by the Cabinet that is essential to our order of things. In the French system there *is* this unity, but it is a short lived and highly vulnerable unity. No Cabinet under the Third or Fourth Republic was or is expected to live out a whole legislative period. Thus the exclusion of the Executive in one case, and its intermittent character in the other, force on the legislatures a substitute for the Cabinet system—and that substitute is the Committee system.

There are, of course, general arguments for a committee system that have their weight. It is possible that they would have led to something like the present system even if there had not been this overwhelming necessity. But it is the necessity that keeps the Committee system in being and keeps it powerful, even at moments when it appears to be working badly and even at moments when the sense of the parliaments and even of the country is against the delegation of so much power, nominally inhering in the Parliaments, to smaller bodies chosen from them.

There are arguments for specialized committees that apply to any assembly; there are arguments against such devolution of power that apply to any assembly. But it is sheer necessity that, in America and France, strengthens the first arguments and minimizes the appeal of the second. It may be objected that the committees in either case are not law-making bodies, that whatever they do in that direction requires the sanction of the legislative bodies acting as a whole. It might be argued that in a day and age when, in all countries, a great deal of what is true law is made by anonymous bureaucrats, it is being hypercritical to criticize usurpations of authority by parliamentary authorities, usurpations which, unlike some bureaucratic decisions, have neither in fact nor form the force of law. But if the formal powers of the committees are limited, their real powers are very great. Had parliaments but world enough and time, it might not matter, but they haven't, and a great deal of what is done in open session is only done because some committee has so decided and a great deal of what is left undone is so left because of a committee decision. Positively and negatively, the committees determine, in great part or entirely, what the general legislative bodies do. And it is not merely a question of what laws are thus made or unmade, but especially in the American system, a question of what laws are discussed or what topics are brought before the legislature—and one of the admitted functions of a Parliament is to educate the public and, as Bagehot said, to provide the subjects of conversation. Conversation today is not so purely political as it was in his time. But the competition from sport, the movies, the crime pages of the popular press, the debates on the air, all make it the more important that whatever diminished share of the public's time *is* devoted to politics, should be devoted to themes already debated, as a rule with more presumable knowledge and responsibility, by the representatives of the people. It would be absurd to suggest that there are no themes worth discussing that have not been or should not be discussed in the legislative body, but most themes should be. And it is not altogether accidental that those countries where much or most effective business is done in committees as a rule are less successful in dramatizing the general debates on the floor of the House. There may be special reasons for that, permanent in the case of the United States, possibly temporary in the case of France. Whenever a President wishes to make a first-class political announcement he blankets, by that fact, all other announcements made that day. As a rule he in fact determines what shall be the theme for a few days and Senators and Congressmen are reduced to saying 'Ditto to Mr. Burke' or issuing stout denials and rebuttals. And this is true whether the President makes his declaration before Congress, in his speech on the 'State of the Union' or at a White House press conference, or at a public meeting. That cannot be helped; it is involved in the basic institutional fact that makes the Committee system necessary, the separation of powers and functions.

In France, it is partly due to exceptional circumstances, that a figure outside Parliament, General de Gaulle, can also dictate, for a few days at any rate, the appropriate theme for political discussion. But even there, the effective business of Parliament is often done or undone in committee and both the Cabinet and the Assembly are to a considerable degree at the mercy of the committees, notably of the Finance Committee who do in fact determine, if not the general shape of the budget, at least those sections of it round which controversy will centre. These obvious limitations or handicaps of the French and American Committee systems account for the repeated efforts to limit its powers. In France, the historical memory of the usurpation of powers by the great committees of the Convention for long hampered the growth of an effective Committee system under the Third Republic and, in America, the rank and file have continually revolted against 'Committee tyranny', often with the benevolent approval of the President who is normally bound to see in the committees an alternative centre of leadership to that provided by the White House. But in Paris and Washington, the nature of things is too much for the sceptics or the critics; basically, the Committee system remains unchanged. It may not be part of the constitution but it is part of its effective functioning in each country.[1]

[1]It is part of the new French constitution in a limited sense. Article 15 lays down: "*l'Assemblée nationale étudie les projets et propositions de loi dont elle est saisie, dans ses commissions, dont elle fixe le nombre, la composition et la compétence*". This is a general grant of power that could be assumed to exist anyway. More important are the provisions for the 'bureau', the general managing committee of the Assembly. Article 11 lays down that: "*Chacune des deux Chambres élit son bureau chaque année, au début de la session, à la représentation proportionelle des groupes.*

"*Lorsque les deux Chambres se réunissent pour l'élection du Président de la République leur bureau est celui de l'Assemblée nationale.*" More important are the provisions that, in the event of the dissolution of the Assembly, the President of the Assembly acts

The disadvantages of this system, from the British point of view (apart from those which have been insisted on by French and American critics), are obvious enough. An effective Committee system means a transfer of some authority from the Ministry to some other body; the transfer, however slight, is an affront to the traditional spirit of the House of Commons which wishes to concentrate Executive responsibility on the Cabinet and legislative responsibility on the House as a whole—even if that responsibility is a fiction and real legislative power is in the hands of the one committee that counts, the Cabinet, with its control of the business of the House. There has been plenty of discussion of ways and means of making parliamentary control effective and these discussions have often, perhaps usually, ended in proposals for reforming or strengthening the private Member. But the Cabinet has preserved its authority and the House has accepted that authority.

Yet it is worth opening the question again, since the immense extension of business, due mainly to the great growth in the scope of governmental functions, has both made the inquisitorial functions of the House far more important and far more difficult than in the days when Mill and Bagehot complained of bad drafting and the absence of a coherent habit of legislation or investigation. If we take the 'grand inquest of the nation' in its popular and erroneous sense, a coroner's jury that was just capable of dealing with one corpse is sure to be swamped when the bodies are to be counted in scores. Since the business of the House has increased, is increasing and is very unlikely to be diminished, since no possible Party change can reduce the functions of government to what they were in 1939, not to speak of 1914 or 1865 (the ideal date of Bagehot's masterpiece), it is not a waste of time to reopen a question that is more urgent than ever and to think out again the lessons to be learned from the dear-bought experience of others.

---

as Prime Minister and nominates the new Minister of the Interior "*en accord avec le Bureau de l'Assemblée nationale*" (Article 52). More important still is the provision that when "the National Assembly is not sitting '*son bureau contrôlant l'action de cabinet, peut convoquer le Parlement. Il doit le faire à la demande du tiers des députés ou à celle du Président du Conseil des Ministres*" (Article 12).

It will be as well to discuss, fairly briefly, the detailed gains
of the American and French systems as far as they are compen-
sations for specifically American and French defects. Although
the two situations are not identical, the general American and
French position affects the young private Member in roughly
similar ways. In Congress, the young Member knows that he
may never get Executive experience, that, indeed, only the
highest Executive offices are worth the ambition of a Member
of either House of Congress; he may, without too obviously
writing himself down a failure, become a Governor or a
Member of the President's Cabinet, but hardly accept any other
office.[1]

It is necessary, therefore, to provide a substitute for the
training that a young Member of the House of Commons gets
as a parliamentary private secretary or junior minister or, even
if he is in opposition, as secretary or aide to a leader of his Party
in the House. The American Committee, as we shall see, does
this with more or less success. In the French Assembly, the
situation is not quite the same. Yet there is not such an inevitable *cursus honorum* as with us. A deputy may become a Minister
without any previous Executive experience. There are also
fewer *quasi* Executive and junior jobs open to deputies; the
Minister may rely on his *chef de cabinet*, brought in from outside
Parliament, rather than on his parliamentary assistant or
assistants. And, since the Party system is far less effective, it is
by no means certain that an aspiring young deputy can automatically hope to be considered for minor office. He may
never get office at all and, if he does, it may be as a result of
some parliamentary upheaval that projects him into full
ministerial rank without preliminary experience—and may
throw him out of office again, in a few weeks, before he has
even begun to know where the ropes are, much less how to pull
them. In both countries, that is to say, the Committee system

---

[1] Two generations ago, an eminent politician refused to be 'promoted', even to
Cabinet rank, on the ground that he would not accept an office from which any
man could dismiss him. And, in much more recent times, it was retorted to someone
who said that Mr. 'X' had left a junior office because he could not afford it and so
a fortiori could not afford to be Secretary of State, "Anybody can afford to be
Secretary of State, but not to be Under-Secretary."

provides a kind of indispensable training in public business that it is not so essential to provide in Britain where the Cabinet system, plus Party stability, make it pretty certain that most really able young Members will (provided their Party gets in) get first-hand experience and even when their Party is out, can have second-hand experience through service to an ex-Minister. But, and here's the rub, a Party may be in Opposition a long time and when the tide does turn, have few young Members with any experience and few or no Members with recent experience. Experience, of course, is not everything. If it were, as Frederick the Great said, an old army mule should make a good general, but it is experience and cannot be got except by practice. If new Ministers are helpless in face of their civil servants (which is often asserted, though not proven and, in some cases, is obviously untrue) the limitations of the political education given to young M.P.s in opposition have something to do with it and, other things being equal, are worth providing a remedy for. Whether other things *can* be made equal and, if they can, whether the price is not too high to pay will be discussed later, but the first thing to note is that, in the French and American systems, there are gains from a device imposed, in any case, by sheer necessity. The House of Commons may do without such an educational system, the Congress and the National Assembly cannot. They cannot, because they do not otherwise automatically provide that training. They should not, because the rewards in pride in work done, in satisfaction of human vanity, in obvious utility given by the American and French parliamentary systems are inadequate *minus* the special chances given by the Committee system, inadequate, that is, to attract enough able and industrious men. Even if it attracted them, it might demoralize them and, after ten years or so in sterile opposition, leave them no longer industrious and only doubtfully able. Or it might confine their industry to what Burke called 'a confused and scuffling bustle of local agency'. The Member of Congress, the Deputy, might end up (as some do end up) as a mere agent for local interest, with his eye fixed exclusively in Buncombe County or on Gonfle-Bonfigue and, should the lightning strike at last, should executive office or

F

legislative power come his way, be totally unfit for either function. Obviously, the situation is not the same with us. But it is surely worth remembering that most private Members stay private Members and that the growth of the social service state has imposed on the average M.P. many of the burdens that, for generations, have lain upon the Congressman and the Deputy and which we were wont, complacently, to use to explain the moral and intellectual inferiority of foreign politicians to our own. True, an M.P. whose sole independent action is to act as a pension agent, as agent for his union or business group, as consul for the local authorities of his constituency, may maintain the Government or support the Opposition by his always ready vote. He may be the delight of the Whips but, if he is only that, he, and others like him, will certainly be unable to control the Executive even in the weak French sense of the word, much less keep an effectively vigilant eye on the activities of temporary Ministers and permanent civil servants or to frustrate the results of their collusion or, in opposition, to lend really effective aid to such members of his Party as are capable of the vigilance that is still the price of liberty. To educate our parliamentary masters, as well as the voters, is one of the functions of Parliament which is better done (at high cost) in the American and French systems. Assiduity, application to a special field, mastery of procedure and of subject matter, all these virtues are more automatically rewarded in Congress or the National Assembly than they are at Westminster. And political virtue that is only its own reward, is likely to be in less abundant supply than in bodies that pay more tangible rewards in prestige and power.

The rewards are often earned by hard and also by useful work. For all but the most secure or brilliant know that in addition to mere parliamentary talent of the flamboyant type, it is necessary to earn a reputation for being useful for something else. Not all Committee Members learn much; not all learn much that is relevant to their duties; but a good many learn a good deal and, above all in Congress, learn to discriminate between real and formal power. Many a silent Committee Member is more feared and respected by the Executive departments than are the Members who make the headlines.

Complaints about the formal deficiencies of parliamentary legislation are an old story and, despite great improvements since the days of John Stuart Mill and Walter Bagehot, they are heard still. It would be quite out of place and beyond my competence to express an opinion on the question raised by Mr. Robert Luce, the question of the alleged superiority, in form, of congressional legislation over parliamentary legislation. But what it is easier and safer to decide is that the private Member (in Congress there are strictly speaking no other kinds of Member) has a chance to learn the trade of legislation more easily than has his British opposite number and, less certainly, the same is probably true of the French Deputy. At any rate there is more parliamentary government in America and in France than there is with us—that is, more legislation planned, originated and elaborated by persons not holding executive office, or office under the Executive, than there is with us where nearly all legislation owes its enactment and often its detailed form to the decisions of Ministers. If we wish to restore to Parliament an effective and independent share in the making and control of laws, then the Committee system of Congress and of National Assembly is one way of doing it.

But is there not a high price paid? Are not the French Ministries notoriously unstable and relations between Congress and the President often strained and seldom cordial? Both statements are true, but the implication is not. The Committee systems in French and American parliamentary life have their power because of the instability of ministries in one country, because of the difficulties of the separation of powers in the other. They are necessary remedies; they are not the cause of the disease. True, a committee often mutilates a 'government' bill, even a budget, beyond recognition, often beyond the power of the administration or the Cabinet to undo on the floor of Congress or the Assembly, but this failure suggests that what is missing is the effective English Cabinet system, not the House of Commons much weaker committee system. We do not need the American or French Committee system to remedy a defect from which our system does not suffer, but to remedy a defect

from which it does suffer—too complete control of the time of
the House and of the processes of legislation by the Cabinet.
And as long as Cabinet control remains firmly based on rigid
Party discipline, only the most outrageous committee sabotage
would interfere seriously with the Government programme—
and that could be remedied by calling in the docile majority
without which, committees or no committees, Cabinet Government will break down.)

To set up a system of committees representing all parties in
proportion to their strength, with subjects allocated to them to
cover and with the power of presenting to the House their own
version of Government projects—and of non-Government
projects may not be worth while and may have serious drawbacks.[1] But it need not and is not likely to upset the basic
principle of British parliamentary government, control of all
fundamental business by the leaders the Commons recognize,
the Cabinet. There are, however, in French and American
practice some real defects that should be noted, though not
overstressed. In France, there is a danger (arising as much
from ministerial instability as from committee usurpation) that
the permanent civil service will have half an eye on the
Committees and their leaders, as much as on the Ministers who
are here today and gone tomorrow. More, in the chief committees, are the ex-Ministers and the future Ministers. Many
a young politician has laid claim to a Cabinet post by a
brilliant report on a bill, a report that did the reputation of the
rapporteur more good than it necessarily gratified the Minister.
No French Ministry lives through a whole legislative term;
committees, in fact usually do.[2] The risks of British civil servants,

---

[1]The representation of the minority parties on the committees is essential. Foreign
affairs, defence policy could be discussed and, perhaps, amended, if confidential
information were given to less than the whole House. Mr. Churchill has been
consulted on defence matters by Mr. Attlee and, a century ago, the Duke of
Wellington was always consulted on military matters by the Whig ministers though
he was Leader of the Opposition in the Lords. (He was also, of course, Commander-
in-Chief.) A more serious problem is created in France by the Communist membership of these committees. No French Government would make really confidential
information available to a committee some of whose members could be relied on
to give it away.

[2]It was quite usual in the Third Republic for a Minister to survive throughout a
series of Cabinet crises and, in such a case he was a match for any committee
leaders. Such were Delcassé, Leygues, Daladier at the War Office.

under the control of firmly established Ministers, being forced to keep one eye on the Committee to the detriment of their disciplined loyalty is remote, not much greater than the danger of keeping an eye on a future Minister when the Government of the day seems to be going out. And, of course, on the other hand, a competent Committee can get behind the official as well as ministerial façade far more effectively than can be done by questions or post-mortems.

If the danger in the French system is that the official may be tempted to help the Committee too much, in the American system the danger lies in the overwhelming preponderance of *expertise* on the Executive side. Things are better since the various reforms of recent years, such as the La Follette-Monroney Act of 1944 which gives to Congress, as a whole, and to individual Congressmen, individually, much better resources for checking the official story than they had. But it is still true that the Cabinet officer is usually much more heavily armed with relevant confidential knowledge than the average Member of a Committee, though *he* is much more heavily armed than is the average M.P. Here the separation of powers again takes its toll, but that is a part of the price paid for the American constitution, a price that Americans (who are, after all, the people most concerned) think not too high.

Other defects have not the same august sanction. There is the so-called 'locality rule' for instance. The constitution provides that Senators and Representatives must be residents of the states they represent; a custom having practically the force of law, insists that Representatives must be residents of the district they wish to represent.[1] This system obviously limits, very seriously, the recruitment of Congress Members of minority parties in safe areas are debarred, permanently, from a congressional career and young members of majority parties have to await the death or promotion of the incumbents before aspiring to enter Congress. The notorious fact that Congress does not, cannot, draw on all the political talent of the country, weakens its efficiency and prestige. But there is no inherent necessity in this limitation, even in a vast federal country, as the

[1] This rule is sometimes evaded but only in very exceptional circumstances.

case of Canada shows. It is something to be avoided not imitated.[1] Another American limitation is the 'seniority rule'. This provides that rank in the committees goes by seniority of *continuous* service. Even the loss of a seat for one term of two years puts the veteran down among the freshmen. This snakes-and-ladders principle has wider effects than are always perceived. The safe seats, whose holders never lose seniority, are inevitably the seats in the solid Republican and Democratic areas. But these areas are those least affected by the movement of opinion that swings the doubtful areas and wins presidential elections, as well as changes the balance of power in congressional politics. It follows, then, that the leading members of committees, being often holders of safe seats in backward areas, more often than not are out of touch and sympathy with the mass of the new members of their own Party and with the President, a handicap bad enough in the case of the Opposition, worse in the case of the Party nominally 'in power'. The efficiency of the congressional committee system is certainly diminished by this rule, which is mere custom and of no overwhelming antiquity. But the practice is modified in two ways. If the majority of the Committee really wants to act, it can force the hand of the chairman and the seniors, if only by accepting their report, confident that, on the floor of Congress, the necessary amendments can alter or totally transform the unpalatable draft. Then special Committees, some of great importance, are often headed by comparatively junior recruits. Thus the most important war committee, that on war expenditure, was headed by the then Senator Truman in his second term and the equally important Atomic Energy Joint Committee is headed by Senator MacMahon, a senator in his second term from a doubtful state. The division of power between the two Houses in America and the very different tenure and size of the Senate and the House of Representatives produce difficulties that could not be paralleled in the British system. It entails the

---

[1] It is perhaps worth noting that Bagehot attributed some of the weakness of the parliamentary representation of the landed interest (before the Second Reform Bill) to the refusal to admit candidates from outside the county whose seats were being contested. Carpet-baggers, Gladstone, Churchill, Mackenzie King, Clemenceau are necessary to the highest parliamentary efficiency.

duplication of Committees, since both Houses must be 'seized' of the proposals and the obvious remedy of joint Committees is not used nearly often enough. This not only causes delay, but imposes an especial burden on Cabinet officers who have normally to explain their projects to and endure questioning from two Committees and, in the case of overlapping topics, to four. Of course, the fact that Cabinet officers (and others) can testify before Committees is especially valuable in a system which denies them a place in either House, but the value of the exposition is much diminished by its duplication. Again, there is nothing in our situation to necessitate any such waste of effort. Whatever happens to the House of Lords, it will never again be powerful enough to force a Cabinet Minister to waste time on it, either before the whole body or a committee.

In the House of Representatives, the comparatively large membership (435) and the short term of service (two years) necessitate far more rigid discipline than is needed in the Senate with only ninety-six members elected for six years, of whom only a third retire at any one time. So, at times, dictatorial power over business has been given to the Speaker or to the Rules Committee, power equivalent to denying the floor to any project or projector not approved of by the leaders of the majority Party, themselves products of the 'locality rule'. But the tendency has been away from this veto power in the hands of a small, and not necessarily very representative body, and the most recent attempt to restore control to the Rules Committee has failed. Yet the absence of a front bench, the consequent absence of automatic discipline, the lack of such a dramatic institution as question-time, the knowledge that, even formally, a vote of the House can be ignored by the President or the Senate, all make the House of Representatives much less dramatic than the House of Commons and the Committee system even more necessary, for there some of these limitations can be circumvented, even the separation of powers that should keep Executive and legislature at polite arm's length. Nor have we much to learn from the American system of presiding officers. The President of the Senate is the Vice-President of the United States, chosen by the voter with no regard for his capacity as a presiding officer and consequently reduced to the minimum of power. Indeed had the Senate a larger membership, it is doubtful if it could do business at all under its present rules and leadership and, sometimes (as during a 'filibuster'), it does not do business. The political character of the Speakership is due, again, to the absence of a Cabinet present in the House. The Speaker is, like the Lord Chancellor, a leader of the House over which he presides and if he is no longer so arbitrary or partisan a figure as were Randall or Reed, that is due to the rise of other centres of authority in the House, not to any very violent demand for a totally impartial moderator.[1] It is basically in the Committee system that the occasional superiority of the French and American systems can be seen, if it is to be seen at all. And even had the system less merits, it would, in both cases, have to be invented. There are not the same reasons for inventing it here, but there is no very apparent reason why some of the merits could not be transplanted without destroying the superiorities that have allowed the House of Commons, for so long, to get on with a rather primitive organization of business. There are minor matters that could be copied of course. Congress, with its vast office buildings and its clerical staff, does recognize how great a burden petty detail imposes on the Member and the House of Commons is still far too modest in its provision for its own efficiency in that respect.

But it is the more serious business of legislation and supervision that concerns us and the Mother of Parliaments might look into the domestic arrangements of her daughters without recoiling in horror at new-fangled political equivalents of a washing machine or even central heating.

[1] The fact that, but for two years, the same party has controlled the House since 1930, means that the Speakership has only once in that period changed hands for party reasons which makes it easier to regard it as an institution partially above party. In the same way, the fact that M. Herriot was for so long President of the Chamber of Deputies and is now President of the National Assembly has helped in the evolution of a non-Party presidency in the French Parliament.

CHAPTER IV

DANGERS OF A SUPREME PARLIAMENT

By J. J. Craik Henderson

WHILST the supremacy of Parliament has many advantages, it is also a serious danger should a Government be formed of men prepared to curtail liberties or to form a dictatorship, as has happened in Czechoslovakia. The methods employed by Communism should make us consider very carefully whether the dangers of a supreme Parliament do not override the advantages of a flexible constitution. Perhaps instead of referring to a supreme Parliament it might be more correct to say that the Cabinet is supreme in the exercise of Executive power and of law making through its control of the majority Party in the House of Commons.

It used to be said in text-books that Parliament controls the executive—the Cabinet. It will be remembered that Bagehot regarded the Cabinet as merely a committee of the Parliamentary majority but neither historically nor in fact is that correct, though there is some excuse for the mistake. The Cabinet, generally speaking, consists of Members of Parliament of the majority party and so has some appearance of being such a committee but it is not appointed by the majority party or by Parliament but in effect by the Prime Minister. The fact that Parliament by a vote of no confidence may bring the then existing Cabinet to an end may also have misled Bagehot. It must be remembered that the Cabinet has many powers which are not derived from Parliament but from the fact that their executive powers, so far as not expressly conferred by Parliament, descend from the prerogative.

In practice the Cabinet consists generally of the leaders in Parliament of the Party constituting the parliamentary majority and, provided it can retain the confidence of that majority, its powers are unlimited. Theoretically it is true that Members of Parliament can ask Ministers to account for their actions and by a vote of no confidence can bring down a Government and force a general election; but it is impossible for the opposition to defeat a Government with a good majority on a vote of no confidence, unless the Government has lost the support of a considerable number of its own followers—and this is likely to become increasingly rare.

It is true that Members of the majority Party exercise in the meetings of their own Parties and elsewhere very considerable influence, but for various reasons the leaders of the majority Party have now more power over their followers than formerly and much more power than Parliament has over the Executive. In the ordinary case even the theoretical control of the Executive by Parliament can only be by the defection of ministerial supporters, though even during the last twenty years or so there have been occasions when Parliament has forced the Government of the day to change direction. Before the war Mr. Oliver Stanley and Mr. Chamberlain had to give way. During the war the opposition of a sufficient number of ostensible followers technically on the Norwegian Campaign, though actually on wider issues, led to the fall of the Chamberlain Government and since the war there have been a number of cases of the Government having to withdraw proposals or amend them materially to meet the views of their own followers—that happened, for example, with regard to National Service and the modification of the proposed charge under the Health Act for spectacles and false teeth.

A minority Party may question Ministers, may criticize but they cannot control in the ordinary case a Government with a reasonably large majority. There can be no control of the Executive where supporters in Parliament are prepared without question to obey the leaders of their Party—through the Whips. All that the minority Party—the opposition—can do without support from Members of the majority Party is to question, inquire and criticize—but whilst this does not amount to control it is an important method of checking abuses of power.

With the support of a majority of Members it would be possible for a Cabinet to suspend the sittings of Parliament, have the minority Members arrested, withdraw all the safeguards of liberty such as *Habeas Corpus*, and freedom of speech, and to establish virtually a dictatorship. All this, too, could be done within the law. It is surprising how few members of the general public appreciate how uncontrolled the Cabinet is where it has the support of a loyal majority in Parliament and that 'the supremacy of Parliament' in this sense is absolute and subject to no real safeguards of any kind.

In the last war and for the best motives, we saw a Member of Parliament arrested and retained in custody without any crime being charged against him. We saw Parliament continue for ten years without an election and Parliament abrogate its powers in favour of Ministers. In a time of extreme emergency this may have been right, particularly as the Churchill Government undoubtedly had a very large degree of public support. In one sphere only was there effective control—expenditure of public money—and the terms of reference to the committee charged with control were wide. This large committee of Members under the able chairmanship of Sir John Wardlaw-Milne exercised a considerable degree of control through the powers of inquiry and investigation and of reporting to Parliament.

It may be asked, why did the Courts not interfere or could they not prevent undue encroachments on liberties? Could they not have enforced *Habeas Corpus*?

There may be some doubts as to the power of the Courts to safeguard liberties, and in the First World War certain eminent judges did attempt to do so, but in the last war the Courts seemed to accept that they had no powers of any kind to interfere, provided the action was done under an Act of Parliament or Order. A good example is Liversidge's case. By Defence (General) Regulations 1939 (Regulation 18 B) it was provided that if the Secretary of State had reasonable cause to believe any person to be of hostile origin or association, etc., the Secretary of State might make an Order against that person directing that he be detained. It was held in that case in the

House of Lords that, where the Secretary of State makes an Order in which he recites that he has reasonable cause to believe a person to be of hostile associations and directs that such a person be detained, a Court of Law cannot inquire whether in fact the Secretary of State had reasonable grounds for his belief. In fact that a requirement that the Secretary of State 'has reasonable cause' is satisfied if the Secretary of State thinks that he has. It may well be doubted whether the House of Commons, when it introduced this safeguard, believed that such a construction would be put on it, but it does show how impotent the Courts may be to safeguard the rights of citizens against possible injustice at the hands of the Executive where a Minister is acting under powers conferred by a statute.

It can be argued that dangers of one kind or another must exist in every system. It is certainly true that a man who is always looking over his shoulder will not progress very rapidly. That is true, but is not a complete answer or possibly an answer of any kind. It is suggested that the test whether safeguards must be introduced against 'dangers' depends on whether the 'dangers' are remote and the remedies so unsatisfactory and irksome as to make it worth risking the possible danger in order to retain our present system which has in the past proved reasonably satisfactory.

Are the dangers remote? Why are the dangers any more threatening today than say fifty years ago? How have things changed in this period and have they made the danger greater? In this period there has been a great change in the financial position and standing of parliamentary candidates. It would generally be true to say that fifty years ago the Member of Parliament was generally either a man of inherited wealth or one who had acquired wealth or a 'sufficiency'. If he ceased to be a Member of Parliament he would be disappointed (a) because he had enjoyed the work, or (b) because he was losing the membership of a very good club, but it would not mean a loss of income. Today for many Members it means a loss of income, unemployment and in some cases poverty. The Member of today very often has chosen Parliament not only as a method of serving his country but as a remunerated occupation. The proportion of 'career' politicians has greatly increased. A career politicianis likely to become a ministerial "yes man." If he is a good Party man in the House, always supports the Government, listens to the Whips and speaks only to order and never says anything to annoy his own front bench, in due course he may rise to the front bench with £5,000 a year and many perquisites. But if he takes the wrong turn, questions the decisions of his leaders, or, horror of horrors, speaks or votes against his Party, he will almost certainly find himself dropped at the next election and without salary or even possibly a trade or business to which to turn. This must lead to the strengthening of the powers of the front bench over the back benches, to the increase in the power of the Executive and to the loss of independence by Members of Parliament.

Also the offices of profit under the Crown and otherwise have greatly increased. All Members receive £1,000 which in fact with free travelling and other perquisites is worth considerably more. There may be eighty or ninety Members in receipt of salaries as Ministers and in addition there are rich prizes: profitable offices of various kinds with the nationalized industries, as governors and judges, and these prizes go to the well behaved Members of the Party. This all builds up the power of the leader of the Party over his followers in Parliament. For good behaviour—titles and jobs; for independence—loss of his seat and often his income and his future. Gold may be the root of all evil but sometimes it makes a man able to be independent and to vote with his conscience and against his interests. Lack of money but possession of a wife and children are very powerful advocates for loyalty to the potential spreader of the morning slice of bread.

Mr. Walter Elliot recently when writing about Sir Alan Herbert said:

"The fact is A. P. H. is a survival, even a throw-back. He is the Member of Parliament, such as nine-tenths were and not more than one-tenth of Members are, the man of whose life Parliament is only a part, the juryman with no desire whatever to sit on the bench; whose verdict is for that very reason the more important and respected; whose loss is deeply to be deplored and may prove fatal to Parliament itself."

Is this tendency towards professional politicians likely to increase or otherwise? Everything seems to point to the tendency increasing and accelerating. It will be a pity. A politician is almost a term of abuse in many countries, but fifty years ago in this country Members were universally believed to be men of principle and of sufficient independence to oppose any measures, from whatever source, that might adversely affect our constitution or parliamentary system.

Here is the first cause that leads to the increasing power of the Executive and which, working through a servile but supreme Parliament, is such a danger. Another is the increasing power of patronage. Where Members are men of established position in business or the professions and/or possess reasonable fortunes, the danger arising from the possession by the Government of gifts to bestow is negligible, but Members are becoming more and more men who look to Parliament for a salary and rewards of office or employment in the nationalized industries or other profitable occupation which the Government is in a position to give to its loyal followers. It may indeed be a good thing that the Executive should be strong, but surely not for this reason, and particularly where it means that the independence of Members is less and accordingly that it would be easier for an unscrupulous Government to carry through measures detrimental to the country.

At one time Parliament acted as a check on the exercise of autocratic powers by the Crown and its Ministers. Parliament through finance was in a position to exercise some effective control of the Executive and when the Executive power passed in fact from the Crown to the leaders of the majority Party, there was still the check of the House of Lords with powers. But fifty, sixty or seventy years ago the danger was not great. It probably did not exist. Everyone then believed in parliamentary government. It was regarded with veneration and no man could have got any following who proposed any measure which tended to destroy or even weaken parliamentary government. Is that the case today?

The Communist Party, for example, may go through the motions of adhering to parliamentary forms and procedure, but Russian-influenced communism has no use for our views of democracy and of parliamentary government. Communism of this kind believes in a dictatorship and in a one Party Parliament where a Member who dared to disagree with the Party line would be liquidated in one way or another. In this country and in Parliament there are 'fellow travellers'. Is it improbable that in the future, and not too remote future, a Party might be returned to power willing to make use of the existing forms of Government in order to achieve results by methods contrary to all parliamentary convention? Mr. Attlee has said that the important thing is not to do things with the most scrupulous regard to the theories of democracy or exact constitutional propriety and Sir Stafford Cripps was even more specific when he said that: "The Government's first step will be to call Parliament together at the earliest moment and place before it an Emergency Powers Bill to be passed through all its stages on the first day. This Bill will be wide enough in its terms to allow all that will be immediately necessary to be done by ministerial orders. These orders must be incapable of challenge in the Courts or in any way except in the House of Commons.

"The devising of the detailed administrative methods for the working out of the (Socialist) Plan are not matters with which the House of Commons need concern itself. Ministers with the advice of their administrative staffs and experts should handle the detailed work. Full powers to that end should be delegated to them. . . ."

No doubt these views expressed before the war may have been abandoned or modified, but the important thing to note is that they are part of the political philosophy of many today.

It is perhaps true that at the moment there are no signs of a Communist Party obtaining power in this country, but no one can say that under certain circumstances it might not be possible for a Prime Minister, avid for greater power, to suspend parliamentary elections and make himself a virtual dictator. It would even be possible for him to arrest political opponents in order to give himself the necessary majority. This may seem far-fetched, but we have the example of Czechoslovakia and other countries to warn us. Even if we admit that the setting-up of an absolute dictatorship is a very remote danger, there are still many invasions of liberty and rights which could be effected contrary to constitutional propriety but within the powers of Parliament. Should there not be some safeguards against abuse of power or is revolution to be the only remedy?

The Greeks and Romans appreciated the dangers and in every country attempts have been made to ensure that there shall be some check on the powers of the majority. Lord Bryce said in *Modern Democracies*: 'That a majority is always right, i.e. that every decision it arrives at by voting is wise not even the most fervent democrat has ever maintained seeing that popular government consists in the constant effort of a minority to turn itself by methods of persuasion into a majority which will then reverse the action or modify the decisions of the former majority.' That is the method and working of parliamentary Democracy, but there are voices which urge a majority Party to make an omelet so that the eggs cannot be unscrambled, and probably there are many in Parliament today who would accept such views. Bryce adds: 'Every people that has tried to govern itself has accordingly recognized the need for precautions against the errors it may commit, be they injurious to the interests of the State as a whole or in disregard of those natural or primordial rights which belong to individual citizens. Some sort of safeguard is required.' What was true in 1921 is even truer today.

Is it not right that some safeguards should be provided here when we see what has happened in other countries? Even if one does not contemplate a Government going to the wildest extreme, is it right that any Cabinet should have power to carry through constitutional or other changes, which might be irreparable, without the country being consulted? We have to remember that no Court of Law or other body can prevent a Government from carrying through changes for which it has neither sought nor obtained a mandate from the electors. It is, of course, right and proper that a Government should seek the approval of the electors for any change of great constitutional or other importance, but at most that is only a convention of the constitution, and has no legal basis.

Whilst the increasing power of the Executive and the absence of any safeguards of fundamental rights are undoubtedly dangers in our Constitution, it would be wrong not to admit that there are certain advantages in a strong Executive and a flexible constitution. Indeed it might be argued that some of the defects we have seen in the Government of other countries have been due to an excess of checks on the Executive and to the Executive consequently not being strong enough.

It is probably a legitimate criticism of the constitution of the United States to say that the Executive is frustrated if the Party of the President does not control both houses of Congress. It might, too, be said that in France few governments since 1918 have remained in power for more than a few months, and that this is the result of the Executive being too weak in relation to Parliament. A more correct diagnosis might be that it is due to the group system of France, but that may only be a different way of stating the same defect, and that under parliamentary government the Executive cannot be strong unless it has the support of a majority and that majority belongs to the same Party as the Executive. The Group system leads inevitably to groups out of power trying to bring down the Government either by forming a majority themselves or by persuading one of the government groups, by promises of office in the new Government, to withdraw support and so bring down the Government.

Perhaps the greatest cause of instability in France is that when a Government there is defeated, it does not involve a general election; nothing is more conducive to loyalty to the Party in power than that Members know that if they bring down the Government, this will probably lead to a general election in which they may lose their seats and their salaries.

Perhaps the result is this: if one could be sure that Ministers could be relied on to observe the niceties and conventions of the constitution and always to act wisely, then a strong Executive and a flexible constitution giving all power to the Cabinet would be best, but unfortunately nobody can be sure of this and accordingly some safeguards ought to be provided. 'History records many a decision whose deplorable results might have been avoided, had there been more knowledge, more time for reflection, more opportunity for reconsideration.' If we were sure in the future to have Members and Parties loyal and faithful to parliamentary traditions and conventions and wise and tolerant, a reasonably strong, or even a strong Executive might be desirable, unhampered by any restrictions on the use of power, except its conscientious regard for the interests of the country. It would, however, be foolish not to realize that there are tendencies in the world today which are contrary to parliamentary traditions. In the last ten years we have seen the growth of Parties who do not believe in parliamentary government. That would not matter so much, were it not that some Members of those Parties today are attempting to infiltrate into Parliament and, if successful, would make use of parliamentary procedure in order to achieve their aim of ending parliamentary government as we understand it. If they believe in parliament at all, it is merely in a one Party system which is used mainly as a form of propaganda for the party itself and fulfils none of the qualities which we consider necessary and which we have fought to secure.

So far, such parties, whether of the Right or the Left, have made little progress in this country; but one can never say that, in certain circumstances and with their camouflage of democracy, such a Party could not gain a majority in the House of Commons, particularly as such a successful Party might even find Members of other Parties willing to support them. It would be too late then to think of safeguards. It may be said that we would have the Royal prerogative of dissolution, but it may be doubted whether an opportunity would be given for the use of such a right, and indeed whether it would now be in accordance with our constitution for such a right to be exercised against the advice of Ministers.

Our electoral system too seems to tend to the successful

Party having a larger majority in Parliament than it would have on a proportional basis, though the results of the elections in 1950 and 1951 were exceptions. That happened in the General Election of 1945 and is quite usual. This, of course, strengthens the power of the Executive and is the main argument either for or against proportional representation, depending on whether you favour a not too strong Executive or believe in a strong Executive. Proportional representation would have the tendency to reduce majorities in the House of Commons, but it is probably a good thing that the Party in power should have an adequate majority and, if safeguards are to be imposed, it would be better to have those through a reformed Second House with powers or the creation of fundamental laws or a referendum.

It is bad for the country to have a succession of governments with inadequate majorities. Such Governments have to devote too much of their time and attention to parliamentary divisions and are forced to adopt a temporizing attitude both at home and abroad. It is true, of course, that even with our present system the majority of the Government Party may be so small as to make it almost impotent, and in foreign affairs in particular that is a tragedy. But the tendency would be increased by proportional representation.

There is the danger that the supremacy of the Cabinet may be used by extremists or fanatics to carry through policies designed to destroy or injure our constitution or to employ parliamentary procedure which, whilst possibly not illegal, is contrary to constitutional practice and convention.

Is it felt by the people of this country that some safeguards are required? This seems doubtful and surprising, considering that nearly every country has devoted much consideration to various expedients to prevent the abuse of power by a majority. May it be that the majority of people do not realize that our Second Chamber is impotent and a Cabinet possessing the loyal support of a majority of the House of Commons is supreme and without any real restraint or restriction on its use of power? Whatever the cause, there is no strong evidence that the country is impressed with the seriousness of the position. No Party has yet proposed safeguards going beyond reform of the House of

Lords; and the man in the street, that elusive if not fictional character, has no knowledge of the nature of our constitution or the dangers. At the moment, apart from Reform of the House of Lords or the establishment of a new type of a Second Chamber, a policy designed to provide safeguards would not seem to be practical politics.

What are the possible methods of providing safeguards? They are a strong Second Chamber with powers or a written constitution with fundamental rights and/or the referendum.

With regard to a Second Chamber, it might be asked in what respect the present House of Lords fails to meet the requirements, as there is no doubt that the House of Lords has been extremely efficient as a revising Chamber, that its standard of debate is probably higher than the House of Commons and that the Members of the House of Lords who take part in the day to day business of the House are men of great distinction who have earned success in many fields—eminent soldiers and sailors, great judges and administrators, Viceroys and Governors, and business men of large experience. But in the event of a conflict between the House of Commons and the House of Lords, the House of Lords has only a right of delay, except with regard to an alteration in the duration of Parliament, and this right of delay is a comparatively short one and means that the House of Commons, except when Parliament has nearly run its course, will always be able to get the particular measures passed in spite of the opposition of the House of Lords.

Even with regard to the provision in the Parliament Act which excludes from the provisions of the Act a Bill to prolong Parliament, this protection can be got over by the Government of the day arranging for sufficient Members to be appointed to the House of Lords to give them a majority.

It will be remembered that Mr. Asquith, as he then was, when he had a dispute with the House of Lords following on Mr. Lloyd George's Budget of 1910, proposed to advise the King to appoint sufficient Members to the House of Lords to give the Liberal Party a majority. It is understood that the list of prospective Peers was drawn up, but the House of Lords did not force the issue.

Mr. Asquith was a constitutionalist, and he obviously believed that this was constitutional and a proper remedy to adopt. The King in such matters is supposed to act on the advice of his Ministers and, though it may be doubtful whether it would be right for the King to accede to a request which is designed to get round a specific provision in an Act of Parliament, it may be assumed that a Government, which was anxious to govern without an election and to carry through measures to which the House of Lords was opposed, would choose the most suitable pretext for requesting the King to make such appointments; and it would be very difficult, if not impossible, for the King in such circumstances to refuse the request.

The position accordingly is that, though the House of Lords has the right to refuse a Bill to prolong the life of Parliament and has the right to delay other non-money Bills, in fact the Government in power can probably give itself a majority in the Upper House with the result that no adverse decision would be given, but even without a majority the present powers of delay are very limited. It may be that it is also a disadvantage that the House of Lords is a purely hereditary body and liable to attack as an aristocratic body out of touch with the 'common people'. This would be an unfair criticism, but it is one which would be used against the House of Lords in the event of a dispute between the Lower and Upper Houses. If our constitution should provide some check on the arbitrary decision of a Government, this should be found in a strengthened Second Chamber which would have the confidence of the country and be given effective powers.

An alternative or additional method would be to have a written constitution, or a partly written constitution, which would provide for fundamental rights which the House of Commons could not abrogate or alter by a bare majority. In such cases it may fall to the Supreme Court in the particular country to determine whether the proposed change is contrary to the constitution or not. In this country a written constitution would be a very far-reaching change. It is doubtful whether there would be support for such a proposal, except after some

invasion of the constitution. The British electorate is unwilling
to foresee dangers. It prefers to adopt an ostrich-like attitude.
The fondness of the British public for locking the stable door
after the event is one of our most cherished and established
political principles.

Another possible safeguard is a referendum which, however,
is a constitutional device which is unfamiliar to our constitution
and has few supporters among constitutional lawyers in this
country. It may be that, with our ancient system, we feel anything not having its roots in Norman or Saxon times is unworthy
of consideration and should be cold-shouldered.

While the referendum is no part of our British constitution,
it is known and used in the Empire. For example, the referendum was used in connection with the Australian federation.
Edmund Barton of New South Wales led the demand that the
Australian colonial parliaments should appoint elected delegates to frame a constitution which should then be submitted
to a referendum in each colony. This, subject to some modifica-
tions, was adopted at a Premiers' Conference and in 1897 a
constitution was drafted and adopted by referendum of the
Australian colonies except Western Australia, and later Western
Australian too came in.

In connection, too, with the more difficult federation of
South Africa, a referendum was held in Natal. Bryce called the
referendum a method of 'direct Popular Legislation, i.e. law-
making by the citizens themselves and not through their
representatives'. In this country, however, the greatest use that
could be made of the referendum would be as a safeguard
against abuse and in order to give the electorate a direct vote on
major constitutional issues.

Switzerland and Australia perhaps have gone further than
other countries in the use of the referendum and Bryce in
Modern Democracies in Chapters XXIX and LXV gives much
interesting information.

It is interesting to note that in Australia between 1901 and
1946 there were ten referenda covering twenty-three proposals
and that only four were carried which seems to show that the
electorate does not favour alterations of the constitution.

How could the referendum fit into our system of parliamentary government? There are probably at least three ways in which it could be used.

(1) Any Government which was meeting with strong opposition on some matter of outstanding importance might itself take a referendum, but this method is optional and gives no safeguard against oppression.

(2) We might adopt a written constitution or a constitution providing that certain rights were to be fundamental rights which could only be changed after a referendum.

(3) We might have a Second Chamber with real powers of rejection of any measures proposed by the House of Commons or of Acts which were contrary to or at variance with certain specified rights or subjects, combined with the right of the Government to a referendum.

The difficulty under (2) is that it would probably be necessary to leave it to the Courts to determine whether for example an Act of Parliament was contrary to some fundamental right, and it is possible for the Executive to appoint judges who are prepared to accept the views of the Cabinet.

An objection which applies to all kinds of referenda is the important question who is to frame the questions? This is very important and some people believe that in most cases the framers could so word the questions as to get the decision they desired. This may go too far, but undoubtedly the method of framing the questions could have some influence on the result. In Australia arguments for and against the proposal are issued to all electors and these arguments form quite a lengthy document. In connection with the referendum of 1946 it consisted of a thirty-one-page pamphlet.

Another problem is what majority should be required and it is suggested that a bare majority of those *entitled* to vote should be sufficient and would be fair. For if a man or woman does not take the trouble to vote, it would not be unfair to say that they cannot feel strongly in favour of the proposed change.

It surely must be admitted that in a country like ours it should be impossible for Parliament to pass constitutional measures of the most vital importance which have not been submitted to the electorate or approved at a general election without some body or method being available to ensure that such act or measure has sufficient support among the people. For example, if the Cabinet wanted to suspend the sittings of Parliament and quinquennial general elections, should there not be some safeguards? If Parliament wanted to form a republic or abolish *Habeas Corpus* or to impose a censorship of the press, is it right that this should be done through a Parliament elected on a quite different programme?

There is much to be said for a written constitution. But probably the reform which is most in accordance with our constitution is to establish a strong Second Chamber, with general powers of rejection of measures which offend against subjects which would require to be specified and which should certainly include those rights which a majority of the people of this country believe to be part of our political heritage—such as freedom of speech and of the press, a freely elected Parliament, *Habeas Corpus* and many others. It might also be provided that if the Government did not accept the verdict of the Second Chamber a Referendum might be taken.

I believe in a two party system and that for its efficient functioning Members must be prepared to support their party loyally and wholeheartedly but not where they have strong conscientious objections to the proposals and where they feel these might involve disaster to the country.

I also believe that one of the greatest problems and an urgent one is, whilst maintaining the strength of the Executive, to provide reasonable and adequate safeguards against abuse of power.

CHAPTER V

CABINET AND PARLIAMENT

By Arthur Salter

THE topic that has been allotted to me is, I think, both important and topical. At this time, the institution, which under our constitution is the ultimate guardian of liberty, needs to be strong, and one of the most notable developments of recent years (I am not speaking only about the last five years but of a considerably longer period) has been a change in the relations between Cabinet and Parliament, a shifting of power from the House of Commons to the Executive.

Before I begin to discuss, as I will in a moment, just what has happened and whether something should be done about it, it is well to remember that we must not measure and assess the position of Parliament in relation to the Cabinet on the assumption that our system of government is or has been a parliamentary democracy in the full sense, the sense in which the government is a Parliament which merely uses a Cabinet as a kind of executive committee. It is not that and it has not been that. Mr. Amery has pointed out very rightly that essentially our government is a government of the Cabinet with the assent, but not under the direction, of Parliament.

When we look at any particular constitution, I think we can see its distinctive and true qualities more clearly if we glance at the constitutions of other countries with Governments of a similar type but with national differences.

On the particular question that concerns me at the moment, namely, the shifting in the balance of power between Cabinet and Parliament, the root of that power is in the ability of one to dismiss the other. It is interesting, to reflect that, if we take the three principal parliamentary democracies, America,

France and Great Britain, we have the three possible alternatives in respect of that power of dismissal. In France the
Assemblée can always dismiss the Cabinet but in practice the
Cabinet cannot dismiss the Assemblée (although there is a
provision for the purpose, hardly ever applied and very difficult to apply, in the constitution). In the case of America, the
Executive cannot dismiss Congress nor can Congress dismiss
the Executive. Each is appointed for a specific term and each
within its own sphere is sovereign—although it is true that
Congress can hamstring the administration by refusing money
for the expenditure it desires to incur. With us you have the
third alternative, that at any moment the Executive can dismiss
Parliament by asking for a dissolution and Parliament can
always secure the resignation of the Government by passing
a vote of censure. That is the formal position. I shall come to
the realities of power a little later, but the difference, which I
have mentioned between these three democracies in this
respect, leads to, and is supplemented by, other differences.

In France, for example, the unilateral power of dismissal by
the Assemblée of the Cabinet encourages the formation of a
number of main parties, sometimes of more or less equal power
and size, and of shifting alliances between them; and the
consequence of those two factors combined is that you tend to
have a comparatively irresponsible overthrowing of the
Government.

Now it is, I suppose, deep in our British tradition that, while
one great Party means tyranny, a number of more or less equally
big parties means anarchy, and that the best foundation for
liberty is the existence of two main parties of comparably equal
strength and importance. That is not upset by the existence of
quite small parties, but normally our system does not work well
unless you have an Opposition and a Government which are
not too unequal and not distorted in their relations to each
other by the shifting alliances of a lot of other fairly important
parties.

Again France and Britain are alike, and unlike America, in
that Ministers are also Members of Parliament. That gives an
exclusive and intimate relationship that is not to be found in

the American system. France and the United States on the other hand are alike, as against Britain, in that their constitutions are written and are only changeable by a much more difficult process than that by which ordinary laws are enacted.

Each of these three systems certainly has its distinctive merits and each of them has a distinctive, inherent danger. The danger of the French system is instability. The danger of the American system is deadlock. The danger of the British system, which is my present subject, is Cabinet tyranny. Whether that exists, and the extent to which it exists, depends upon all sorts of conditions, that change from period to period.

I might take as a text for my subject as a whole, the saying of Abraham Lincoln—it is indeed the crucial problem of government in free countries—"Must a government of necessity be too strong for the liberties of its people or too weak to maintain its own existence?"

For a long period, especially perhaps from about the middle of the nineteenth century until the outbreak of the First World War, Britain seemed to have solved this problem. Its flexible, elastic, unwritten constitution, the presence of Ministers in Parliament, their dependence upon the electorate, seemed to give the solution, and the British solution was widely admired and widely imitated. Its actual success, however, to an extent to which the countries that imitated it did not as a rule realize, was due to other facts, other institutions and other factors— for example, the strength of local government and of voluntary institutions and societies of all kinds, to the character of the national press and its influence on government, to the practical sharing and dispersal of power, not the separation of powers as in America, between the legislative, judicial, administrative authorities, etc.; the recognition by each institution of the rights, authority and the appropriate responsibility of the others. There are also the national temperament and tradition, which include a disinclination to push any single logical principle to an extreme; a respect for the rights of minorities; a passion for personal freedom, fortified by memories of many centuries of constitutional struggle and also by the continuity of political development, which is only possible in an area exempt, as no other area in the world has been, for nearly a thousand years from foreign invasion.)

Other countries, imitating what was visible on the surface, have failed to realize the extent to which the British success, in combining personal freedom with efficient government, was dependent upon these deeper roots. Our own generation, I think, shows signs of a similar delusion.

It is in the blend of the factors I have just named that we find constituted and expressed the distinctive quality of British democracy and the British conception of liberty.

There is, I think, as anybody who has either studied foreign constitutions or lived under other parliamentary systems will realize, something distinctive about the particular British conception of what constitutes the right of an individual in a free country. I remember how this was impressed on an American friend of mine by one small incident. He called on me one day and said, "You know, I am now convinced that you British do believe in freedom of speech." I said, "Certainly, but why do you suddenly realize this now?" He said, "I will tell you. I was driving my little car across Hyde Park and saw people standing on barrels, with crowds round them. I saw one man with a very fine voice obviously denouncing something with very great effect. I drove up my car and stopped on the edge of the crowd, without stopping my engine, to listen, and what he was saying as I got there was 'this brutal and corrupt Metropolitan police'. That seemed a very popular sentiment and the people cheered. To my delight I saw a member of the brutal and corrupt police, a mountain of a man, stalking across in our direction. I thought I would see some fun. I expected to see him collaring the man and taking him off, but as he came nearer he went not to the man on the barrel but to me and said quite politely, 'Would you mind turning off your engine, sir, people can't hear what the gentleman is saying'." There is indeed something distinctive in the particular British conception of what our rights as individuals ought to be.

British constitutional history consists of the emergence of successive forms of tyranny or excessive privilege, and in turn of successful challenges to them. Against Norman Kings feudalism secured the rights of Magna Carta. Against feudalism monarchy itself became in some degree the champion of the people. Against monarchy, again too powerful, the Parliaments of the seventeenth century established liberty. The later excessive privilege of the landed aristocracy was countered by the extensions of the franchise in the Reform Bill of the early nineteenth century. And when power and privilege then passed to the industrial and trading plutocracy, it was met first by further extensions of the franchise in the later nineteenth century and now, in this century, by adult suffrage, distributive taxation and social reform.

The danger of today, as I have suggested, is the tyranny of the Cabinet and the bureaucracy. My successor in the Gladstone Chair at Oxford in his inaugural lecture termed our system of government a parliamentary bureaucracy. That was some years ago and developments come along fast. I am not quite sure I should not now call our system of government not so much parliamentary bureaucracy as cabinet bureaucracy. In the years ahead, it is not inconceivable, though I trust we shall not reach that point, that successors of ours might prefer the term 'party bureaucracy' to describe the domination of all parliamentary and cabinet institutions by an external party organization. We are not there yet, but that is a danger that may lie ahead of us. I will refer to it in a moment.

The causes of what I may now call 'cabinet bureaucracy' are these:

1. We have had two great wars in which extra power had to be concentrated in the Executive, and the whole economy controlled by the State. In both cases profound consequences remained after the war was over.

2. Apart from wars, we have had the long-term tendency to replace laissez-faire competitive enterprise by planned control, with consequent extension of the State's responsibility.

3. The extension of the social services has a similar result.

4. As a consequence of that, we necessarily have had the development of a very great growth of delegated legislation, where Parliament only gives the enabling powers that are translated into specific laws or regulations by a process that

may come before Parliament but not in a way which secures adequate supervision or debate.

5. Then you have in addition to that the growth of party discipline and Party organization. That is a natural development from the very great enlargement of the electorate.

6. Then next you have the semi-professionalization of the House of Commons—that is, the increase in the number of Members whose main source of income is their parliamentary salary supplemented, as it is, in a number of cases, by payment from external bodies who desire them to exert a certain influence in Parliament. It is obvious that when you have a House of Commons so semi-professionalized, Party discipline becomes much more effective and the Party Whips have a much easier task. The threat or hint of premature dissolution, with all the expense and uncertainty and risk to Members involved, is bound to be more effective now than it was in earlier Parliaments in which all Members derived their income from other sources.

All the above causes were in operation before the advent of the Labour Government in 1945. A further cause has now been added in the recent heavy legislative programme, which has resulted in truncated debates on legislation and administration, and the almost complete cessation of private Members' opportunities for initiating legislation, such opportunities as my colleague at Oxford, Sir Alan Herbert, for example, used so successfully a decade ago.

I referred just now to the possibility that what I have called 'cabinet bureaucracy' might in future be replaced by Party bureaucracy. That is a very real danger to parliamentary democracy. It is a very real possiblility. We have had examples in the British Commonwealth, though not yet in this country, in which an external Party organization has been able not only to appoint the Prime Minister but to dictate to him what Ministers he should appoint and then to dictate exactly and in detail what the Government should do. When you have dictation of that kind by an institution external to the constitution altogether, parliamentary government has almost been destroyed. That has been a phase in the parliamentary systems

of certain Dominions in the British Commonwealth. We have
not got there, but already here the Party conferences have a
different relation to Government from what they have had in
the past. This is not a subject I can pursue in the limited space
available to me, but I would suggest to those studying the
subject to read a very interesting leader in *The Times* on this
subject on 21st January, 1950.

The next result of all the causes I have referred to is that
Parliament does not now effectively debate or control legislation, administration or finance, and I might add that, to a
large extent, the Courts have also been excluded. The great
bulk of legislation is now in the form of Orders in Council
outside the effective control of Parliament, the great bulk of
administration is carried through without any real supervision
or knowledge of Parliament, and the great bulk of decisions of
a judicial character are now taken, not by the Courts, but by
various judicial or semi-judicial bodies set up by the Administration. The fact is that the increase in the bulk and complexity of
what is now attempted in the way of government is much too
great for such a body as the House of Commons working
through its present machinery. I would like to give one or two
illustrations of what has happened, sometimes almost without
being noticed. First of all, as to the truncating of debate. In 1947
there was a very heavy legislative programme including the
Transport Bill, Town and Country Planning Bill and other
measures. In order to get the whole of that legislation through,
the Government introduced what, in the circumstances and in
the form in which it was introduced, was a novel form of closure
and guillotine. Some of us thought that if Parliament could not
get a proper opportunity of debate, obstruction apart of course,
the legislative programme ought to have been lightened, but
we recognized that at least the genuine reason for the closure
and guillotine was to give Parliament time to get all the measures
through.

That was in 1947, but look at the next year, the 1948–9
session. There was then no pressure on Parliament's time, there
was only one measure of first-rate importance—the Iron and
Steel Bill. But again debate was restricted. Tennyson said that

"Freedom slowly broadens down from precedent to precedent."
But it is not only freedom that broadens down. Its opposite
may do just the same. The precedent of restricting debate
having been established in 1947 (where there was at least a
genuine reason, namely, that time was required for other
measures), the time was again restricted in 1948 when Bills
were being dug out of musty pigeon-holes, of no urgency or
importance, to clutter up Parliamentary time. That was the
suppression of debate for the sake of supressing debate. That
way lies the death of Parliament and of all of which it is the
guardian.

I was greatly disturbed then, not as a person who has
particular views about the Iron and Steel Bill, though I have
some, but as a Member of Parliament. When you get action of
that kind, it is no use for Members of the Opposition to make
their protests or for persons opposed to the Bill to make their
protests. I was disappointed that there were no protests from
supporters of the Government and of the Iron and Steel Bill.
They might have said, as Voltaire said about his great anta-
gonist, "I deeply differ with everything he says but I would
defend to the death his right to say it."

Whatever Party is in power, you may get a danger of
Cabinet tyranny. The only safeguard is that the people generally, and Members of Parliament of every Party in particular,
should have a real understanding of what Parliament and its
traditions mean for the country; and that there should be
immediate protests from all sides against any attempt to
suppress debate. I would like to quote a few words of what I
said myself in the House in March 1947, as to the way in which
Parliament's rights are being destroyed. "This proposal" (to
closure debate on the floor of the House and in Committee) "is
completely without precedent and is not only a grave assault
upon Parliament's legislative function, as we have known it in
the past, but a completely novel assault. . . . I deplore it all the
more because it is only one of a long series of such assaults
within the last eighteen months. We must consider them in
their cumulative effect. Time after time, in the Borrowing Act,
the Exchange Control Bill, and I might quote many others"

(I am now coming to the second way in which parliamentary authority has been undermined) "clauses have been drafted so widely, that it has been easy for us to demonstrate that quite fantastic abusive action could be taken within the powers of the Bill. When this has been demonstrated, the Minister has always said: 'That is not what I intend to do. I intend to do so and so. I have quite a reasonable policy.' We may agree that the Minister is sincere and that his policy is reasonable, but we cannot properly accept such assurances as alternatives to drafting the law in such a way as to define his powers. We are concerned in this House, as legislators, with the legal intention which is to be inferred from the words of a Bill, and not with ministerial intentions or assurances which do not bind even their successors of the same Government and still less their successors in another Government, while the measure itself, with all the powers which were given originally, still survives."

That is a second way in which, in my view, the real authority of Parliament is being filched away. The Government draft a Bill with an extraordinarily wide definition of powers; a critic then gets up and says that under these powers the Government could do fantastic things. The Minister replies: "You know me, I have told you what I want to do. You know I am a reasonable man." The House believes him and time after time the Bill goes through in that form, on that assurance. But that is not legislation; it is giving a blank cheque to a person who may be worthy of credit but who has the power to pass it on to someone who may not be worthy of credit. It is not legislation.

That is the process by which power shifts from Parliament to the Executive. I would like to suggest one barometer of the change in the authority of an M.P. as such and the Executive; this is the extent to which you find M.P.s trying to get what they want, not by exercising their legitimate influence through debate, through public discussion, but by getting favours from individual Ministers. The habit of deputations is increasing. Of course, at any time and under any system we must have deputations as a part of our system, but it is a bad sign if we find Members increasingly saying, "It is no good raising that in the House, it will irritate the Minister and make it more difficult for

H

him to give way if we criticize him in public. Let us go on a deputation." It reflects a shift in the relations between Members and Ministers. You remember the aphorism about deputations: 'a deputation is a noun of multitude signifying many but not signifying much'. There is some danger of deputations now taking an unduly large part in the working of our institutions.

I think at this stage I had better not spend further time in illustrating what I think has happened and why, but come to what I think might be done about it, if we agree that this weakening of Parliament is undesirable. We want, in any reform, to bear in mind the double purpose, first to make the machine of Government efficient for its greater mass of business and second to restore and safeguard the reality of parliamentary control and an adequate respect in majority decisions for the opinions of different classes and interests. I make the following suggestions.

To begin with, I do not think that either real parliamentary control or the essentials of a free system are compatible with either the pace and scale of legislation in recent years or the extent, scale and character of our present state control of the economic system. I say that not as a controversial point, because I do not think in any case, whatever Government is in power, that legislation is likely to proceed at as great a pace as we witnessed in the early years of the recent Government. It is only on the assumption that both the pace and the scale will be reduced in the years ahead that I think the suggestions I am going to make are of any value.

First, better ministerial organization is required, in order to secure a 'Cabinet Policy' which is not merely an imperfectly reconciled conflict of departmental policies. The line of progress is quite clearly, I think, the further development of the 'Cabinet Committee' system, as urged by Sir John Anderson in his Romanes lecture some years ago and as urged recently by Mr. Amery.

Second, each of these Cabinet Committees should be served by an adequate research and planning staff, not self-contained but, like the Joint Intelligence and Planning Staffs developed during the war, composed of members of the intelligence staffs of the several offices and departments.

Each of these Cabinet Committees might perhaps, I would suggest, have the Prime Minister as its formal Chairman—and he would preside wherever he found it desirable, but normally I think each should be presided over by a Cabinet Minister of high status.

At this point I differ from Mr. Amery. He thinks you should have a small number of superior Cabinet Ministers without departmental responsibilities and that they should, each of them, be chairman of a group of Ministers, each of whom would have a Department. The great objection to that proposal, I think, is that under peace conditions a Minister not supported by a powerful Department would not in practice be able to make his views or those of his Committee prevail over the powerful Departments—a 'super-Minister' for example, such as Mr. Amery proposed, presiding over an Economic Committee of the Cabinet would scarcely prevail over a powerful Chancellor of the Exchequer backed by the Treasury. I think myself the right course is to group the departmental Ministers in Committees, each of which would be presided over by the Minister in charge of the most important Department of the group. The objection that such Chairmen-Ministers would be overburdened and would be unable to find time to consider general policy could be met by the appointment, in each of these more important Departments, of a Minister of State (as now in the Foreign Office) and the delegation of greater responsibilities to him.

I should myself envisage an inner Cabinet composed (apart from the Prime Minister) of the Defence Minister, the Foreign Secretary, the Chancellor of the Exchequer, and perhaps one or two others, each normally having a Minister of State in his Department and holding a superior position over other Departments in his group by virtue of his Cabinet position and his presidency of the Cabinet Committee.

Each Cabinet Committee would, of course, invite particular Ministers, not among its permanent members, when dealing with problems of current administrative action. Out of such problems general policy would largely develop, as it does now and must, 'inductively' so to speak. But the Committee would also meet on other occasions without departmental Ministers except its own Members, for more general consideration of wider long-term policy.

I think in that way you would get what Mr. Amery considered so essential but with an authority that you would not get if you tried to give non-departmental Ministers authority over the most powerful departmental Ministers.

At such 'policy' meetings, a Committee might sometimes invite Dominion representatives (Ministers or High Commissioners) to participate. It might also on questions less involved in current political controversy, where continuity of policy is possible from one Administration to another (e.g. Defence and Foreign Policy), invite leading Members of the Opposition. Our system is mainly based on a clear responsibility of the Government on the one hand and a critical and powerful Opposition party on the other, but I do think that there is a very considerable area over which a very considerable measure of shared responsibility as between Government and Opposition is possible and is desirable. America has found a solution in the development of a bipartisan policy on foreign affairs—Senator Vandenberg co-operating on behalf of the Opposition Party with President Truman and Mr. Marshall on the side of the Executive. Although we have no similar system here, something of the kind is visible in embryo. Quite obviously there has been more sympathy between Mr. Bevin and the leader of the Opposition than between Mr. Bevin and his own left-wing supporters. In actual organizational procedure, there has been quite recently a development under which at a certain stage (not merely on the eve of war when it was the practice in the earlier years but long before that) the Prime Minister has consulted with the leader of the Opposition. There have been one or two meetings of that kind recently and I think that practice might be developed further.

Next I suggest there might be a deliberate policy of decentralization and the assignment of a greater range of independent decisions to local authorities. There has been a growing tendency, while increasing the bulk of work imposed on local authorities, to reserve more and more of the actual policy decisions for Whitehall. I think we should reverse that tendency and also the tendency which has been undermining the authority of voluntary institutions, the centralizing tendency of Whitehall which has been reflected for example in the attitude of the National Health Insurance Department to the Friendly Society officials. The same attitude is expressed over a wide sphere. I think if you take a combination of the financial policy and Whitehall's centralizing policy, you will see that a great deal of what was been one of the foundations of British democracy as developed in this country, namely, voluntary institutions that are real and powerful, has been undermined. I think every effort should be made to reverse the process.

Then I think a determined effort should be made to increase the general understanding by the public of the extent to which the British system has in the past combined freedom with order through a sharing of power between different centres of authority and influence, with respect by each for the other, and restraint in the exercise of the majority vote.

This involves, in my view, the acceptance in our general system of a combination of different principles, without pressing any one of them to its logical extreme to the exclusion of all the rest. You have for example such principles as 'one person one vote', 'one vote one value', 'stake in the country', the 'representation of classes and interests', 'representation of the electorate as a whole', the 'right of the majority', 'respect for the rights of minorities'. If you press any one of these principles to its extreme, you may get what may be called a 'logical system', but you destroy what has been the strength of the British constitution, its tolerance and its balance.

Let me illustrate my point by the reason given for the abolition of the University seats, one of which I occupied for thirteen years. It is that the University franchise is 'anomalous' because it is based upon a second vote. True; but a vote is nothing in itself, apart from its effect. The principle 'one person one vote' is unmeaning unless it is combined with the principle

of 'one vote one value'. But no one proposed to press this
principle to its logical extreme. More seats are for example,
even under the latest electoral act, assigned to Scotland and to
Wales, as compared to England, than the number of voters
would justify, on the ground that there must be some recognition of the fact that both Wales and Scotland are in a real
sense 'separate communities'. Even more important is the fact
that if the principle of 'one vote' were to be pressed to its logical
extreme, we should obviously have 'proportional representation'—and to that the two main parties are both opposed.
We therefore have the absurd result that the 'one vote' principle
is considered by the Labour Party to have an absolute sanctity
when they are dealing with the University seats, a partial
sanctity when they are distributing seats between the different
parts of the United Kingdom, and no sanctity at all when they
are faced with the problem of proportional representation. In
other cases the consideration that a departure from the 'one
vote' principle is justified by utility and convenience is allowed
to prevail. Only in the case of the University seats is every other
consideration except the 'one vote' principle said to have no
validity.

Next I would suggest that the Enabling Acts which give
power for subordinate delegation should be drafted so as to
lay down all the main principles clearly, and to define closely
the limits of the delegated power. If that were done the present
Committee whose duty it is to supervise and report to the House
on Orders in Council might have a measurable and manageable
task. I think, however, that this committee should be enlarged,
and the staff and organization by which it is assisted enlarged,
and that it should be regarded as having the same status as the
Public Accounts Committee.

I have one other main proposal. I should like to see
unofficial committees of Members of Parliament (about the same
size as the present official standing committees and like them
reflecting the Party Membership of the House) formed for
each main group of subjects. These would be recognized as
important and Ministers would be expected to attend, but they
would be unofficial in the sense that their deliberations would

in themselves have no legal effect. In practice, you would have
a group of members in the House specially interested for each
particular subject constituted in practice by a self-selective
process; they would be the members interested in the particular
questions dealt with by each committee, colonial questions,
foreign affairs, financial policy, Board of Trade questions, etc.
The Minister would come and explain his problems and his
policy and he would have with him his higher officials. The
official debates would, of course, be as at present on the floor
of the House, but if they had been preceded by informal and
expert discussions upstairs, they would be less discursive and
uninformed than they are at present; and Members with special
experience would be much better able to exert an influence on
the Departments.

That would be a very important way of restoring some
reality to the role and influence of the ordinary private Member.

Another more radical reform is the interesting one proposed
by Mr. Churchill in his Romanes lecture of 1930. This is that
Parliament should choose an Economic sub-Parliament consisting of say one-fifth of its members in proportion to Party
strength, composed of persons of high technical and business
qualifications to discuss in public all the most disputed questions
of Finance and Trade. "The conclusions of such a body, although themselves devoid of legal force," he says, "might well,
if they commanded a consensus of opinion, supply us with a
comprehensive and unified view of high expert authority, which
could then be remitted in its integrity to the political sphere."

That in principle is an enlarged and more important
example of the kind of Members' committee that I have been
suggesting, but this particular one would have a higher status
and greater importance. That is, I think, an interesting suggestion, but I have no time to discuss it further now.

These proposals, taken all together, would I think do a great
deal to arrest the present very dangerous tendency of parliamentary authority and control to become an unreality.

Again, however, I would repeat in my final words—I do not
believe that any system of Parliamentary-Cabinet-Bureau-
cracy, such as we now have, can be so reformed, by any

devices or improved machinery, as to combine the reality of parliamentary control with efficiency, without a great reduction in the mass of work now falling upon central government. A combination of decentralization, reduction of new legislation, and restriction of the area of detailed state control are indispensable if other reforms are to be effective.

My concluding word is this. The British Parliament has a past of glory, a present of frustration, a future of uncertainty. Our destiny turns largely, I think, upon our ability, without making the Executive impotent or ineffective, to restore the traditions and the authority of Parliament so that it can be once more the effective guardian of our liberties.

CHAPTER VI

PARLIAMENT IN RELATION TO THE CIVIL SERVICE[1]

By H. E. Dale

THE title at the head of this chapter might be held to cover a wide range of interesting subjects. It might include, for example, the constitutional law, written and unwritten, which governs the relations of Parliament with the Civil Service; or the history of parliamentary dealings with the Service from the time when there was anything that could be described by that name; or the large questions implicit in such phrases as 'administrative law' and 'delegated legislation' If only for. reasons of space, however, no attempt is made here either to recount history or to examine theory. This chapter is concerned primarily with existing facts and their consequences. It endeavours to provide some sort of answer to the questions: 'What is, in fact, the present relationship between Parliament and the Civil Service? What influence does Parliament (which in this connection means almost exclusively the House of Commons) in fact exert upon the Service? And, conversely, what is the influence of the Service upon Parliament?' The answers to such questions are clearly not matters of statistical certainty or even probability; but the main facts are familiar

[1] In previous writings, the author of this chapter has already dealt to some extent with its subject. Not having changed materially the views stated in those writings, he has felt at liberty to use again appropriate parts of them (with a few minor alterations) when it seemed convenient. These constitute about one third of the chapter; the remainder is new.

He is indebted to the Association of Barnett House, Oxford, for permission to use in this manner a passage of about 1,200 words (pp. 123–7 of the chapter) from his Sidney Ball lecture 'The personnel and problems of the Higher Civil Service' (delivered at Oxford in 1943, and published that year by the Oxford University Press as No. 26 of the Barnett House Papers), of which the Association owns the copyright.

to persons well acquainted with the House of Commons and the Service, and the inferences to be drawn from the facts do not as a rule appear doubtful.

On the surface, the relation between the two bodies seems to be purely one-sided, or rather (for it might be objected that a purely one-sided relation is a contradiction in terms) to be entirely active on the one side and passive on the other. Parliament, as the supreme authority of the realm, can do or cause to be done substantially whatever it pleases with the Civil Service, as with anyone or anything else within the realm; and it does from time to time cast a roving eye and stretch out a powerful hand towards the Service. It is graciously pleased to emit year by year legislation providing the salaries and wages of civil servants, and, at fairly long intervals, to modify the conditions of the pensions and gratuities which cheer or depress them on their retirement; it can debate at any time such fascinating topics as methods of appointment and promotion in the Service; and it can inquire, by questions addressed to Ministers or even by a set debate, into the actions or words of individual civil servants down to the casual remarks of one of H.M.'s Inspectors of Schools to the head mistress of a school he was inspecting. On the other hand, the Civil Service, and individual civil servants, have as such no means of expressing directly to Parliament their opinions and desires.[1] His Majesty's Government—the Ministers of the Crown for the time being—stand completely between them and Parliament, and cut them off from all contact with the supreme authority (as a corporation). No civil servant ever appears in either House;[2] the official galleries (the pews at one entrance to the House of Lords and to the right of the Speaker's Chair in the House of Commons) are technically outside the House. No civil servant can be a Member of the House of Commons without resigning his

[1] No doubt civil servants can legally address Parliament by petition; but this is, of course, a general right of all British subjects, not of civil servants as such. How, far it would be 'proper' (in the official sense of the word) for a body of civil servants to exercise this right, is another question.

[2] The staffs of the two Houses are servants of those Houses, not of the Crown. The Comptroller and Auditor-General is a special case; though appointed by the Government, he is an officer of the House of Commons. Even he never appears on the floor of the House.

official appointment; if (as does sometimes happen) a civil servant acquires a peerage by inheritance or otherwise, he must not exercise his full parliamentary rights in the House of Lords while he is a civil servant. The only occasion when a civil servant comes directly into contact even with a representative emanation of Parliament is appearance as a witness before a committee of one or both Houses. Before such Committees, of which the Public Accounts Committee and the Estimates Committee of the House of Commons are the most important, he appears only as the mouthpiece of his Minister. He can answer from his own knowledge or opinion concerning facts and figures, and the reasons (legal and administrative requirements, the practice of the Department, the policy of the Minister, and so forth) why such and such things were done or not done; and he may explain the grounds of the Minister's policy. But if he is asked, directly or by implication, "What do you think yourself of the policy?" and the question is not disallowed by the Chairman, he must either decline to answer or say he has no opinion other than his Minister's.

This in brief is the appearance; the reality is very different. In fact, the House of Commons and the Civil Service exert constantly a mutual influence which produces results certainly momentous on the Service, and probably not insignificant on the House. It is exerted partly through the intermediacy of the men who are leading members of the first body and undisputed masters of the second, i.e. Ministers; and partly through the personal contacts, in some degree random contacts, of individual members of the one body with individual members of the other. Of these two connecting wires, the former transmits, both ways, currents of far more continuous, powerful, and pervasive influence than the latter. Those currents cannot be measured; but their description must be the substance of any attempt to exhibit the facts.

From one point of view, British Cabinet Ministers may be regarded as Directors of one of the two or three greatest businesses in the world, far surpassing any private business in scale and complexity, and surpassed, if at all, only by the central administrations of the United States and Russia. The business is conducted under conditions so familiar to us that we seldom realize how remarkable they are. It is subject to the supreme control of a committee of several hundred shareholders (including the Directors themselves) of whom a large proportion, maybe nearly one half, are bitterly opposed to the existing Directors and to much of their policy, and are perpetually seeking to turn them out and substitute a Chairman and Board chosen from their own Party. Any fairly large section of the committee is able to raise a set debate on any part of the firm's business, or on any particular transaction they may select. The leaders of the minority are at liberty, whenever they think a serious mistake has been made, to propose that the Board, or at least the Director responsible for the mistake, shall be reprimanded; and if the proposal is carried, that Director, and perhaps the whole Board, will have to resign at once. Any member of the committee is entitled to ask at any time any question he chooses about any matter of the firm's business, from issues of broad policy down to the least detail, and ordinarily to have a full and accurate reply within a few hours or at the most within two or three days. Finally, the committee, with these rights and powers, sits at the firm's headquarters in London for several hours a day, on seven or eight months of the year.

This is a loose and incomplete but not unfair representation of some of the main conditions under which the vast business of modern government is conducted here; they may be comprehended in one phrase—the existence, powers, and habits of the House of Commons. It is outside the scope of this chapter to consider, save incidentally, their effect upon Ministers; but it is clearly essential to consider their transmitted effect in relation to the little *corps d'élite* of high officials,[1] the men who

[1] It is a reasonable conjecture that the total number of the 'higher civil service' (defined as the officials who are in a position to exercise a real and direct influence upon government policy in important matters) is now between 1,000 and 1,500— a tiny fraction of the total number of civil servants, even after excluding industrial and manipulative staffs and minor staff such as messengers and charwomen. Even of these high officials the great majority appear but seldom in the region of policy, because their powers and influence are confined to a limited province of their department's work; only a small proportion of them, perhaps one-seventh or one-eighth, are in close and regular contact with their parliamentary chiefs—members, so to speak, of the little cabinet which forms almost inevitably around every Minister at the head of a large department, for the discussion both of general policy and of particular matters requiring his immediate attention.

stand close to Ministers, give them advice and receive instructions from them, and are responsible to them for the detailed
working of the administrative machine; and in relation also
to the subordinate staff, numbering hundreds of thousands, for
whose countless and mostly obscure doings Ministers are ultimately responsible to Parliament. Let us take first the effects
upon the high official.

First, parliamentary business normally takes precedence of
everything else in his estimation, as (and because) it does in
his Minister's. Apart from his professional duty of loyal service
to the Minister (whose present position and future career depend
largely on his performances in the House), the Department itself, as an entity distinct from the Minister for the time being,
suffers some temporary loss of influence if its chief makes a bad
speech on an important occasion or is severely battered at
question-time. Conversely, the possession of a Minister who is
a 'good parliamentarian' strengthens a Department's arm in
many ways, not least in its dealings with other departments.

Second, Ministers require in their high officials two
qualities which have few or no analogies in private business,
however large: judgment of the probable attitude of the House
towards new actions and proposals, and skill in marshalling
justificatory facts and arguments.

Third, business must sometimes go more slowly than it
would if the House of Commons did not exist; for the official
is cautious about deciding without reference to the Minister
some things in themselves trivial, if they are likely to provoke
discussion in the House. It is not that he doubts the wisdom of
his own views or is afraid to act on them; it is the feeling of fair
play. "This may mean trouble in the House, and my chief
will have to face it, not I; it is not fair to run him in for it
without giving him a chance of objecting."

Fourth, both Ministers and officials are in general less willing
to take large risks in their enterprises than magnates of private
business—the officials from loyalty to their Ministers, the
latter because even one mistake may do serious harm to their
reputations in the House and the country. The ultimate reason
is simple. Directors who have to face only an Annual General

Meeting are judged on the record of the whole year; failures can be covered up, or set off by successes. But with the House of Commons meeting nearly every day for months together, a big mistake is taken by itself—it is the hot event of the day and a heaven-sent chance for the party in opposition, invective is concentrated on it, and appeals to successes gained months before in quite different fields have little persuasive force. Even if the Government as a body survive attack, there remains a black mark against the particular Minister responsible.

Fifth, for a similar reason, officials are strongly inclined to follow regulations and precedents, even when they are embarrassing. Defence is then easy.

Sixth, the high official must have at his command full records, always quickly available—which means 'paper work' in quantity, for his subordinates if not for him. Unlike his compeer in private business, he has to fight on two fronts at once, so to speak; he has to do the work or see that it is done, and he has to provide for its public defence, in detail and at short notice, against questions and attacks from a numerous, acute, and well-organized body of professional critics.

These are the principal consequences to the high official which follow from the impact of the House of Commons as transmitted through Ministers. The qualities and habits so developed may sometimes, like other necessary qualities and habits, pass beyond the golden mean and become vices, or at least failings. Reluctance to take risks may become timidity; the insistent question "Will the House like this?" may sometimes lead officials as well as Ministers to defer action that ought to be taken, particularly when the true grounds of action cannot be publicly stated; a proper regard for precedent may degenerate into a rigid formalism. The only safeguards are natural energy and common sense, and high officials are not generally lacking in these antiseptic qualities—if they were, they would scarcely be where they are. But the main point is that, good or bad, many of the principal characteristics of the high official spring inevitably from those of the House of Commons. If in a great department whose work is often a battle-field of party politics the higher staff were suddenly and entirely replaced by men imported from science or industry or commerce, it is probable almost to the point of certainty that within three years many of them would have transferred themselves or been transferred elsewhere, and the remainder would have developed the qualities of their predecessors in office.

The influence of the House, transmitted through Ministers, is naturally attenuated as it passes through the higher officials down to the lower ranks of the Civil Service; but it remains powerful and pervasive in one most important respect. A quite insignificant act or remark of any civil servant in his dealings with the public may cause entirely disproportionate trouble, culminating perhaps in a question in the House or even a heated debate; it may be very unlikely, but it is always possible. A Minister is constitutionally bound to defend his subordinates, and will discharge his obligation with complete loyalty, even though he never before heard of the official who has caused the trouble, knew nothing of his action, and personally thinks it ill-advised and stupid. But to put it at the lowest, he will not be amused by such entanglements, and it is the duty of his higher staff to save him from them. Accordingly, the complaints of individuals, however obscure, are sure to be taken seriously at headquarters if they have any semblance of reasonable foundation. If, as many do, they reach the department through the Member of Parliament for a complainant's constituency, they are seen by the Minister himself; for a Member is entitled to a reply signed by the Minister or (in his absence) by his private secretary.[1] But whether a complaint comes direct from the aggrieved person or through some intermediary, it will be carefully investigated, and if there has been any official misdoing, 'suitable notice will be taken'. All this is well known to

[1] No implication is intended that a complaint made to a Member and sent on by him to the Minister (or made to a high official through a personal friend) will be treated more favourably than a complaint made direct by the aggrieved person to the Department; such an implication would be incorrect.

Incidentally, these personal communications to Ministers and high officials—if they do not become too numerous—are useful as enabling them to see how the executive machinery of the Department is working, to judge whether a general policy is being properly applied in individual cases and to consider whether general instructions given to branch officers require to be altered or amplified.

the Civil Service itself. Every official of any experience, down
to the village postman, is aware that if he has done anything
wrong or silly in his official capacity (sometimes even if he
hasn't) a bolt from the blue may burst upon him in the shape of
an urgent request from his superiors for a full report on what
he did or said, and why; and that if his report does not give a
satisfactory account, there will be trouble. That knowledge is
a powerful restraint upon any tendency of the proud official to
abuse the little brief authority in which he is drest. The
ultimate origin and sanction of such salutary discipline is the
House of Commons.

Let us turn now to the converse question: "What influence
does the Civil Service exert through Ministers upon Parliament,
and particularly the House of Commons, as a corporate body?"

As stated at the beginning of this chapter, the answer is
"On the surface, none"; the House is indisputably master, the
official indisputably a subordinate, the separation between them
is apparently complete. But all Ministers are in fact both-
way transmitters (so to speak), though some are better
transmitters than others; and through them some influence
from the Civil Service does reach the House. Its importance
must not be exaggerated; it is only one of the many currents
of thought and feeling that converge on the supreme authority
of the realm. Nevertheless it is reasonably certain that it is not
negligible.

Almost every considered communication made by a Minister
to Parliament, whether in print or orally (Bills, statutory regulations, set speeches, answers to questions, parliamentary
papers, and so forth) is seen by at least one civil servant
(usually by several) before it is made; as a rule a draft has been
prepared in the department—of course, in accord with the
general policy of the Minister as known to his officials—and
often accepted by him without substantial amendment. It is
impossible to examine in detail the part played, and the
influence exerted, by civil servants in these (and other) dealings
between Ministers and Parliament; but as legislation is the
supreme exercise of parliamentary power, it may be taken as an
example, and a summary account given of the processes through

which a long and elaborate Bill has usually passed before it reaches the House of Commons.

If it is a principal item of the Government's policy and highly contentious, the first step will probably be a conference or series of conferences between the Minister, or even a committee of Ministers, and three or four of the highest officials of the department primarily concerned, from which there emerges a memorandum stating the purposes, limits, and general lines of the Bill. Then the Treasury is formally asked to instruct those very important persons, Parliamentary Counsel to the Treasury, to place themselves in communication with the department; and about the same time other departments interested are told what is in the wind if they do not already know. By arrangement among the Parliamentary Counsel themselves, of whom before the war there were generally four or five and are now nearly twenty, the Bill is assigned to one particular counsel; he gets into touch with the Legal Adviser of the department, and together they produce a first draft. Now comes the real labour. The first draft is no more than a rough framework which must be converted into a finished structure. The Parliamentary Counsel, the Legal Adviser of the department, and the two or three administrative officials immediately concerned go over the draft, clause by clause and word by word, proposing and discussing additions here and deletions there, searching for ambiguities and possibilities of evasion, raising every conceivable point which can occur to acute and experienced minds. After one or two such discussions counsel produces a second draft, and the process of minute and exhaustive examination is repeated. Even of a small Bill there will probably be ten or twelve drafts before its terms are finally settled between the lawyers and the administrators; a big and complicated Bill may run into fifty drafts or more. Certainly at some stage, and perhaps at every stage, copies of the drafts go to the particular persons in the Treasury and other departments who deal with the subject of the Bill so far as it touches their departments; their criticisms and suggestions must be fully considered, and met if at all possible. On some clauses there may arise a fierce inter-departmental battle, only to be decided by higher

I

authority—perhaps even by the Prime Minister or the Cabinet if the point at issue is of great political, financial, or administrative importance; other clauses may require confidential discussions, not always short and easy, with outside bodies such as local authorities, trade unions, or the great commercial and industrial associations. Finally, after weeks or months of labour the Bill emerges from the little working gang of civil servants, administrative and legal. Every clause, every word in it has been thoroughly examined and its effect considered; all the departments concerned have been 'squared'; all the outside interests conciliated so far as the policy and principles of the Bill permit. It is then submitted to the Parliamentary Secretary and the Minister with a brief explanation of its provisions. Unless (as is quite possible) the Minister has been often consulted during the period of gestation and therefore already knows the points of real doubt and difficulty, he will probably summon a little meeting at which the framers of the Bill will explain the crucial points, the reasons for any provisions which look queer, and in particular the reasons for any clauses that are likely to arouse opposition in the Cabinet or among the Government's own supporters in Parliament. The result of the meeting may be yet more alterations and one or two more drafts; but probably the Minister will accept the Bill as it stands or with only trivial amendments, and it is sent at once to the Cabinet Office with a memorandum over the Minister's initials, setting out in words as few and simple as can possibly be employed the reasons for the Bill and its main provisions, and asking the Cabinet to approve its introduction into Parliament. The draft Bill and the memorandum are referred automatically to a Cabinet Committee, if there is an appropriate committee and if there is time; otherwise they go straight to the Cabinet. Then the Bill is out of the hands of the civil servants who framed it; the Minister himself must acknowledge paternity and watch tenderly over his offspring. Since, however, the other Ministers concerned have all been committed by their departments during the preliminary discussions, it is not likely that there will be any serious difficulty in the Cabinet. If the Bill involves expenditure from public funds (few indeed are the bills which do not) and is to be introduced in the Commons, a memorandum giving an estimate of that expenditure must accompany it; the estimate must be agreed with the Treasury—not always an easy matter. When this memorandum has been settled, it remains only for the Minister's private secretary to speak to the Whips and arrange with them a date for the first reading (purely formal), and for the second reading which is the real start of the Bill's parliamentary voyage.

It will be clear that any statute enacted on the proposal of Ministers must be in great part the work of civil servants—in far the greater part, if the criterion is simply the number of clauses or words. Nevertheless the Service may reasonably claim to be absolved from Sir James Stephen's condemnation, old but perhaps not entirely out-of-date: "To make laws is the single employment of adult life which is supposed to require no preparatory study; which may be one of the reasons why the studies of half a life are too little for the right interpretation of such laws as our legislators make." In proposals for legislation, as in the other work of Government, Ministers determine policy, and determine also many of the important matters lying in the wide field between high policy and purely administrative detail; in such decisions the influence exerted by an official upon a Minister varies not only with the nature of the particular question to be decided and the Minister's opinion of the official, but also with the political pressure concentrated on the point. Again, it may become evident during or after the second reading of a Bill that the feeling of the Government's own supporters about some particular clause or part is so strongly adverse that it must be altered, whatever the effect on the rest of the Bill. Thirdly, in the arduous process of conducting a highly contentious Bill through committee of the whole House, the Minister in charge is likely to be suddenly confronted from time to time with novel criticisms and suggestions, *prima facie* reasonable, to which he has to give an answer off-hand, with little or no chance of consulting anyone; if, as may happen, the criticism or suggestion is supported by some Members of his own party and the point at issue does not seem important, he may well accept an amendment that carries within it the seeds of much future trouble. Finally, under pressure of time and in order to get a Bill on the Statute Book at once, a Government is sometimes forced to ask the House of Commons to agree to unwelcome and inconvenient amendments proposed by the other House. For such reasons, a long and contentious Bill presented for the Royal assent is not likely to exhibit in all its important provisions and in all its phrasing the influence of the professional qualities of the civil servants who originally drafted it; but it does not follow that that influence has been ineffectual. The same remark applies to the proceedings of Parliament other than legislation.

What then are the relevant qualities of the Civil Service— 'relevant' in this context meaning the qualities of apparent value by which it may be expected to supply something that is needed by a large popular assembly? Clearly those engendered in the high official by the conditions of his life and work in which he differs most markedly from a Member of the House of Commons. The differences may be summed up in four words— non-political appointment, permanence, privacy. A full discussion of the effects of these conditions on the high official would be out of place here; it will suffice to indicate three principal qualities or habits of mind which are developed in him, and transmitted in some degree from him, through Ministers, to the House of Commons.

At this date no defence is required for the non-political method of appointing civil servants, nor for their permanence of tenure; together these involve the well-known consequence of political neutrality, at least in public. Such conditions tend to repel from the Service the youth who is an ardent advocate of one party and its doctrines, and to attract candidates whose thoughts and ambitions do not turn naturally towards politics. Most entrants into the Administrative Class of the Service are likely to have in them by nature something of the 'mugwump', a creature who has his uses although he may be an abomination to politicians. Life in the Service fosters this coolness of mind and character; the higher a man rises, the less inclined he becomes to think that all the arguments, whether of principle or of expediency, are to be found on one side of a complicated question, or that the merits of a proposal have necessarily any close relation to the sincerity and vehemence of its advocates. Little need be said on the third point, the 'privacy' of the Service. The rule that the high official's dealings with his parliamentary chiefs above him (as with his subordinates below) are completely hidden from the public eye[1] is absolutely necessary if he is to do his duty, viz. advise Ministers with complete candour, argue freely with them if he thinks them wrong, and yet retain his office and do his utmost for the execution of their decisions if he is overruled. These conditions of the official life foster three cognate qualities to which the life of a politician does not offer similar encouragement—impartiality, a certain cool prudence, and adherence to principle as against immediate expediency.

These qualities are by no means confined to the civil servant. They are to be found in all professions, including politics; but political life does not favour their growth. Except for a very few 'independents', Members of the House of Commons hold their seats as party men. They are constantly exposed to the demands of their own constituents and of sections of the electorate banded together in leagues, unions, and associations of all kinds, as well as to the exhortations and reproofs of the Press; Ministers are exposed to all these, and also to the emotions and prejudices of the House itself. All Members desire to do what will give immediate pleasure to the majority of the electorate, and to avoid anything that will displease it—a desire that the approach of a General Election blows into flame. Nor is it merely a case of material benefits. The leaders of a party must maintain the enthusiasm of their followers, and the power to inspire enthusiasm does not often in politics go with an impartial mind and a cool prudence in word and deed.

---

[1]Very rarely, some confidential minute or memorandum by a civil servant emerges in a statement made by or on behalf of a Minister; but it appears only by mistake, and, if noticed, it is at once withdrawn with apologies. One old story goes that a Minister, reading mechanically a long and dull reply to a question in the House of Commons, electrified the House by concluding with the sentence "The Honourable Member is very tiresome; the more information we give him, the more he wants." (The official, now a distinguished Member of the House of Lords, to whom the authorship of this remark is attributed intended it, of course, only for the Minister's eye; by a typist's error it was copied as part of the reply to the question.)

It would be quite untrue to say that British politicians always take short views, but it is true that they are always under that temptation. It is one from which the civil servant is relatively free. Probably by nature, and certainly by training, he stands somewhat aloof from political parties. He has no personal motive for any but an impartial judgment on doctrines and schemes. During his time in the Service before he attained high rank—twenty years or so—he may well have had some inside knowledge of legislative or executive measures, perhaps originally welcomed with enthusiasm by most of the House and of the country, which have not had the desired results and have had results not at all desired; and he may have seen also the troubles they leave behind them, to be faced by other men than their authors. He is not likely to forget such lessons when he has risen to be one of his Minister's principal advisers. Lastly, by virtue of its security of tenure the Service is one representative of the principle of continuity in Government; the high official is a link between successive Ministries, and the repository of principles and practices which endure while Prime Ministers come and go. He tends to see the British people as a permanent entity, and the individuals now alive and active as single cells among the hundreds of millions which have been, are, and will be the body of the nation. To the party politician as such these individuals are of paramount importance; the dead and the unborn feel no hardships—nor have they votes. Most politicians and most civil servants are sensible enough to be conscious of the truth in the others' line of thought; but there is between them a difference of emphasis which may become crucial when a Government has to face the question, whether in great matters or in small, "How far is the present to be sacrificed to the future?"

The impartiality and cool prudence which belong to the high official by nature, or at least by second nature, lead directly to the third characteristic ascribed to him above; adherence to principle, even at the cost of immediate expediency. Except when the fundamental principles of party policy are involved, a Minister does not always share this attitude of mind with his officials. It has its drawbacks; it

tends to slow down business (a consideration often decisive
in times of crisis), and it provokes irritation in the House of
Commons and among the public when it forbids some small
concession, apparently reasonable enough in itself. The
officials have perhaps another ten or fifteen years to serve,
probably in the same department; they know that they will
have to cope with the distant effects of the decision now to be
taken; from their point of view it is mere common sense to
face a difficulty at once, rather than refuse the fence and
follow a course leading to future complications not to be foreseen in detail but certainly troublesome. This reasoning is
naturally less cogent to a Minister, and to the supporters of the
Government in the House. He has to bear the immediate
responsibility, e.g. of refusing a strongly backed demand for a
small increase of pay or pensions, and to face the consequent
clamour, knowing that within a year he may be holding another
office or be out of office altogether; they have to vote on his
side, knowing that at the next election in their constituencies
their votes may provide their opponents with admirable
propaganda. Nevertheless, it is fair to say that if a Minister is
convinced that something he wishes and is pressed to do is
contrary to sound principles of administration or finance, he
will almost always accept the official view, and argue it in the
House if necessary. But he may need a good deal of convincing.

In what degree the three qualities ascribed above to the
Civil Service are transmitted through Ministers to Parliament
and modify its work and character, there is no means of
ascertaining; but most persons fitted to give an opinion would
probably agree with the view suggested earlier in this chapter,
that this influence of the Service is not negligible, and would
agree also that it is least negligible when it is least obtru-
sive.

Transmission through Ministers, however, is not the only
method by which Parliament and the Service exert a mutual
influence; there is personal contact between individual
members of the two bodies. At first sight this would seem the
more effective way for them to act on one another, but in fact
it is not so; it is a less continuous and pervasive method,

governed more by the characters of individuals and (on the side of the civil servant) by the feeling that dealings with Members of Parliament are the special province of his parliamentary chiefs. Nor are its consequences in any material point discrepant from the much larger consequences of the contact through Ministers; on the contrary the two reinforce one another. Nevertheless, it does add something to the general picture, and requires a brief account.

Its origin for an individual may be either within or outside his profession. A high official, especially if he was educated at Oxford or Cambridge, is likely to have in Parliament a fair number of old acquaintances, and some friends, perhaps men whom he has known from boyhood or early youth, and calls by their Christian names or nicknames. He meets them at his club or in private society; he may stay with them at their country cottages (if they possess such amenities) during weekends, or take holidays with them. Apart from these purely private intimacies, during his official career he acquires a steadily widening acquaintance in Parliament, and particularly in the House of Commons—first perhaps as secretary to a committee which includes one or two M.P.s, then as Private Secretary to a Minister, finally as one of his Minister's principal advisers. It is not too much to say that the permanent head of a great department which has much parliamentary business knows by reputation most of the active Members of both Houses, is personally acquainted with many of them, knows some well, and may be on terms of intimate friendship with one or two. Such a relationship is by its nature reciprocal; knowledge of high permanent officials, by reputation and personally, is widespread among the active Members of both Houses.

Apart from purely social meetings, individual civil servants and M.P.s see most of one another, and most informally, during the committee stage of a long and contentious Bill, extending perhaps over several days and nights. It is then that each side is most likely to renew or extend its acquaintance with the other. The atmosphere is less exciting than during a set debate of one or two days. A certain *camaraderie* grows up among all engaged night after night upon a big Bill—Government, Opposition, and civil servants alike; it is legitimate to escape from the debating chamber to the terrace or the smoking-room and indulge in cheerful conversation while some notorious bore is moving an amendment which everyone knows to be impossible. Even then, however, and even with Members whom he knows and likes, the civil servant will keep the conversation away from the Bill (and other official business) if he can; and if he cannot, he will confine his remarks to commonplaces. He knows that he must say nothing to suggest that his opinion differs from his Minister's; and equally he knows that within a year or two, perhaps within a few months, he may be serving a Minister who is at the moment one of the Bill's most violent critics and opponents. On the other side, the Member can scarcely be unconscious that he is part of the supreme authority to whom the civil servant is ultimately subordinate. But at 2 or 3 a.m. such hidden reservations need not interfere seriously with genial if somewhat sleepy conversation.

We have already observed that this personal contact neither adds anything material to the mutual influence transmitted both ways through Ministers, nor detracts from it; that influence, so transmitted, arises from causes too powerful for it to be affected by such relatively minor incidents. Yet the personal contact is not without its value. For one thing, it mitigates any tendency on either side to generalize about the other, or to think that failings which are, perhaps correctly, attributed to politicians or civil servants in general are necessarily to be found in a particular member of the profession. Politicians discover that high officials are often quite human, and the officials that politicians may be disinterested and candid. The esteem and liking which personal acquaintance occasionally generates is sometimes useful in the conduct of ordinary business; to take a small example, the appointment of a civil servant (instead of a business man or trade unionist) to the Board of a nationalized industry may be received with acquiescence or even approval in the House of Commons, if he is known to Members on both sides of the House as an able and fair-minded man. But the case need scarcely be argued in detail; when two different sets of men are both closely engaged in one great enterprise, it is surely obvious that (within the limits imposed by the nature of the enterprise and of the other partners in it) the better they know one another and the more clearly they understand one another's idiosyncrasies, the greater the chance of success.

Besides the relations of the Civil Service with Parliament which arise through Ministers or by personal contact, there are other means by which the Service might be supposed to exert influence on Parliament; they are mostly unimportant, and need only a brief mention. In one or two constituencies civil servants (e.g. employees in naval dockyards) are a large part of the electorate and make themselves felt at elections; the parliamentary representatives of such constituencies are, of course, bound to have regard to their interests, but it is a representation of purely sectional and material interests, with little or no bearing on the larger questions discussed earlier in this chapter. The same remark applies to the non-localized trade unions or similar associations into which many civil servants have organized themselves; they hold periodical conferences which receive some notice in the Press, and they publish journals which may sometimes be read by Members of Parliament,[1] but outside the Service itself the total effect appears to be insignificant. Until recently there was one Member of the House of Commons who for a time was regarded as representing and speaking for a part of the Service as well as for his constituents; but if anyone were to ask what influence he exercised on his fellow-members in general, perhaps the best answer would be "What is one among so many?" Far more important are the men, not numerous but compensating for their fewness by their distinction, who have entered the House after being permanent officials of the Administrative Class— such men as Sir Henry Craik and Sir Francis Acland in the past, Sir John Anderson, Sir James Grigg, and Sir Arthur

[1]The Institute of Public Administration and its Journal are, of course, on a totally different footing from these societies and their publications. The Institute offers opportunities to politicians and civil servants to meet and discuss common problems; but it is not confined to those two classes, and it is primarily a scientific body.

Salter among the living.[1] They do not appear to have regarded themselves, or been regarded by others, as representing the Civil Service and speaking on its behalf; but their presence in the House, even apart from the ministerial offices which nearly all of them attained, must have done something, perhaps much, to bring together the parliamentary and the official mind.

The argument of the preceding paragraphs evokes a final reflection—a reflection which if thoroughly pursued would take us far beyond the permissible limits of this chapter. There is a fundamental difference of nature between the influence of the House of Commons on the Civil Service and that of the Service on the House. The former, it has been said, is strong and pervasive, reaching down to the lowest ranks of the Service, and (for the higher ranks) modifying profoundly mind, character, and daily life; but it is, so to speak, primarily self-regarding; in exerting it, the House of Commons is promoting its own interest. The House demands for its proper working that Ministers should satisfy quickly and efficiently its desires for information, action, and explanation; its influence is directed to producing in the Service the qualities and methods that will make it a fit instrument for the use of Ministers to that purpose. Yet at the same time Parliament, by a kind of self-denying ordinance, maintains the 'anti-political' conditions of the Service, fostering qualities very different from, even opposed to, some of the qualities fostered by parliamentary life; it has created an agency both delicately responsive to some characteristics of its creator, and corrective of others—a remarkable combination of attributes, which goes some way to justify Graham Wallas's well-known dictum that the Civil Service was 'the one great political invention in nineteenth century England'. It is not perhaps a paradox to suggest that in the long run the corrective influence of that invention on its creator, though naturally weaker than the converse, may have larger and more permanent results. Politics everywhere is, and seems likely long to remain, an affair not of pure intellect but

[1]High officials on their retirement are sometimes given peerages; but they seldom take a prominent part in the proceedings of the House of Lords, and in any case a seat in that House is for the present purpose quite unimportant as compared with a seat in the House of Commons.

of intellect merged in emotions, prejudices and interests; in that region at least, few impartial observers would venture to answer Hazlitt's question, "O Reason: when will thy long minority expire?" with anything more than the good old official phrase "In due course". Both question and answer imply that reason does not yet occupy its rightful place in human affairs. If the influence of the Civil Service is correctly described here, it may justly claim the merit that so far as it avails it strengthens the intellectual element in politics, and diminishes the power of the irrational. It is not an insignificant thing to provide, in however small a degree, something that is needed by the governments of all countries at all times, not least in the stormy politics of the twentieth century.

CHAPTER VII

PARLIAMENTARY PROCEDURE, OLD AND NEW

By Gilbert Campion

IN an earlier chapter in this book an attempt is made to interpret British Parliamentary Democracy, at its present stage, in terms of an analysis into two distinct components—a traditional element and a democratic element—the democratic element having been superimposed during the last seventy or eighty years on to, and only imperfectly merging with, a long-established and still vigorous parliamentary tradition. In this chapter I propose to inquire how far this situation is reflected in the procedure of the House of Commons—the methods and machinery by which the House carries out its functions—which it must necessarily adapt to changes and developments in those functions. The subject might be called the 'democratization' of procedure—a process which has been described as 'the converting of the comfortable old parliamentary coach into an up-to-date, streamlined legislative engine'.

In the procedure of the House the traditional and modern components are called the 'practice of the House' (or the 'ancient practice') and the standing orders, respectively.[1] I will have to describe these components more fully, but for the moment it is a sufficient indication of their character to say that 'practice' covers the body of rules which grew up, chiefly by precedent, during the early and middle period of Parliament and may be likened to the common law; while the standing orders, characteristic of the democratic period, being deliberately imposed, may be called the 'statute law' of Parliament. Just as the democratic element in politics arose and developed in a traditional setting,

[1] I am concerned here only with the standing orders of *public* business.

so in procedure the standing orders were imposed upon a pre-established practice. Neither our kind of democracy, nor the book of standing orders is intelligible except as a modification of a long-established system which still lives on, and is very much alive.

The corpus of practice of the House of Commons is rightly called the practice of *Parliament*, for it was originally followed in both Houses and it still regulates the procedure of the House of Lords. Some of its rules are very ancient. For instance, the procedure on a Bill, with its three 'readings', and probably also the use of small committees for work of preparation and review, were already in existence before 1547 when the House began to record its proceedings in its Journals. The greater part of the rules which govern debate and regulate behaviour in the House, besides such machinery as the Committees of Supply and Ways and Means, with their financial functions, were established in the early part of the seventeenth century. The development of practice can be studied in manuals compiled by Members, such as Hakewil, and parliamentary clerks, such as Scobell and Elsynge, in the seventeenth century; in Hatsell's collection of precedents made at the end of the eighteenth century; and in the early editions of Erskine May's famous *Treatise*, first published in 1844.

The character of practice is well marked. It was leisurely, ceremonious, cumbersome; it was individualistic, giving wide scope to the initiative of members and affording no special facilities to the Government; it was designed to protect the rights of minorities in debate and to encourage opposition to the Executive. Since the formative period of practice lay during the first half of the seventeenth century, when the majority of the House was in chronic opposition to the government of Charles I, it acquired the characteristics of 'the procedure of an opposition'; and it retained these characteristics permanently, in spite of the fact that by the middle of the eighteenth century the establishment of the Cabinet system had turned the majority of the House from opponents to supporters of the Government. Arthur Onslow, the famous Speaker (1727 to 1761) who did so much to fix the traditions both of his office and of procedure, is reported by Hatsell as saying 'that nothing tended more to throw power into the hands of Administration and those who acted with the majority of the House of Commons than a neglect of or departure from these rules. . . .' One of these rules—a rule of fundamental importance—was that no decision could be reached or action taken in the House—even such formal actions as the reading of an order of the day or the Speaker leaving the chair for committee—except on a question to which every member had the right to speak, if only once. Occasions for putting questions seem to have been multiplied beyond reason. For instance, the number required on the stages of a bill—apart from any questions on amendments to the text—were reckoned by Speaker Shaw Lefevre in 1848 to be eighteen.[1] Many other examples could be pointed out of a system deliberately designed to prevent the House being caught napping—the minority required protection from themselves as well as from the majority.

Arthur Balfour put his finger on one of the chief grounds of difference between the traditional practice and standing order procedure. Speaking in 1902 in recommendation of his plan for a further tightening up of procedure, he said: "In the middle of the eighteenth century, and indeed to a much later period, the difficulty was not to check the flow of oratory, but to induce it to flow at all. . . . With the change in the circumstances of the House, in itself revolutionary, our rules which were originally framed to promote a fertilizing and irrigating flow of eloquence are now, it appears, required to dam up its vast and destructive floods. . . ."[2]

The eighteenth century was not a period of constructive legislation and the area of administrative authority was very small. Even so, it is hard to see how Ministers (who had to compete for time as ordinary members and were always liable to find their business forestalled by one of a multitude of technical forms), made any progress with government business. It could only have been, as Parnell suggested when he helped to destroy the old free ways, through the 'connivance' of

[1] Redlich, *Procedure of the House of Commons*, i, 65.
[2] Redlich, *Procedure of the House of Commons*, i, 64 and 198.

individual members. That the endless opportunities were not abused was due to the social atmosphere, which was against political fanaticism or ungentlemanly disregard of the spirit of the game. Even when opposition was unusually heated, as it was against the minority government of Pitt in 1784, heroic measures, such as the refusal of supplies, though threatened, were not in fact employed. There was one famous case of obstruction in the eighteenth century. In resisting proceedings against newspapers which had published the debates of the House, Edmund Burke in 1771 divided the House no less than twenty-three times, remarking later, "Posterity will bless the pertinacity of that night." He could not foresee what his compatriots would be capable of a hundred years later.

It would be misleading to say that the standing orders are grafted on to the trunk of practice; they are more like shears pruning the overgrowth of leaves and branches. But either metaphor expresses an important fact (which I have already alluded to) that the standing orders everywhere presuppose practice. They are in no sense a code; they are amendments of the rules of practice.

The purpose of the standing orders is almost the opposite of that of the traditional practice; it is not to preserve the rights of the minority in debate, but to help the Government to get business through the House—and, ultimately, to get more and more business through quicker and quicker. In their process of development the standing orders may be divided roughly into two groups: (1) those adopted between 1832 and 1878, the purpose of which was to give the Government rights over the order of business and the distribution of the time of the House commensurate with the increased importance of the Cabinet in the parliamentary system, and (2) those passed since 1878, which reflect the impatience of democratic governments in the face of obstacles to the achievement of a vast annual output of legislation.

(1) After 1832 the problem of the distribution of the time of the House began to outgrow the old arrangements for sharing it fairly between Ministers and private members. A daily programme was drawn up and notified in advance and different

days of the week were allotted to particular kinds of business. But the opportunities left by the old practice for raising un-notified subjects on the plea of urgency were so ample that it was in the power of a few members to forestall and interrupt the prearranged programme of business and destroy any prospect of its being carried out with certainty. For instance, a favourite device was the presentation of a petition, since the discussion of it took precedence of other business. This became a serious rival to all other kinds of business. Petitions were multiplied a hundredfold between the beginning of the century and 1840. The discussion of petitions was first restricted and finally, in 1842, practically abolished by standing orders.[1] Other technical devices for seizing the initiative in debates were: to move an amendment to the question for reading the Orders of the Day for the purpose of springing an entirely new subject on the House; or an amendment to the question for the Speaker to leave the chair for committee on a bill, for the purpose of re-debating the merits of the bill (already decided on second reading); or to the similar question for Committee of Supply for the purpose of introducing a new topic under the plea of dis-cussing grievances. These devices were all the more effective because the choice of a subject to raise was not limited by any rule requiring it to be relevant to the question on which it was raised. These devices were countered in this period by a series of standing orders which applied the same simple remedy, namely, to dispense with the proposal of the question for the reading of the Orders of the Day or for the Speaker to leave the chair, and so to deprive the enterprising member of the neces-sary 'peg' on which to hang his interposition.

(2) Early in the democratic period, and particularly in the ten years from 1878 to 1888, the House of Commons was faced with the challenge of Irish obstruction. The systematic attempt of a comparatively small group to bring the business of the majority to a standstill is, as other instances in modern

---

[1] As the franchise was extended and all varieties of opinion began to find expression inside the House of Commons, the practice of petitioning, which was most valuable for bringing the grievances of the unrepresented before Parliament, lost its *raison d'être*; public petitions, though still presented, are intended merely as demonstrations, since no parliamentary action is now possible on them.

K

Chambers have shown, one of the most serious threats to parliamentary institutions. It is a very difficult threat to cope with—particularly difficult for the House of Commons of that period which had only recently been brought with great reluctance to curtail individual liberty to the extent necessary to have a tolerably watertight agenda. Among the devices which Parnell and his group of sixty or seventy used in order to help out their native prolixity were the motions for the adjournment of the House and of the debate—the so-called 'dilatory motions' which previous reforms had left untouched (in order to leave the House some latitude for debating matters of unforeseen urgency). After Speaker Brand had been driven to put an end to a debate (which had lasted forty-two hours) on his own responsibility and without any warrant from the practice or standing orders of the House—the famous *coup d'état* of 2nd February 1881—the House provided itself in the course of the next few years with a defensive equipment of restrictions on debate which left a great deal to the discretion of the Chair. By these means obstruction was reduced to manageable proportions. Since the disappearance of Irish representation in 1918 the House of Commons has hardly seen any organized 'strategic' obstruction. But the drastic restrictions which defeated Parnell still continue as methods, used with varying frequency at different periods, for reducing debate and thus permitting a greater volume of legislation to be forced through the House than would otherwise be possible. The efficacy of these methods has been increased by the system of standing committees, established in 1907, which on the principle of the division of labour relieves the House of the committee stage of all bills (with a few exceptions) and permits four or five bills to be proceeded with simultaneously outside the Chamber, while the House itself is occupied with other business.

These standing orders have deprived the minority of the long-recognized right to use obstruction as a tactical weapon, i.e. to threaten to keep the majority up all night as a protest against an unduly speeded-up time-table, or to talk at length on uncontentious business in order to defer progress on more obnoxious items. The majority is thus spared the need to compromise, since it can count on carrying out its plans in full, after reasonably (or unreasonably) short discussion, by sheer weight of numbers.

This brief account of the development of House of Commons procedure is sufficient to show that its forms and rules fall, broadly, into two distinct groups, based on different kinds of authority and representative of two distinct stages of political development. I propose now to review in greater detail some aspects of the evolution of procedure during the last seventy or eighty years. It will be convenient, and give firmer body to what is rather an abstract subject, if I treat procedural forms as methods by which the House discharges its various functions. I will try to show how far the changes of function brought about by the growth of democracy—and the changes in the relative importance of the Government, the Opposition and individual members—are reflected in the standing orders.

The basic forms and rules suited to a large deliberative body, the factors which make for reason and fairness in discussion and for decisiveness in decision, belong to the traditional procedure of Parliament. Among these factors are (1) the physical arrangements of the 'forum' of debate, (2) provisions for focusing discussion and removing all uncertainty from decision, and (3) an impartial judge or umpire to see that the rules are observed.

(1) It is a commonplace that the seating arrangements of a Chamber both influence and reflect its character. As Mr. Churchill has said: "We shape our Houses and our Houses shape us." Among aristocratic bodies, such as the Roman Senate or the House of Lords, it is natural for members to sit in the order of their rank.[1] In the House of Commons the notion of equality between members—a sort of domestic democracy—from early times left members free to sit where they pleased except on the benches reserved for privy councillors. Hooker, describing the Elizabethan House of Commons for the instruction of the contemporary Irish Government, wrote: "Upon the

---

[1] The order of precedence in the House of Lords was laid down by an Act of Henry VIII, which is no longer observed; the standing order consequential on the Act was last enforced in 1771.

lower row on both sides of the Speaker sit such personages as be of the King's Privy Council, or of his chief officers; but, as for any other, none claimeth ... any place, but sitteth as he cometh. ..." The arrangement of benches in two sets of rows confronting each other is probably due to the elongated shape of St. Stephen's Hall (if it is not earlier). This arrangement is thus not the result of the two-party system (the germ of which cannot be traced beyond the reign of Charles I); but it has contributed powerfully to the maintenance of that system. It was natural for members of the same party to sit together, and so for the two parties to sit on opposite sides; but when exactly the Government Party took to sitting on the Speaker's right and the Opposition on his left is not certain. One version of the familiar story of Pulteney's bet against the accuracy of Walpole's Latin makes him toss the guinea *across the floor*. This, if correct, would prove that by 1740 the two front benches were occupied by opposing parties.

Another traditional peculiarity of the Commons' debating chamber is its small size in relation to the number of members. 'None claimeth any place, but sitteth as he cometh', because there has never been room to give him a place of his own (as places are reserved in Washington, Paris and most other deliberative Chambers). Inconvenient as it is for the individual, the confined space of the Chamber has played a part in forming the distinctive quality of House of Commons debate. Taken with other arrangements, such as the rule for speaking from where one sits instead of from a tribune and the rule against the reading of speeches, it tends to keep debate on a conversational level, practical and reasonable rather than rhetorical. On ordinary occasions quite a number of members can be engaged elsewhere without making the Chamber depressingly empty; while on great occasions, the sense of drama is, as Mr. Churchill has observed, enhanced by the crowding of every place where a member can sit or space where he can stand.

Keeping political differences at a temperate level is the object of most of the formal rules regulating the conduct of members in the Chamber, and the reason why, in spite of their elaborate courteousness and occasional quaintness, they have been religiously preserved during the two or three generations of parliamentary democracy. Only a few examples need be given. The ancient rule, mentioned by Sir Thomas Smith in his account of the Elizabethan Parliament, banning allusion to a member by his own name and requiring a formal periphrasis has the effect of discouraging personalities; so also has the rule which makes a speaker address the Chair instead of directing his remarks to individuals. The old rules about the management of the hat (when the hat was worn) were full of significance; they survive only in the requirement of a hat for a member raising a point of order during a division—a rule which has lost its meaning, but is still clung to. One may also mention the rule that a member should not be attacked in his absence; the insistence on withdrawal of, and apology for, imputations and 'unparliamentary language'; and the prohibition of 'unparliamentary noises' calculated to drown the remarks of a speaker. All these rules, backed up as they are by the disciplinary powers of the Chair, have created an atmosphere which, in spite of occasional breakdowns, remains characteristic of the House of Commons and compares favourably with that of any democratic assembly. It is an atmosphere in which argument is listened to, however unpalatable to the majority, and the minority are neither shouted down nor driven to making scenes in order to secure attention. This atmosphere is the condition as well as the expression of a fundamental tolerance and reasonableness which has come to the aid of Parliament in many crises during its long history. These qualities form an important part of the traditional parliamentary spirit which British democracy has had the good fortune to inherit and the good sense to preserve.

(2) I hesitate to plunge into the technicalities which regulate the process of parliamentary debate. Enough to say that by the end of the seventeenth century the House of Commons had evolved a simple type of process, applicable to all forms of proceeding—bills, motions, etc.—which consisted in beginning a debate by the moving of a motion, carrying it on on the same motion repeated as a question, and concluding it by a decision on the same motion-question. The fundamental

rule is that there is one question, and one question only, before the House at one time. No other deliberative body, past or existing, seems to have evolved this simple rule independently. They fell into confusion either by allowing a number of questions to be presented simultaneously—in which case, instead of a straight Aye or No, there is a competition between a number of Ayes—or, more frequently, by starting discussion on a vague 'subject' and not formulating a question until the conclusion of the discussion. The House of Commons followed the latter method until the seventeenth century but abandoned it because it gave the Chair (to whom the duty of formulating the question was entrusted) too much power to influence decisions. Some Continental Chambers throw the formulation of the question at the end of the debate open to all comers; and then have to decide which question shall be first decided. Further confusion is introduced by the fact that the process of amendment, which should follow the same simple pattern, tends to take the form of long-winded and extemporized new motions. Without the technical rules peculiar to the House of Commons, relevancy in debate is hard to maintain, and there is often uncertainty as to what has been actually decided. It is undoubtedly one of the reasons why most Continental Assemblies refer everything to committees and limit themselves to discussing their reports,[1] that they have not evolved a method of debate which will enable a large body to discuss matters of detail or complexity without falling into confusion.

(3) The most valuable achievement of the parliamentary spirit was the agreement by both parties in the period between the Reform Acts of 1832 and 1867 to take the Speakership finally out of politics. This was the second milestone in the evolution of the modern Speakership. Till towards the end of the seventeeth century the Speaker had been the 'king's man'—in effect nominated by the king, though formally elected by the House. After 1679, when Charles II refused his approval to the election of Seymour, no king has opposed the choice of the House. After ceasing to be a courtier, the Speaker came to be

[1]Except for the practice of 'interpellation' for which there is a special stereotyped procedure involving the formulation of a question *at the end* of the debate.

regarded as a party leader. The City of London thought it worth while to secure Speaker Trevor's support for a bill by a bribe of a thousand guineas; and the aid of eighteenth century Speakers was solicited by the more respectable method of deputation. Arthur Onslow, the prototype of the modern Speaker (though his example was lost sight of for the best part of a century) was the first to take independence of Government as his guiding rule and to give up a valuable sinecure in order to prove his sincerity. "Ministers," he wrote, "seldom love Parliament; never bring business there for counsel, but to carry points that must have the authority of the Legislature." It was against the Government that he consistently upheld the ancient rules and forms of proceeding as 'a protection to the minority against the attempts of power' and 'against the irregularities and abuses which . . . the wantonness of power is too apt to suggest to large and successful majorities.'

Onslow was able to maintain a standard so far in advance of his time partly no doubt because his period of office (1737 to 1761) was a quiet time for party politics. The increase of party bitterness after the accession of George III had the inevitable effect of making Speakers stronger party men. Opposition to the re-election of the serving Speaker, which had lapsed for a hundred years, was reintroduced in 1780 to get rid of a Speaker whom the king disliked. Speakers re-entered active politics after their term of office. Addington left the chair in 1801 to form an administration, and as late as 1832 (during the Reform Bill crisis) the sitting Speaker, Manners Sutton, was offered, but refused, the premiership. His successor, Abercromby, came from the Cabinet to the chair. It is not surprising that the dangerous practice of making political speeches in committee and elsewhere was revived.

After the election of Shaw Lefevre, Speaker from 1839 to 1857, the principle has been observed that the Speaker is not only impartial but abstains from anything which could cause the slightest suspicion of partizanship. He does not intervene in committee or make political speeches outside Parliament; he keeps aloof from party contacts, does not even enter a political club. After resigning from the chair, he also retires from the House, being rewarded by the Crown with a peerage. He is not opposed on re-election in the House as long as he wishes to serve,[1] nor in his constituency during a general election.[2]

It is fortunate that these conventions were established while the party system was still fluid. The value of a non-partizan Speaker increases, while the chances of finding such a figure (if he is not already there), diminish, in proportion with the hardening of the lines of division between parties and with the growing difficulty and delicacy of holding the scales even between the Government and the minority. The House of Lords is happy in the enjoyment of an atmosphere which dispenses with restrictive rules and disciplinary powers, and can afford to have as its Speaker a prominent member of the Government in office. Most democratic Chambers still waver uncertainly between two conceptions of the Speaker which we have experienced in succession—the majority leader and the impartial umpire. In the American House of Representatives— with good reason, since the Executive is constitutionally excluded from membership—the Speaker is the natural leader of the House. But he has recently lost some of the powers through which leadership was exercised, and more attention is paid to his role as a moderator. In France the President of the Chamber or Assembly has generally been a prominent party politician, an ex-Minister and a future Minister. But the long tenure of the chair by several Presidents of the former Chamber, and now by M. Herriot, has tended somewhat to place the office above party. In Australia and New Zealand the conception of the Speakership and the conventions relating to it, inherited from the House of Commons, have made a brave struggle for survival. But the strength of party feeling has been too great to allow the office to be left in the hands of a member of a party which has fallen from power; few Speakers hold office long enough to grow out of their party attachments; the Speaker's vote is too

[1] The most striking instance of this convention is the re-election by the Conservatives of Speaker Gully in 1895, though he followed an unbroken series of Liberal Speakers and they had just failed by a narrow margin to defeat his election in the dying Parliament of the previous year.

[2] Once or twice recently, an unofficial Labour candidate has contested the Speaker's seat.

valuable in a small Chamber for his party to be willing to dispense with it in committee; the chair is too often regarded as a consolation prize for a disappointed ministerial candidate; and, as some Speakers do not refrain from party speeches and votes when out of the chair, their impartiality in the chair is sometimes, however unfairly, regarded with scepticism.

The general confidence of the House of Commons in the impartiality of the Speaker has been used since the 1880's as the basis of a new and restricted procedure of debate. The most drastic of the new restrictions, and the most repulsive to the old school of members, was the closure—or, as Randolph Churchill called it to mark its alien origin, the 'clôture'. This rule, worked out in 1887 and 1888, enabled a member to cut short debate, even while another member was speaking, by moving 'that the question be now put'. This power, so valuable to itself, the Government sought to recommend to the House by the provision of safeguards. First and most important, the Speaker had to be convinced that the motion was not 'an abuse of the rules of the House or an infringement of the rights of the minority'; at least one hundred members were to support the closure, if divided against; further, the closure could not be moved in the House, if one of the Speaker's deputies and not the Speaker were in the chair, or in committee if a temporary chairman were in the chair. Refinements of the rule added provision for securing a decision on the main question, when the closure was moved on an amendment; and, in committee on a bill, for comprising a whole clause with all its amendments in a single motion—so drastic a power that it has seldom been used. It may fairly be said that what prevents the closure from being used to destroy freedom of debate is that it cannot be imposed without the Speaker's acquiescence. It is very different in Chambers where the closure is not dependent on the Speaker's acceptance. Strange cases of democratic intolerance could be quoted even from the Dominions.

Most of the other restrictive rules will be better dealt with in connection with legislation and other specific functions rather than in relation to the general rules of debate. One must, however, mention the powers given to the Chair to check persistent irrelevance and 'tedious repetition' by ordering a member to discontinue his speech; to refuse dilatory motions or put them to the question without debate; to substitute a vote by rising and sitting for a division, if the division is unnecessarily claimed; and, finally, to distinguish genuine from pretended urgency among the constantly arising claims to secure precedence for 'definite matters of urgent public importance'. These powers would be liable to gross abuse in unfair hands; they are, however, as a matter of fact, gently handled and sympathetically applied by the Chair. For instance, a group of three members was for long permitted by Speaker FitzRoy to divide the House, instead of being called on to vote by the quicker process of rising to be counted in their places, because they claimed to constitute a separate party (and no division-list giving their names would have been published if the more summary procedure had been adopted). Only in the case of 'emergency adjournment motions' has the trend of Speakers' rulings been criticized as unduly restrictive. It is generally a question on which opinions differ whether a particular subject proposed to be raised is sufficiently definite, urgent and publicly important to justify its discussion in preference to the business previously fixed for the day. If the Speaker were too easily satisfied, the urgency adjournment motion might become a method of obstruction and the House slip back towards the time when it did not know from day to day what it was going to discuss. As it turned out, a series of Speakers took the opposite line and read so much into the conditions for accepting the motion that it became very difficult to satisfy them.[1] Recently, however, there has been a reaction. It would have been regrettable if this modest amount of elasticity in the daily programme had not been preserved for the cases for which it was intended.

I have referred in the preceding paragraph to Speakers' rulings, and before going any further into the development of the standing order system I must explain briefly how far that system owes its workableness and consistency to the interpretation of the standing orders by the Speaker, chiefly, but

[1] Select Committee on Procedure, Third Report (1946), pp. 54, 55.

also by the other occupants of the chair. Some standing orders give the Chair discretionary powers—with regard to these it is convenient that they should be exercised on consistent lines which commend themselves to members generally as reasonable. Other standing orders lay down mandatory rules which it is the duty of the Chair as of other members to follow; but cases, even with regard to these, constantly arise which contain some element of doubt, some feature which was not foreseen or provided for by the standing order in question. In such cases there is apt to be disagreement among members as to the application of the standing order, and it becomes the duty of the Speaker in the House, and of the Chairman in committee, to explain the interpretation he puts upon it (including, where necessary, its relation to other standing orders and the general practice of the House), or in other words to 'give a ruling from the chair'. Such rulings are sometimes asked for in advance outside the Chamber by members who anticipate difficulty with regard to some item of the business of the House. All rulings, when made, are classified and preserved for future reference as precedents—a new parliamentary 'precedent' now almost always means a ruling from the chair. During the hundred years since the systematic collection of rulings began many volumes of such precedents have been printed for official use, and the most important find their way into the successive editions of Erskine May and form a valuable supplement to the recognized sources of procedure—the rules of practice and the standing orders. Speakers' rulings are thus the third main basis of procedure. As they are all concerned with concrete cases which have actually arisen, they may be called by analogy the Case Law of Procedure.

After the restrictions imposed on debate, generally, it remains to consider the further restrictions applicable to the process of legislation, specially. With the opening of the democratic era and the embarking of the ship of state on the shoreless seas of social and economic amelioration, two things happened. First, the volume of legislation progressively increased and, second, its specialized complexity and the burdens it imposed on public funds concentrated it in the hands of the Government. The elimination of political abuses—the earlier goal of reform—had not been beyond the comprehension of individual members. Now the Government was expected to justify itself by the magnitude of a programme of legislation which it was alone competent to handle. Whereas under the old system of unrestricted debate one big controversial bill was as much as a Government could hope to pass in a single session, now Ministers began to be more ambitious; and it became clear that something more was needed than the closure and the other methods of restricting general debate, mentioned in the preceding paragraph, in order to speed up the committee and report stages of bills, where the multiplication of amendments was the problem. The goal of speedier legislation was approached by different methods. There were at least three of these: they may be called the 'slimming process', the 'squeezing process' and the 'purging process'.

By the 'slimming process' I mean getting rid of superfluous stages during the progress of a bill—those eighteen questions, for example, stated in 1848 as having to be put on the main stages of a bill, and each of them debatable. Standing orders passed since then have reduced those eighteen questions to two—the questions 'that the bill be read a second time' (when the principle of the bill is open to debate) and 'that the bill be read the third time' (when its acceptability, as amended, may be reviewed). (There still remain, of course, all the questions on possible amendments at the committee and report stages.) Debate on a motion to recommit a bill, as a whole has been restricted to two ten-minute speeches, one for and one against. There is still the possibility of proposing instructions to the committee receiving a bill in order to extend its powers of amendment. This once handy method of delaying a bill has almost lapsed since Speakers of this century have taken to propounding a kind of 'Morton's fork', which is fatal to most instructions—'Either the instruction is out of order, as beyond the scope of the bill, or it is unnecessary, as the committee can do what the instruction suggests without the instruction.'

The 'squeezing' process is effected by the method of 'Allocation of Time' Orders (nicknamed, generically, the

Guillotine') together with the power, which the Chair now has, of 'selecting' amendments. Like the closure, the guillotine originated in the rules of urgency procedure, which Speaker Brand was authorized to make in order to counter Irish obstruction to the Coercion Bill of 1881. Like the closure, also, the name and notion of 'urgency' were borrowed from France. In origin, it is a charmingly simple idea—that a bill, declared urgent, should be reported and disposed of by a certain date, with or without discussion. But, with our more elaborate procedure and tendency to compromise, the idea has been complicated into a time-table, first of all, allotting so many days or portions of days—quite a considerable number in all— to each stage of a bill and, secondly, in the case of the committee and report stages, squeezing a number of clauses, with all the amendments proposed to them, into the compartment formed by a day or portion of a day. Provision is made in a comprehensive way for preventing any rule of the House or other business from interfering with the attainment of all the objectives to be attained on an allotted day. It is naturally in the periods of most strenuous legislative activity that the guillotine has proved its use, and indeed its indispensability— its democratic indispensability—namely, from 1906 to 1914, and 1945 to 1950. During the latter period it was for the first time applied to standing committees (see below).

Since the guillotine is essentially a denial of free debate, it has, not unnaturally, been resented by Oppositions. The tactics first employed to discredit it were to spend as much as possible of the allotted time on the first few amendments to the first clause in each compartment, cry 'Gag! Gag!' when the guillotine fell, and write to the Press about the number and importance of the clauses and amendments which had fallen under the guillotine without a word of discussion. This outraged attitude has changed during recent years, partly, through familiarity (for all parties have found they could not do without the guillotine), partly, through the use which the Chair has made of the power to select amendments. (A standing order of 1919 conferred on the Chair the power to disallow amendments without assigning any reason for the refusal.) By this means the

Chair has done much to humanize the blind working of the guillotine and make the best use of the limited time available under it. After ascertaining the views of parties and groups as to the points they consider of most importance, the Speaker or Chairman chooses the amendments which raise these points most clearly and divides the time available as fairly as possible between them, ignoring all other amendments. The organization of a debate is worked out with great care, and the Opposition as a rule is glad to make the best of a bad job and fall in with the Chair's arrangements. On their side, the Government Whips help by discouraging the intervention of their backbench supporters, so that a debate in committee under the guillotine often becomes a business-like exchange of arguments between the Opposition and the Ministers in charge of the bill (which is more rational and as likely to produce concessions as the old-fashioned methods of attrition by all-night sittings which crop up again on bills which it is not the practice to guillotine, such as the Finance Bill).

What I have called the 'purging' process is the relieving the House of business that can be done by smaller bodies. Down to 1882 the committee stage of practically all public bills was taken in Committee of the whole House. This is the lengthiest stage of a bill; under the old unrestricted rules of debate controversial bills have taken fifty or more days to pass through committee. Reluctantly, under the pressure of Irish obstruction, the House agreed to refer this stage in the case of certain bills to two standing committees. In 1907 the number of standing committees was raised to four; in 1919, to six; and in 1947, to 'as many as shall be necessary'. (For practical reasons, at most five standing committees can sit simultaneously; the number of members, staff, reporters and accommodation, available, are all limiting factors.) There is no resemblance whatever between the House of Commons type of standing committee and the American or Continental type—bodies of relatively stable membership specializing in particular aspects of public policy. A standing committee of the House of Commons has no permanence or individuality; its members are constantly changing; it is distinguished only by a letter of the alphabet; and it does not receive one type of bill more than another. It is a miniature committee of the whole House, preserving relative party strengths, brought into existence by the simple calculation that four standing committees sitting simultaneously can get through four times as much work as the single committee of the whole House—and also leave the House free to make progress with other work.

The weakness of a standing committee from the Government's point of view was until recently that, as it sat only two hours a day on two days a week, it was apt to take an inordinately long time to dispose of a big controversial bill. In 1947 the guillotine was made applicable to proceedings in a standing committee; the House prescribes a day by which a bill is to be reported and leaves it to the committee itself, assisted by a business sub-committee of its own members, to work out an acceptable time-table. It has become necessary for a committee considering a bill under the guillotine to sit longer hours and more days in the week to fulfil its assignment. Greatly increased pressure has thus been put upon the energies of members, but the Government by this latest and probably last turn of the screw (for what other expedients remain?) has achieved its objective of increasing the output of legislation.

It is impossible accurately to compare the relative speed of the legislative process at different periods, but a rough-and-ready method is possible which may give results not very wide of the mark. One may divide the number of pages in the statutes of a session by the number of days (and portions of days added together) spent in the House on the consideration of bills; the result will give the average number of pages disposed of on each 'legislative day'.[1] On this basis the speed of legislation has increased from an average of five pages per legislative day during the period 1906 to 1913 to an average of sixteen pages per legislative day in the session 1945–6.

It is in the legislative function of the House, principally, that the traditional facilities for full debate have been restricted

[1] In this calculation only the time spent in the Chamber is taken into account; standing committees are treated as a device for increasing the output of legislation without adding to the burden on the time of the House.

during modern times in the ways I have described. Legislation has become the special province of the Government and ways and means of speeding up progress, with the help of its faithful majority, are always in the minds of its advisers. But there is a great block of business in which the Government has no such interest. It consists of a number of items which recur session after session without much variation—forms of proceeding, chiefly devised to deal with finance, which are now used principally by the Opposition for the purpose of criticizing administrative policy.

In this part of the proceedings of the House debate is comparatively unrestricted and the forms of the older practice survive with comparatively little change, although by a mixture of conservatism and ingenuity, which is characteristic of the House, some of these forms are applied to purposes very different from those for which they were devised.

The most important business outside the government programme is that by which the House discharges its functions of controlling finance and administration. To a large extent these functions are concentrated in the seventeenth century machinery of the Committee of Supply and the Committee of Ways and Means, and the bills founded on their reports. So far as the control of expenditure is concerned, the functions of the Committee of Supply, which were originally financial, have experienced a gradual change during the last hundred years until they are now almost entirely concerned with the control of administrative policy.

Before describing how this change has taken place, it will be as well to look at the way in which the House carries out its function of controlling revenue and taxation in the Committee of Ways and Means. The Finance Bill, though it is an essential part of the parliamentary machinery of control, is also a Government bill. But it has been much less subjected to the 'reducing process' than a bill which forms an item in the Government's programme. It still originates in 'Budget' resolutions which are discussed in Committee of Ways and Means for the best part of a week. The debate at this stage has become a general review of national finance—the discussion of individual imposts, both in committee and when reported as resolutions, being prohibited by a recent standing order. On the other hand, debate on the Finance Bill, itself, is designed to cover both principles and details and is comparatively un-restricted. It is expressly reserved for consideration in Com-mittee of the whole House; progress on it is not interrupted at the normal hour for the conclusion of business; it is rarely subjected to a guillotine.[1]

Turning now to the Committee of Supply—two processes, working together, have resulted in changing its functions from those of an instrument for the scrutiny of expenditure into those of an instrument for criticizing administration. (1) As national expenditure grew and took charge of more 'services', it became evident that the attempt to control it in detail was defeating the machinery devised by the House. It had been possible for the Committee of Supply to scrutinize a royal demand and decide whether to satisfy it in whole or in part. But the insistence of the House on prescribing the detailed application of grants led to the presentation, as a basis of their discussion, of estimates which grew more and more complicated and voluminous. Soon after the middle of last century, when annual expenditure had reached the enormous total of seventy millions, the Committee of Supply virtually gave up the impossible task of controlling expenditure by public debate, agreeing tacitly to leave it to the Treasury to enforce departmental economy and to the Audit Office, checked by its own Committee of Public Accounts, to enforce the parliamentary scheme of appropriation. Other considerations tended in the same direction. The estimates reach the House in a form to all intents and purposes final, which it cannot change because, on the one hand, constitutional practice debars it from *increasing* a single item and, on the other, the whole strength of the majority party machine is behind the Government's resistance to the *reduction* of a single item. Consequently, as there was nothing the House could do about the figures, it turned its attention entirely to the *policy* of the estimates.

[1]Only the Lloyd George Finance Bills of 1909–1910 and the Finance Bills of the crisis years, 1914 and 1931, have been guillotined.

L

(2) In the last quarter of the nineteenth century the growing claims of the Government on parliamentary time and the loss of other opportunities for criticizing administration made the opponents of the Government more and more dependent for their chances on the procedure connected with Supply. One of the most venerable Commons' slogans, 'Grievances before Supply', had long been used to justify the habit of discussing administrative shortcomings on the question, required under the old practice, to be put on every occasion when the House resolved itself into Committee of Supply. This opportunity was found so useful by critics of the Government that it became more and more difficult to 'get into' committee and actually vote supply until the tail-end of the session. No Government dared entirely abolish a practice based on 'grievances before supply', but a compromise was reached. On all but three occasions every session the House would, under standing order, go into Committee of Supply without a question being put—the three occasions being those when the three main branches of the estimates (army, navy and civil) were first put down for discussion. This compromise had the effect of accelerating progress on the estimates. But it did nothing to promote genuine financial discussion in place of criticism of administrative policy; it merely transferred the occasion for the latter from the House to the Committee.

The fact that the Committee of Supply had become primarily an instrument for debating administrative policy was generally accepted when in 1896 Arthur Balfour had the idea of bringing the estimates under a comprehensive guillotine like that used for bills. Briefly, leaving certain estimates outside the scheme, he allotted twenty days before the 5th of August each session for the consideration of all the rest with a provision for voting all, whether discussed or undiscussed, on the last two days of the allotted twenty. Twenty days he claimed to be the average amount of time devoted to the estimates during previous sessions. The estimates had now reached proportions which would have required the whole time of the House for their due consideration by the method of unrestricted debate. The Committee of Supply abandoned the pretence. The understanding which resulted had its advantages for both sides of the House. The Government, being assured of having supply completely voted by a date before the normal end of the session, gracefully conceded to the Opposition the right to choose which of the 150 or more votes of the estimates should be put down for discussion on each of the days allotted to supply; and the Opposition used this facility to furnish themselves with a procedural peg on which to hang an attack on the Government on any question of administration which happened at the moment to be topical. This has had the effect of emphasizing the official status of the Opposition. The days allotted to supply and to the legislation giving final authority to votes of supply— now some thirty days every session—have come to be reckoned as 'Opposition Time', a commodity which the leader of the Opposition can use as an asset in bargaining with the leader of the House about the arrangement of business. In the Labour Government's procedural reforms of 1947 and 1948 another step has been taken which has made the original financial function of the Committee of Supply recede still further into the background. It has been provided that, subject to the assent of the Government, the old procedure of raising 'grievances' on the question for going into Committee of Supply shall be revived whenever the Opposition think an explicit motion is a better peg for the topic they wish to raise than a more or less relevant vote or set of votes. Further, this form of proceeding is available throughout the session, whether there are estimates for the Committee of Supply to consider or not. These developments have resulted in giving more form and body to the rights of the Opposition.

I must now mention briefly the other forms of proceeding which are used for the purpose of criticizing administrative policy. The principal are: the Address in reply to the King's speech, Substantive Motions, Substantive Motions for the adjournment of the House,[1] Questions to Ministers.

The King's speech at the opening of each session is a venerable form descending from the allocutions made by the

---

[1]'Substantive' because moved independently and not in the course of proceedings on other business, in which case they are classed as 'dilatory' motions.

medieval Chancellor, or other official cleric, for the purpose of explaining to a Parliament the cause of its summons. Since the establishment of the Cabinet system the King's speech is used to set forth the policy of the Government and its programme of legislation for the session, and the Government takes responsibility for its contents. The address in reply is a motion in stereotyped form limited to the expression of humble thanks for the gracious speech. The debate on the speech, which occupies the best part of the first two weeks of every session falls into two parts: the first part provides an occasion for a general review of Government policy, while the second part takes the form of amendments generally expressing regret for the omission of particular items from the programme of legislation.

Substantive motions provided the form chiefly used under the traditional procedure for full-scale attacks on Government policy. The vote of censure is an example. Because of the control which the Government has acquired during the last fifty years over the time of the House, the substantive motion is not as frequent or important as it used to be. Ten or twelve days at the beginning of the session are reserved under standing orders for private members' motions. The Government itself sometimes submits items of policy, usually drafted as a 'White Paper', for consideration in the form of a motion expressing the concurrence of the House. Also the Opposition occasionally prefer to criticize the Government on a motion instead of on a vote of supply; but when they do this, it is generally at the expense of forfeiting one of their 'allotted' days.

The substantive motion for the adjournment of the House is another traditional form. It seems to have originated in a combination of two ideas, (1) that the House should not rise without giving an opportunity for the discussion of outstanding grievances, (2) that the House should be persuaded to rise in order to give members who act together an opportunity to consult in private on the action to be taken on some contingency, usually of an urgent nature. Under (1) may be classed the motions before the periodical holiday adjournments, also the motion which is needed to close the daily sitting and which, under a recent standing order, is debatable for half an hour. Under (2) may be put the 'emergency adjournment motion' (already described) and also motions for the adjournment of the House moved at the instance of the Opposition and in lieu of a supply vote on one of their allotted days.

Parliamentary questions are probably the best known feature of the House of Commons; they are the one procedural invention of the democratic period. During the 'question hour' on four days a week seventy or eighty questions on an average, together with many supplementary questions, are disposed of; but many others are not reached by the end of the hour and are left over to be answered in writing. Although members are rationed, the flow of questions seems inexhaustible; they are handed in at the rate of about two hundred a day. As no debate is permitted on questions, strict rules have been evolved by Speakers' rulings to ensure that they are not in fact short speeches but genuinely interrogative and concerned with matters for which the Ministers to whom they are addressed are responsible. Supplementary questions, arising out of questions on the Paper, which may be put at the Speakers' discretion, afford a searching test of a Minister's grasp of departmental business. In spite of the short time which can be allowed to each single question, the question hour has proved an effective way of controlling the departments in their day-to-day administration; members who are dissatisfied with the answers they receive have an opportunity of pressing for fuller explanations during the half-hour adjournment motion referred to above.

All these proceedings which together account for about half the time of a session, are methods by which the parliamentary function of controlling government is exercised. In respect of some, the private member is still free to take an individual line rather than act as a unit in a party organization; he makes his own opportunities; in questioning Ministers, particularly, but also in choosing a subject to raise on a motion for the adjournment, he can act as the representative of his constituents, irrespective of party. Other proceedings, such as the Address in reply to the King's speech and particularly the proceedings connected with the grant of supply, are, as already stated, the special province of the Opposition, or Oppositions, acting as parties. The total amount of time given to these matters is fixed by standing orders or conventional arrangements; but within these limits Opposition leaders can choose the subjects to be raised and the time to be allotted to each subject, at their own discretion. The only restriction, on debate in the case of two of the more important forms—Supply and Adjournment Motions—is that, as these forms are specifically designed for the control of administration, they may not be used for the purpose of raising matters of legislation.

I have tried to show that the restrictive effect of the modern standing orders is confined to a part only of the field of parliamentary debate. They are devised mainly to benefit the Government which has by their means so far reduced opposition as to treble the speed of the legislative process, during the last fifty years. But there remains a great block of business, taking up on the average half the time of a normal session, the discussion of which is used for the criticism of government policy. In this field the Opposition have no temptation to delay progress, nor the Government any motive to speed it up. It retains the characteristics of the traditional practice of the House, free of restrictive standing orders and serving the purposes of the minority. Unlike legislation, in which the House is confined to the subjects which the Government initiates, it affords opportunities to the Opposition to raise matters of its own choice, while they are still fresh, and to discuss them at reasonable length. It must be admitted that these opportunities have accrued to the organized Opposition at the expense of the individual member, who is progressively deprived of the rights which the old procedure gave him. But it is worth noting that of the whole field of parliamentary business a considerable portion remains which is governed by the spirit of the traditional procedure rather than by the standing orders. The up-to-date streamlined legislative engine symbolizes only a half of Parliament.

A hundred years ago the procedure of the House of Commons was still essentially the same as that of the Long

Parliament. It is this 'ancient practice', and not the standing orders, which remains the essential basis of procedure. Modern standing orders have restricted the working of some of the basic parliamentary forms; some have been diverted to purposes for which they were not originally intended—a fact, among many, which shows that, in spite of their age, they remain adaptable to changing circumstances. A distinguished Clerk of the House, Sir Courtenay Ilbert, has written: "The House of Commons is not only a workshop; it is a museum of antiquities." He might have added: "And all the exhibits are still in working order."

CHAPTER VIII

THE ORGANIZATION OF
BRITISH PARTIES

By Ivor Thomas

THE origins of the British Party system can be traced to the reign of Charles II, when those Members of Parliament who supported the exclusion of James, Duke of York, from the throne were dubbed Whigs and those who opposed it were nicknamed Tories; and for a century and a half such Party organization as existed was confined to the precincts of Westminster. Candidates made their own arrangements for securing election, the most convenient being to win the favour of a powerful patron able to influence votes. The enlargement of the electorate brought about by the Reform Act of 1832 made Peel see that a new approach was necessary, and with his encouragement associations began to be formed in the country to secure the return of Conservative Members. As their primary duty was to ensure that men of known Conservative views were not omitted from the lists of voters they were known as registration associations.

This was the modest beginning of party organization in the country, and every subsequent decade has seen a strengthening of that organization until it seems to some observers at the present time that the party machine is all important and that the individual counts for virtually nothing. The example of Lloyd George in the Liberal Party, of Ramsay MacDonald in the Labour Party and of Mr. Winston Churchill in the Conservative Party shows that even in these latter days a powerful personality in a position of authority can still exercise a tremendous influence, destructive or constructive, on his party's fortunes, but the general election of 1950 certainly showed how powerful party organizations had become. In no previous election had the main party machines been so well prepared, and in no previous election had their influence been greater.

It may surprise some readers accustomed, and not without reason, to regarding Great Britain as a two-party country to realize that the 1,868 candidates who contested the 625 seats stood under as many as thirty-three different labels.[1] It is true that not every label indicates a separate organized party; nevertheless, on a minimum reckoning, that is if we group together parties which support each other's candidates and omit those whose organization is too rudimentary to be considered, there are eleven British organized parties or groups of parties. Their fate at the general election of 1950 is given in the table on page 170.

The list of eleven parties given in this table looks remarkably like the analysis of a cricket eleven's innings, with a long string of 'ducks' following a big stand by the opening pair and a slight contribution by the first wicket down; one player has retired hurt, and there is a little wag in the tail. Two main features of the election were the rout of all Independents and all the candidates of minor parties. Even the Liberal Party, though able to put 475 candidates into the field, was not able to get more than nine of them elected, two of them with Conservative support. Public opinion polls had made it clear that few votes would separate the Labour and Conservative

[1]The following labels were used, and are here arranged in groups:
Conservative, Unionist, Conservative and Unionist, Ulster Unionist; Independent Conservative; National Liberal, Conservative and Liberal, Conservative and National Liberal, National Liberal and Conservative, Liberal and Conservative (10).
Liberal; Independent Liberal (2).
Labour, Co-operative and Labour, Northern Ireland Labour (3)
Independent Labour, Labour Independent, Independent Socialist, Socialist Party of Great Britain, Irish Labour (5).
Communist (1).
Social Credit (1).
Scottish Nationalist, Scottish Self-government, Scottish Home Rule, Welsh Nationalist, Independent Welsh Nationalist, Welsh Republican, Irish Nationalist, Irish Anti-Partition, Sinn-Fein (9).
Christian Democrat (1).
Independent (1).
In addition the Speaker stood without any label. Common Wealth did not put up any candidates at this election.

Party or group of parties	Candidates	Total votes	Percentage of total poll	Candidates elected
Labour and Co-operative	617	13,295,736	46.21	315
Conservative and National Liberal	621	12,501,983	43.45	298
Liberal	475	2,621,489	9.11	9
Communist	100	91,815	0.32	0
Independent Labour	2	3,005	0.01	0
Socialist Party of Great Britain	2	448	—	0
Common Wealth	—	—	—	—
Social Credit	1	551	—	0
Scottish Nationalist	4	10,347	0.03	0
Welsh Nationalist	7	17,580	0.06	0
Irish Nationalist	2	65,211	0.23	2
Total	1831	28,608,165	99.44	624
All others ..	37	161,312	0.56	1
Grand totals ..	1868	28,769,477	100.00	625

parties; therefore every vote counted, and on this occasion more perhaps than in any previous election, the voters tended to vote for parties rather than for individuals. The general election of 1950 was a battle of two gigantic party machines, in which both the Independents and the minor parties fared badly.[1]

In view of the enhanced importance of the party machines it is worth while giving some attention to the way in which the various parties are organized. At the outset it may be explained that both the Labour Party and the Co-operative Party are elements in wider associations. The Co-operative Party is a department of the Co-operative Union, Ltd., which is an association of local co-operative societies whose main business

[1]So much so that in the General Election of 1951 most of them did not stand again and there were far fewer Liberal and Communist candidatures, As the proofs of this chapter are being corrected while the general election campaign of 1951 is being waged, it is not possible to take account of it, but clearly it reinforces the general conclusions.

s 'mutual trading' rather than politics. The Labour Party and the Co-operative Union together with the trade unions affiliated to the Trades Union Congress make up what is commonly called the Labour movement. The only organ of the Labour movement as a whole is the National Council of Labour, consisting of seven members from each of the three constituent bodies. It is the duty of the National Council to 'consider all questions affecting the Labour and Co-operative movements as a whole and make provision for taking immediate and united action on all questions of national emergency'; but its pronouncements are not binding on the constituent bodies until ratified by them. There is also a certain amount of interlocking between these three bodies, many trade unions and one co-operative society (through its Political Purposes Committee) being affiliated to the Labour Party.

With the exception of the Communist Party, the bodies with which we are concerned are purely British. The Communist Party of Great Britain is unique in being an integral part of an international organization and in accepting directions from outside this country. Some other parties have international associations, but not such as to limit their freedom of action. The Labour Party, in pursuance of Articles 6 and 7 of its constitution, maintains cordial relations with the Labour Parties of Australia and New Zealand and with the Co-operative Commonwealth Federation in Canada, and it is a member with other European Social Democratic parties of the International Socialist Conference; but it is free to differ from its allies if it chooses and has done so, for example, over the Schuman Plan. The Co-operative Union is affiliated to the International Co-operative Alliance; but this body includes the most diverse elements, and it would not be possible for it to reach a common political policy, much less to make it binding on its members. There is a Liberal International which holds conferences attended by leading British Liberals in an individual capacity, but the Liberal Party as such is not affiliated to it, and has no international connections. There are Social Credit parties in other countries, and in Alberta there has long been a Social Credit Government, but the British

Social Credit Party's links with them are purely ideological. The Conservative Party eschews formal oversea alliances though naturally individual Conservatives may have their sympathies.

As a main object of party organization is to secure the return of Members to the Parliament of the United Kingdom, the two biggest parties are organized over the whole of Great Britain and Northern Ireland. This may be regarded as the goal of all party managers except for the Nationalist parties, whose organization is naturally confined to their own regions, but so far only the Conservative and Labour Parties have been able to cover Northern Ireland as well as Great Britain. Even the Liberal and Communist Parties are obliged to confess the Unionist hold on Northern Ireland too strong to break, and have no organization there. But as Northern Ireland is a geographically separate entity, has a Parliament of its own, and has many separate problems, the Conservative and Labour Parties find it convenient to have a separately organized Ulster Unionist Party and a Northern Ireland Labour Party—each a party within a party, so to speak.

In a lesser degree the same problem exists for Scotland, and both the Conservatives and the Liberals have felt it incumbent to have a distinct organization north of the Tweed under the names of the Scottish Unionist Party and the Scottish Liberal Party. Each of these parties is organized independently of its English counterpart and holds a separate annual conference, though there is some interlocking between them. The National Liberals have also an organization in Scotland—the Scottish National Liberal Association—separate from that in England. The Labour and Co-operative Parties have not felt it necessary to have separate national organizations in Scotland; their local Scottish organizations are regional in character, corresponding to their regional organizations in England and Wales, and the annual conferences are attended by delegates from north of the Tweed on the same basis as those from the south. The Communist Party also makes no distinction between England and Scotland. In the case of the smaller parties the question hardly arises.

Of the parties covering the whole of Great Britain, only the Liberals have felt it necessary to have a separate organization in Wales. But 'the Liberal Party of Wales' is largely a name and nothing more; it has not the distinctive character of the Scottish Liberal Party, and in such matters as representation on the party's Executive Committee Wales is put on the same basis as an English area, whereas Scotland has no representative.

What follows will normally have reference to party organization in England and Wales, but in most cases it may be applied to Scotland also with the necessary changes in nomenclature. It would be rash without further inquiry to make any application of English and Welsh conditions to Northern Ireland.

Membership of a party is normally effected by individual subscription to its principles and its funds. The Conservative, National Liberal, Liberal, Communist and minor parties are all composed of men and women who have individually assented to its principles and paid the requisite financial contribution. Perhaps we should add to the last sentence the words 'or are deemed to have done so', for only the Communist Party makes much inquiry into the orthodoxy of the applicant's beliefs, while minimum subscriptions are low and often casually collected. A British Party is not an *élite*, as the Russian Communist Party confesses to be, but welcomes all comers.

The Labour and Co-operative Parties have a fundamentally different basis. Since the adoption of a new constitution in 1918 the Labour Party has had individual members recruited in the manner described above, but they are a small part of its total membership. The present position is thus defined in clause (2) of the Party's constitution:

"1. There shall be two classes of members, namely:
   (*a*) Affiliated members.
   (*b*) Individual members.
2. Affiliated members shall consist of:
   (*a*) Trade unions affiliating to the Trades Union Congress or recognized by the General Council of the Trades Union Congress as *bona fide* trade unions.

    (b) Co-operative societies.

    (c) Socialist societies.

    (d) Professional organizations which, in the opinion of the National Executive Committee, have interests consistent with those of other affiliated organizations.

    (e) Constituency Labour parties and central Labour parties in divided boroughs.

    (f) County or area federations of constituency labour parties.

*   *   *   *   *

4. Individual members shall be persons of not less than 16 years of age who subscribe to the conditions of membership, provided they are not members of political parties or organizations ancillary or subsidiary thereto declared by the annual conference of the Labour Party . . . or by the National Executive Committee in pursuance of conference decisions to be ineligible for affiliation to the Party."

According to the report of the forty-ninth annual conference of the Labour Party, in 1950 there were eighty-eight trade unions affiliated to the Labour Party, one Co-operative society, four socialist societies and professional organizations, 667 constituency and borough Labour parties[1] and twenty federations.

As the representation of the affiliated bodies in the counsels of the Labour Party is roughly based on the number of members on whom affiliation fees are paid, and as the membership of the trade unions is so much greater than that of the constituency Labour parties or the affiliated bodies, they can always dominate the party if they act together.

The eighty-eight trade unions affiliated to the Labour Party in 1950 ranged in size from the Enginemen and Firemen's Union with sixty members on whom affiliation fees were paid in 1949

[1]The number is greater than the total number of constituencies (625) because it includes many borough parties as well as the constituency parties in the borough, e.g., Gateshead as well as Gateshead East and Gateshead West.

to the Transport and General Workers' Union with 830,000 members on whom affiliation fees were paid. Other giant unions with the number of members on whom they paid affiliation fees were the National Union of Mineworkers (650,096), the Amalgamated Engineering Union (594,339), the National Union of General and Municipal Workers (400,000), the National Union of Railwaymen (365,386) and the Union of Shop, Distributive and Allied Workers (317,000).

An energetic constituency Labour Party may recruit as many as 5,000 members, but the normal membership of local Labour parties is below 1,000. It will be seen that a single union, the Transport and General Workers' Union, is able to amass almost as much voting strength in the Labour Party as all the constituency parties put together. The one co-operative society affiliated to the Labour Party (through its Political Purposes Committee) is the Royal Arsenal Co-operative Society Ltd., which paid affiliation fees in 1949 on 33,600 members—about the membership of one of the smaller trade unions. The socialist and professional societies with the number of members on whom affiliation fees were paid in 1949 are: Fabian Society (3,216), Jewish Socialist Party (Poale Zion) (2,200), Socialist Medical Association (1,800) and the National Association of Labour Teachers (300). As far as voting strength goes, these figures are negligible.

The most accurate picture of the balance of power in the Labour Party is provided by the voting strength at the annual conference, which is roughly based on affiliated membership, as will be explained later. Not all affiliated bodies were represented at the 1950 conference, but the number of those who were so represented and their voting strength were as follows:

	Number	Delegates	Votes
Trade Unions	69	567	4,998,000
Socialist societies	4	4	10,000
Co-operative societies	1	6	34,000
Labour parties	588	606	992,000
Federations	17	17	17,000

It may be urged that the trade unions are composed o
individual members like constituency Labour parties, and tha
it is immaterial whether a man or woman becomes a membe
of the Labour Party through his trade union or through hi
local party. This would be a sounder argument if all member
of trade unions on whom affiliation fees are paid were keen
supporters of the Labour Party. It may be presumed that
persons who have gone to the trouble of joining a constituency
party or a socialist society are keen supporters; but no such
presumption can be made about the members of trade unions,
especially since 'contracting out' was substituted for 'contracting in'. A member of a trade union who does not want to be
reckoned a member of the Labour Party now has to take the
positive action of signing a form under the eyes of trade union
organizers who may be able to make life unpleasant for him.
It is not surprising that millions of trade unionists take the line
of least resistance and pay the political levy without query.
As a result of the repeal in 1946 of the Trade Disputes and
Trade Unions Act, 1927, the percentage of members of all
trade unions having political funds who were liable to contribute
to those funds rose from forty-five at the end of 1945 to ninety-
one at the end of 1947. In consequence, those who control the
trade unions are able to cast votes in the name of many
members who have never given a thought to the subject and
might vote differently if they did.

This does not mean that the system is not empirically
justified. The trade unions, who embody the solid good sense
of the British working man, have had some reason to fear the
consequences if ultimate control should slip from their hands
into that of the constituency Labour parties or socialist societies.
It is not the case that on most issues at the Labour Party
conference the trade unions are ranged on one side and the
constituency parties on the other. On almost all issues the
majority of the constituency parties vote the same way as the
big unions, but it is often a very precarious and incalculable
majority, and large numbers of constituency parties are
capable of embracing very strange causes. It has probably been
to the advantage of the Labour Party, and it has certainly been

to the advantage of the country, that the trade unions should in the last resort be able to dominate the Labour Party by this artificial system of voting. But there is no point in disguising its artificial character, which is shown by the fact that a man may be counted a member of the Labour Party in as many as five different ways—as a member of his constituency Labour Party, as a member of the federation to which it belongs, as a member of the Fabian Society, as a member of the Royal Arsenal Co-operative Society and as a member of his trade union— and he may have votes cast in his name at the party conference on opposite sides.

The trade unions may not only be affiliated nationally to the Labour Party, but local branches may be affiliated to the constituency Labour Party, which is built up in much the same way as the National Party. But trade unionists are generally casual in their attendance at local party meetings, except when a matter of real importance is under consideration, such as the selection of a parliamentary candidate, and the individual members' section normally shows much greater activity. For this reason those who have been frustrated by the national 'block vote' of the trade unions have suggested that they should be affiliated only to constituency Labour parties, and that the national party should be built up of local parties; but for the same reason the trade unions have received the suggestion coldly, and as they have the power in their hands nothing has come of it.

Membership of the Co-operative Party is not so complicated as that of the Labour Party, but it is of the same type. The individual co-operator does not decide for himself whether to become a member of the Co-operative Party by paying his subscription and expressing his adherence to its principles. The Co-operative Party is a federation of local societies which have decided by a majority vote to affiliate. Out of 1,050 societies 671 were affiliated in 1950, covering eighty-seven per cent of the membership.

Individual membership of a party is normally effected through the local body (association, branch or party) in the district where the member lives, but in most parties members

M

may be centrally enrolled at the national headquarters if they so desire. In the minor parties, which do not have an organization covering the entire country, this is a virtual necessity, though an applicant might be put on the lists of the nearest local branch to his place of residence. It is only in the Labour Party that the question is acute, and except in the case of persons temporarily resident abroad an individual member must be a member of the constituency Labour party in the area where he resides. At one time the party headquarters wished to have the power of central enrolment, but the party conference firmly rejected it.

Minimum subscriptions and the fixed affiliation fees are not onerous. Many Conservative and Liberal associations have a minimum subscription of one shilling a year. This low rate comes down from a time when the value of money was different from what it is today, but the associations have generally resisted national efforts to get it increased. In the Labour Party constitution it is laid down that each affiliated trade union, socialist society or co-operative society shall pay to the headquarters of the party an affiliation fee of sixpence a member annually. Each individual member of the Labour Party is required to pay not less than sixpence a month to the constituency party of which he is a member, and of this sixpence a year is remitted to Transport House as an affiliation fee in respect of that member. Those co-operative societies which decide to affiliate to the Co-operative Party are required to pay to the party a levy of one halfpenny a member annually. The Communist Party has a subscription at a much higher rate, as befits a small party with a zealous membership—1s. 4d. a month, reduced to 8d. a month for old-age pensioners, the unemployed and housewives.

The minimum subscriptions of the Conservative and Liberal parties would not carry them very far. Most members pay higher subscriptions of their own free will, and funds are raised by jumble sales, fetes and similar 'efforts' arranged largely by devoted bodies of women workers; occasional special appeals to finance national or local work may also be made. The Labour Party makes use of the same methods, but it relies for the greater part of its central work on the steady income which flows from affiliation fees. The trade unions are, of course, much the biggest contributors, and among the sums paid in 1949 were: Transport and General Workers' Union, £20,750; National Union of Mineworkers, £16,273; Amalgamated Engineering Union, £14,858; National Union of General and Municipal Workers, £10,000; National Union of Railwaymen, £9,134; Union of Shop Distributive and Allied Workers, £7,925. The substitution of 'contracting out' for 'contracting in' when the Trade Disputes and Trade Unions Act, 1927, was repealed in 1946 gave a big and immediate fillip to Labour Party finances, the total affiliation fees paid by trade unions rising from £51,261 in 1945 to £91,930 in 1947 and £113,695 in 1948. Large additional contributions are paid by the trade unions to the Labour Party's General Election funds.

As a main object of parties is to return members to Parliament, the unit of organization is normally the parliamentary constituency. The constituency unit is variously known as an association (constituency), party or branch. The Communist Party is not organized on a constituency basis but has branches in towns and factories. The minor parties frequently have town or district branches also, but this is usually because their organization is not sufficiently extensive to cover the whole constituency or because they have no prospect of fighting a parliamentary election in that area; usually the minor party in an area revolves round one active adherent. The Communist organization seems, however, to be dictated by a different conception of popular representation; the factory branches in particular suggest that the Communists would prefer to see in place of a Parliament consisting of members elected on a geographical basis, a soviet consisting of deputies chosen by the 'toilers' in the various industries.

A Conservative or Liberal constituency association is composed of individual members who live or are entitled to vote in that division. Men and women take part in its main activities on the same basis, but there is usually a women's organization (called among Conservatives the Women's Divisional Branch or Women's Divisional Committee) with activities of its own;

and there are few constituencies which would not admit that the work of the women's organization, generally humdrum and behind the scenes, is indispensable. There is also usually a Young Conservatives' or Young Liberals' section with activities of its own. The Labour Party system is rather different. A local Labour Party is a microcosm of the national party, that is to say it consists of affiliated organizations (mainly local branches of trade unions, but perhaps also the local branch of a socialist society such as the Fabian Society) and individual members. The individual members' section will generally include a women's section with activities of its own, but the several attempts of the Labour Party to organize its youths have not had a happy history, as the organizations have generally been captured by the Communists.

The ultimate authority in a Conservative or Liberal association rests in the whole body of members, each member having one vote. In the Labour Party it rests in a delegate conference composed of delegates chosen by the affiliated organizations and individual members in proportion to their numerical strength; in the conference each delegate has one vote but some sections have, of course, more delegates than others. The whole body of members in a Conservative or Liberal association, or a delegate conference in a constituency Labour Party, is convened only occasionally, and an executive council or an executive committee is chosen to carry out the ordinary business of the association. The officers are normally a president, who is a figurehead, a chairman, who is expected to be active, one or more vice-chairmen and a treasurer, all elected at the annual general meeting. An association or local party normally has one salaried official—the agent, who acts as secretary to the executive council or committee and on whose personality and efficiency the smooth working of the organization to a large extent depends. Some constituencies may not be able to afford a full-time agent, though the party headquarters are ready to help in such cases, while others may not only have a full-time agent but a paid woman organizer or an assistant agent.

For the purposes of organization constituencies are subdivided into wards (in boroughs) and polling districts (in county divisions). This is not simply to secure the benefits of decentralization, but because these are units of local government representation; and although party organizations were first formed to secure the return of Members to Parliament, the winning of local government elections has now assumed almost equal importance. The Labour Party does not carry the system of affiliation down to the ward level, and therefore the ward or polling district section of a constituency Labour Party, as of a Conservative or Liberal association, is composed entirely of individual members.

In most parties the constituency units are grouped into area or regional organizations. The Conservative Party has twelve areas in England and Wales; the Liberal Party divides England into ten areas, and Wales is also treated as an area; and the Labour Party divides England, Scotland and Wales into eleven regions. These do not correspond to any electoral divisions and are merely convenient groups between the constituencies and the head office. In each area the Conservative Party has an Area Council of the National Union[1] which provides representation for every constituency and every unit of the party organization within the area; and the Central Office[2] has an office with an area agent and deputy in each area. The Liberal and Labour parties have similar arrangements. The Labour Party may have two or more federations of constituency parties within a region and has a number of regional councils. The areas chosen by the three parties are shown in the following table on page 182; the order is that given in official publications.

The Communist Party organizes its branches into *districts*, of which there are twenty in Great Britain, e.g. London and Yorkshire. In some places *area committees* are interposed between the branches and the districts, e.g. the London boroughs. In some large towns, e.g. Sheffield, there is a *city committee*.

The national organization of the Conservative and Liberal Parties has a dual aspect, the one side being built up from the constituency units, the other created at the top to give help to

[1]See below, p. 182.
[2]See below, p. 182.

PARTY AREA ORGANIZATION

Conservative (England and Wales) Area	Liberal (England and Wales) Area	Labour (England, Wales and Scotland) Region
1. London City and all London boroughs	1. Devon and Cornwall	1. Northern Cumberland, Durham, Northumberland, North Riding except Scarborough and Whitby
2. Northern Cumberland, Durham, Northumberland, Middlesbrough	2. Eastern counties	2. North-western Cheshire, Derbyshire, Lancashire, Westmorland
3. Lancashire, Cheshire and Westmorland	3. Home counties	3. Yorkshire East Riding, West Riding, York, Scarborough and Whitby
4. Yorkshire (excluding Middlesbrough)	4. Lancashire, Cheshire and North-western	4. Southern Berkshire, Buckinghamshire, Hampshire, Kent, Middlesex, Surrey, East Sussex, West Sussex, Isle of Wight
5. East Midlands Derbyshire, Leicestershire, Lincolnshire, Nottinghamshire, Northamptonshire, Rutland	5. London	5. London
6. West Midlands Gloucestershire, Herefordshire, Shropshire, Staffordshire, Warwickshire, Worcestershire	6. West Midlands	6. South-western Cornwall, Devon, Dorset, Gloucestershire, Somerset, Wiltshire
7. Eastern Bedfordshire, Cambridgeshire, Hertfordshire, Huntingdon, Norfolk, Suffolk	7. East Midlands	7. Eastern Bedfordshire, Cambridgeshire, Isle of Ely, Essex, Hertfordshire, Huntingdon, Norfolk, Suffolk
8. Essex and Middlesex	8. Northern	8. Wales
9. Kent, Surrey and Sussex	9. Western counties	9. Scottish
10. Wessex Berkshire, Buckinghamshire, Dorset, Hampshire, Isle of Wight, Oxfordshire, Wiltshire	10. Yorkshire	10. East Midlands Derbyshire, Leicestershire, Lincolnshire, Northamptonshire, Nottinghamshire
11. Western Cornwall, Devon, Somerset, Bristol	11. Wales	11. West Midlands Herefordshire, Oxfordshire, Shropshire, Staffordshire, Warwickshire, Worcestershire
12. Wales and Monmouthshire		

the constituency. This dichotomy has historical origins, but it continues to exist because it corresponds to a genuine division of functions.

The National Union of Conservative and Unionist Associations is a federation composed of constituency associations and central associations in divided boroughs. The governing body is the Central Council which includes the leader and other principal members and officials of the Party; Conservative Members of Parliament and prospective Parliamentary candidates; and representatives from constituency associations, central associations of divided boroughs, and provincial area councils and their advisory committees; the Scottish Unionist Association and the Ulster Unionist Council are also represented. The Central Council is constituted annually and elects a president, a chairman and three vice-chairmen of the National Union. In order to carry out the ordinary business of the National Union between meetings of the Central Council there is an Executive Committee composed of the Leader and other principal members and officials of the party and four or more representatives appointed by each provincial area; Scotland and Ulster are also represented.

The Liberal Party Organization is the body corresponding among Liberals to the National Union among Conservatives. It has a Council and Executive Committee analogous in scope and composition to the similarly named bodies in the National Union. In addition there is a Liberal Party Committee whose 'prime purpose is to express the Liberal attitude on questions of immediate urgency as well as to act on matters of long-term policy', and which has the further duty of maintaining contact with the parliamentary party.

Side by side with this organization built up from the constituency units is a central organization not depending on a complicated system of annually changing popular representation. In the Conservative Party this central organization is known as the Conservative and Unionist Central Office and in the Liberal Party as the Liberal Central Association (or Whip's Office). In the Conservative Party the Chairman of the Party Organization, who directs the work of the Central Office, and his two vice-chairmen, as well as the two treasurers, are appointed by the Leader of the Party. The primary task of the National Union is to assist in the democratic formation of a collective opinion in the Party and to enable it to find expression, above all in the annual conference; the Central Office is not concerned with the task of forming policy as such, but with winning adherents for it in the country and securing the election of members who will get it carried out in Parliament. Its main business is therefore to carry out the national propaganda of the party, to give constituencies all possible help in carrying out their own propaganda, to ensure that candidates of good quality are available, to advise the Leader on the state of the organization and on political trends in the country, and to provide any help needed by the party in Parliament. It is, of course, impossible to draw a firm line between the work of the National Union and the Central Office, and it is essential for them to work harmoniously. In the Liberal Party the dividing line between the Organization and the Central Association is even more difficult to draw.

In the Labour Party this duality in organization is not so apparent because the federation of constituency parties is not carried beyond the area level. The party headquarters at Transport House does the work done in the Conservative Party by both the Central Office and the National Union. But the party headquarters, and indeed all the extra-parliamentary activities[1] of the party, come under the authority of a National Executive Committee which is elected at the annual conference, which is in turn composed of delegates from the affiliated organizations and constituency Labour Parties. As the National Executive Committee is the highest authority in the Labour Party between annual conferences, and far excels in importance the place held by the similarly named bodies in the Conservative and Liberal Parties, it will be worth while to glance at the way it is made up. It is composed of four divisions, and the following rules are laid down in the Party's Standing Order No. 4:

[1]The extent to which the parliamentary activities of the party come within its purview has been a matter of some controversy.

"Division I shall consist of 12 members, to be nominated by trade unions, and elected by their delegations at the annual party conference.

"Division II shall consist of one member to be nominated by Socialist, Co-operative and professional organizations, and elected by their delegations at the annual party conference.

"Division III shall consist of seven members, to be nominated by federations, constituency Labour parties and central Labour parties, and elected by their delegations at the annual party conference.

"Division IV shall consist of five women members, to be nominated by any affiliated organization, and elected by the annual party conference as a whole."

The Leader of the party, who is not elected by the conference, and the treasurer, who is elected by the conference but usually without a contest, are members of the National Executive Committee *ex officio*.

It will be observed that the trade unions have in Division I only twelve of the total membership of twenty-seven, but as they could, if they so chose, nominate all five women members in Division IV, and secure their election, they have the balance of power firmly in their hands. But they do not abuse it, and in fact the seven members elected by the constituency parties tend to be more prominent in the committee. The annual election for these seven places is keenly contested and closely watched, as it gives an index of rising and falling fortunes among Labour politicians. The committee chooses as its chairman the member who has served longest on it and has not previously 'passed through the chair'. This automatic rule has sometimes given the committee an embarrassing chairman at critical periods.

In the Communist Party the highest authority is also a national congress, but it meets only once in two years, and in between authority resides in an Executive Committee of thirty-six members elected by the congress. The party's chief officers are chosen by the Executive Committee from among its own members and are the chairman, vice-chairman, general secretary, assistant general secretary and head of the organization department. These officers are all members of a Political Committee of eleven chosen by the Executive Committee from its own ranks.

The climax of party organization is the party conference, usually held annually. The Conservative and Labour conferences are now huge affairs which only a few towns such as London and Blackpool have halls sufficiently large to accommodate. Over five thousand persons are entitled to attend the Conservative conference and the number who do so, with visitors, is not far short of that figure. An attempt by the party chiefs to limit the numbers, partly in order that the conference might be held in other towns for missionary purposes, was defeated in 1950 by the rank and file, perhaps through misunderstanding of the objective. About 1,500 persons are entitled to take part in the Labour Party conference, and with visitors double that number may be present. Even the Liberal Party Assembly, as its conference is called, musters an attendance of about 1,500. The Co-operative Party and the Independent Labour Party also hold annual conferences.

It should be obvious that binding decisions on policy cannot safely be taken at such huge meetings. The complexities of policy cannot properly be considered in such large gatherings, nor is the atmosphere always favourable to the cool consideration which is necessary for a right decision. In some cases the members of the conference come with instructions how they are to vote, instructions which are often framed by ill-informed bodies in circumstances which may largely have ceased to be relevant.

The position of a Government is particularly embarrassing if it is bound beforehand by the decision of a party conference taken perhaps on inadequate information and bad advice in very different circumstances. This is an old problem, accentuated by the rise of the Labour Party, but antedating it. Mr. Gladstone's last Government, for example, was seriously embarrassed by the Newcastle programme endorsed at a party conference in 1891. Commenting on this fact, Mr. A. Lawrence Lowell wrote:[1]

[1] *The Government of England*, vol. ii, p. 20.

"So long, therefore, as government by a ministry responsible to the Commons endures, it is obvious that policy must be formulated by the Cabinet alone, and that this is inconsistent with any serious effort to formulate it by means of a party organization."

The Conservative Party accepts this point of view. Every constituency association is entitled to send seven persons to the conference—two men, two women, two Young Conservatives and one trade unionist—apart from its Member of Parliament or prospective candidate and certified agent and certified organiser. They are styled representatives, and are expected to use their own judgment on the issues debated. Each representative has one vote. The resolutions have been sent in by associations some time beforehand, and if approved are communicated to the Leader of the party, but are not binding on him. They are useful to him for getting the feeling of the party, but the announcement of the Conservative policy and programme is his prerogative. This can easily be represented as undemocratic, and often is by other parties. But the Leader of the Conservative Party does not, of course, act without advice. He receives much advice from many quarters, in particular from the National Union's Advisory Committee on Policy. This consists of a chairman and deputy chairman appointed by the Leader, five members of Parliament appointed by one of their own committees, two peers and seven persons appointed by the Executive Committee of the National Union. In the light of such advice he formulates the party's policy or programme unfettered by any body outside Parliament. If his formulation were not acceptable to his parliamentary colleagues and their confidence were withdrawn, he could not, of course, survive as Leader.

The members of the Labour Party conference are termed delegates, and are frequently, indeed normally, instructed on how they shall vote on major issues. Affiliated organizations and constituency Labour parties are entitled to send one delegate for every 5,000 members or part thereof on whom affiliation fees have been paid. The delegates of each affiliated organization or constituency party are given a card with a number on it representing so many thousand votes according to its membership. A constituency organization will normally have only a figure '1' on its card for 1,000 votes, whereas a member of a big trade union delegation may be able to pull out from his pocket a card with 500 on it for half a million votes. This is known as the block vote system. Debates are generally very keen, as they may well be since the decisions are binding on the party.

These are the respective theories of the Conservative and Labour conferences, but in practice the difference, though very real, is not quite so sharp. In office the Labour Government has not infrequently acted in a sense different from conference resolutions. Mr. Ernest Bevin, as Foreign Secretary, repeatedly ignored embarrassing resolutions on Palestine; and it has become a regular procedure of the conference to elect Mr. Aneurin Bevan at the head of the constituency section of the National Executive and then to defeat him on some question of policy. In the Conservative conference of 1950 the assembled representatives insisted on putting into a resolution on housing a figure of 300,000 houses a year as the minimum which should be built; and this was accepted immediately by the 'platform' and later by the Leader of the party. In practice, therefore, the Labour Party may ignore conference decisions and the Conservative conference may give advice of so forceful a character that it will be accepted, but over the broad range of policy the distinction is true that the Labour conference decides and the Conservative advises.

The members of the Liberal Assembly are for the most part chosen by constituency associations in proportion to their number of paying members; and there are other members such as Liberal M.P.s and prospective candidates. The Liberal view is intermediate between that of the Conservative and Labour Parties; the official formula is that nothing is regarded as binding on the Party until passed by the Assembly. No one who has studied the voting record of Liberal Members of Parliament could accuse them of being hampered in the independent exercise of their judgment.

In the last resort Parties must choose between having policy formed by their representatives in Parliament or by a party organization outside. Over the course of many centuries we have developed in this country a highly sensitive system of parliamentary democracy, in which the Government is formed of persons having the confidence of a majority of the elected Members of the House of Commons. It is our traditional system to choose representatives who we think will serve us well in Parliament, to let them get on with their job without undue fetters, and to get rid of them at the next opportunity if we do not like the results. It is another possible system to have a chain of delegate conferences to formulate policy and administer the country; but this is not our traditional system and cannot well be grafted on to it.

The success of a party conference, and indeed of all party organization, depends very much on the permanent officials of the party. The salaried officials of the older parties follow the tradition of civil servants in avoiding publicity. They regard themselves as the advisers and executants of the political chiefs of the party, and do not themselves enter into public controversy over policy. It may be doubted whether the outside public is aware of the names of the chief officials of the Conservative Central Office. There is a marked difference in the practice of the Labour Party and it is still more marked in the Communist Party. The secretary of the Labour Party frequently makes controversial speeches in public. In the Communist Party the general secretary is the party's effective leader, and no question of his right to make controversial speeches on policy is ever raised. This marks a difference in outlook between the older parties and the Socialist and Communist parties. It will be recalled that Stalin held no post except that of general secretary of the Central Committee of the Communist Party of the U.S.S.R. from 1922 until 1941, but the reality of power was always in his hands. It is the triumph of the professionals over the amateurs, the ousting of the gentlemen by the players.

The relationship between the central organs of a party and its constituency associations or other local units calls for careful handling. In theory all parties are built up of autonomous constituency associations or other local organizations, and the theory corresponds to the facts in a surprising degree. The great development of party machines has so far taken place without destroying or even impairing the vitality and independence of the constituency associations. Constituency associations have control of their own finances, which are normally self-balancing; and although the head office may make a contribution to a needy association as part of its missionary work, it does not thereby gain or seek control. The annual affiliation fee of 6d. paid to the headquarters of the Labour Party on behalf of every member has been mentioned. In the Conservative Party each divisional association pays an affiliation fee of two guineas a year to the National Union and contributes a quota to the central funds of the Party. The head offices of the parties draw up model rules for constituencies, but these are only part of the general guidance given, and the local association, subject to certain minimum requirements, is able to draw up its own rules and conduct its own business.

The most conclusive test of the independence of constituency organizations lies in the selection of agents and parliamentary candidates. The agent has probably passed a test under arrangements approved by the head office.[1] He is the channel of communication with the head office and by reason of his training he is expected to guide his organization along sound Party lines. But he is very definitely the servant of the local association, appointed by its Executive Committee and paid out of constituency funds even if the head office makes a contribution. Although he may not always wish to stay in the same constituency or may aspire to promotion, almost invariably he gives a wholehearted loyalty to his local association. Head offices rarely attempt to secure the selection of a particular person as agent, though they may be ready to suggest names.

The head offices of all parties have from time to time attempted to secure the selection of particular individuals as prospective parliamentary candidates, and the reaction is

[1]In the Conservative Party the certification of agents is done by the Conservative and Unionist Examination Board, which consists of representatives of the National Union, the Central Office and the National Society of Conservative and Unionist Agents.

strong proof of the real independence of the constituencies. There are from time to time persons whom the head office wants to get into Parliament and whom the constituency associations are glad to select. But when this identity of views does not prevail the local body can always reject the nominee of the head office and frequently does so. Constituency associations prize their independence so greatly that in such circumstances the nomination of the head office may be a disadvantage against a local candidate.

When it becomes necessary to select a prospective parliamentary candidate, the executive committee of a Conservative association usually sets up a selection committee consisting of the chairman and a few other leading members. Applicants are not usually lacking even for the least hopeful seats, and the Central Office is approached for suggestions. It is the business of one of the two vice-chairmen of the party organization, who is usually a Member of Parliament himself, to answer such approaches. After making inquiries the selection committee rejects some names without more ado but may decide to give interviews to a few persons, who are asked to appear one after the other, make brief speeches and answer questions. The applicant's wife is sometimes asked as well, as she is nowadays almost as important as the candidate. In the past a very pertinent question at such interviews was, "How much are you prepared to contribute to the party funds?" but this is a question that may not now be put to applicants in the Conservative Party. After selection candidates are not allowed to contribute more than £25 a year to the constituency association and Members of Parliament £50; the association must assume responsibility for all election expenses. After the interviews the selection committee generally recommends one name to the executive committee; the recommended person makes a brief speech, perhaps his wife also, and it is very rare for the executive committee not to accept the recommendation. Sometimes the selection committee makes a short list for the executive, which hears the applicants speak in turn and chooses one. Finally the person selected appears before a general meeting of members to receive their approval as prospective parliamentary candidate. When the election approaches and the candidate ceases to be 'prospective', his adoption takes place at a general meeting designed to rouse the maximum enthusiasm.

Among the Liberals the sifting of the applicants is normally done by the constituency executive committee, which then usually recommends one person to a general meeting. No limit is placed on candidates' contributions.

In the Labour Party also the sifting is done by the executive committee, which is a smaller body than its Conservative namesake. Applicants must be nominated by an affiliated organization or polling district section, or must be put in by the head office (technically by the elections sub-committee of the National Executive). The list is reduced and a small number, say six, are asked to appear before a delegate conference and make brief speeches. This is commonly known in the party as 'the singing competition'. The question "How much are you or your organization prepared to contribute to the party funds?" may be put and usually is, either at the interview or privately beforehand. The words 'or your organization' must be added because trade unions who sponsor candidates are prepared to finance their election expenses heavily and to make substantial annual contributions to the local Party. This places individuals not sponsored by trade unions in a difficulty, and often they feel obliged to pledge more than they would like in order not to jeopardize their chances, more particularly as, in the delicious language of *The Times House of Commons*, 1950,[1] "trade union candidates nearly always contest the safer seats because the sponsoring unions feel that they would not be justified in using their members' contributions to support candidates in constituencies where the prospects of success are doubtful". In the 1945 election, according to the same guide, 120 out of 125 trade union candidates won their contests and formed thirty per cent of the parliamentary Labour Party; in the 1950 election 111 out of 140 candidates sponsored by trade unions were returned and formed thirty-five per cent of the Labour Members of the House. The Labour Party is conscious of the disadvantage in which unsponsored candidates

[1]P. 284.

are placed, and the demoralization of local parties that may result from large subventions, and has imposed limits on contributions, but as the ideas of the trade unions and individuals about what is reasonable are different the limits are high. An affiliated organization or an individual (whether a parliamentary candidate or not) may not pay to the funds of a constituency Labour Party for organization and registration purposes more than £200 in a parliamentary borough or £250 a year in a parliamentary county, and may not contribute to the expenses of an election more than eighty per cent of the actual election expenses nor more than eighty per cent of sixty per cent of the maximum expenses allowed by law. When the interviews are over the delegates vote on the applicants by a system of successive ballots in which those who do not get the requisite quota at each ballot are rejected until one gets a clear majority. It is usually known how delegates will vote on the first round, and the anxiety of applicants is to know how a trade union or ward delegation will vote when its own man is knocked out.

In the Communist Party the local organization is not usually on a constituency basis, and when an election is announced it is often necessary to form an election committee *ad hoc* to run a candidate. This has also to be done by the smaller parties.

In all parties it is laid down that the candidate selected by the constituency organization must be approved by the appropriate national body—in the Conservative Party the National Union's Standing Advisory Committee on Candidates and in the Labour Party the National Executive Committee—but if it should disapprove, the local association may very well run the candidate all the same. In no field is the independence of local associations so marked; and few fields of inquiry would so repay the social historian as the way in which those who are ambitious for parliamentary honours are selected. We must now turn to those who have surmounted all obstacles and have taken their seats at Westminster.

As Parliament is the sovereign body in this land, and has traditions and privileges which far antedate the organization of parties in the country, the relation of constituency bodies

N

and national headquarters to the people's representatives in Parliament is a matter of some delicacy.

The attitude of the Conservative and Liberal Parties, which crystallized in the great days of parliamentary government, is unambiguous. Neither the constituency associations nor the head offices claim any right of control over a member's action in Parliament; as far as they are concerned, he is free to speak and vote as he pleases. Like all other citizens he must abide by the consequences of his actions, and if his conduct in Parliament displeases his Leader, his constituency association or his head office may feel under no obligation to select or approve him as the candidate at the next election. At an election a constituency association is married to its candidate, if elected, for better, for worse, for richer, for poorer, but only till the next general election do them part. It is open to the association at any time in the lifetime of Parliament to select a prospective Parliamentary candidate other than the sitting Member; and although a sitting Member is normally readopted without question if he wishes to stand again, this power of reopening the candidature is the one sanction possessed by a constituency association, and has not infrequently been exercised. If the Leader of the party is displeased with the Member, the only course open to the head office is to try and persuade the local association to employ this sanction; but in such cases the local association will as often as not stand by its Member.

The attitude of the Labour Party is not quite so unambiguous. Some imprudent speeches by the late Professor Harold Laski led Mr. Churchill in the general election of 1945 to assert that a Labour Government would be under the control of an extra-parliamentary body, namely, the National Executive Committee of the Labour Party;[1] and the issue by the same body in 1950 of a document on "European Unity" revived these doubts, which were not wholly removed by Mr. Attlee's disclaimers.

The National Executive Committee of the Labour Party does not claim to be able to direct a Member of Parliament

[1] See *The Times*, 22nd June, 1945, and for Miss Ellen Wilkinson's rebuttal, *The Times*, 25th June, 1945.

how to speak or vote, but clause 9 of the party constitution lays down:

> "9. No person may be selected as a parliamentary Labour candidate by a constituency Labour Party, and no candidate may be endorsed by the National Executive Committee, if the person concerned:
>
>   *   *   *   *
>
>   (d) does not undertake to accept and act in harmony with the standing orders of the parliamentary Labour Party."

These standing orders require members not to speak or vote in a sense contrary to decisions of a meeting of the parliamentary party, though their right to abstain on matters, such as religion and temperance, on which they have conscientious scruples, is recognized.

It is unnecessary to labour the point, as the standing orders are strongly criticized within the party and have been suspended since 1945; but in strict theory under these standing orders the only parliamentary action allowed to a Labour Member without consultation is to put down questions. When constitutionalists raise their eyebrows, attention is drawn to a note added to the standing orders, which says, "Members should take advantage of party meetings in suitable instances to raise questions of party policy concerning which they may have doubts." But the effect is to transfer the real debate from the public discussion on the floor of the House of Commons to the private conclaves of the party, which the party managers are generally able to control.

Each of the parliamentary parties holds such a regular meeting—usually weekly—in a committee room of the House of Commons to discuss its attitude to the approaching business. But the Conservative and Liberal meetings differ from the Labour meetings in that no attempt is made to bind members to speak and vote otherwise than as they feel. It is obvious from the division lists that the Liberal members speak and vote as they please, and in this case the real question is whether the freedom is not so great as to make them a group of Independents rather than a party. Among the Conservatives, with whom the sense of party solidarity is stronger, there are enough divagations in speech and vote to show that no rigid party line is laid down for everyone to follow. A noteworthy feature of the Conservative Party meeting is that it is essentially a private members' committee, and is indeed so called.[1] It is rare for the party chiefs to attend, and no attempt is made to bind members. A general discussion takes place, and the sense of the meeting is conveyed to the Leader of the party or the front-bench Members who may have to speak in the House on the subject. The Labour Party meeting always has a good attendance of front-bench members, and even the cares of office are not allowed to prevent the Prime Minister and the Leader of the House from frequent attendance. The reason is that the Labour Party meeting not only holds a general discussion of the approaching business, but decides the party's attitude towards it, and by a majority vote if a division is demanded.

For these reasons Labour Party meetings are much more lively and much better attended than Conservative meetings, and attract much greater interest in the press, though it came as a shock to most members to learn that two newspapers were prepared to pay, and two members to receive, financial subventions for revealing what took place there.[2] But there is an obvious threat to the constitutional relations of the Government and the House if ministers indicate their policy to a party meeting before they do so to the whole body of members; and there is a clear danger to the status of members if a private decision taken upstairs, perhaps by a narrow majority, reduces them to acquiescence against their judgment. Perhaps we could have a Parliament run on these lines, but it would not be Parliament as we have known it, with its 'cut and thrust' of open debate and decisions taken on the floor of the House.

[1] It is commonly called the 1922 Committee from the initiative it took in 1922 in bringing Mr. Lloyd George's Coalition to an end.

[2] I believe that attendance at, and interest in, meetings of the Parliamentary Labour Party have to some extent subsequently waned, largely because Members who attended found they were expected to listen to lectures on economic theory for which they were in general neither qualified nor inclined; and meetings are now normally held only once a fortnight.

Students of other constitutions may wonder how far these facts indicate an invasion of the House of Commons by the caucus system as known in Australia and New Zealand. In these countries not only is party policy settled at a party meeting (or caucus), but the caucus of the dominant party actually chooses the persons to fill the ministerial offices.

In describing the New Zealand system[1] Sir Gilbert Campion (now Lord Campion) has given the warning:

"The logical end of the process seems to be the transfer of power without individual responsibility to the caucus, with the reduction of Cabinet ministers to the status of its spokesmen in Parliament. . . . Democracy should think again before it ties itself to a system under which free and open debate in Parliament, the cutting edge of political progress during three centuries, will be reduced to a pretentious and expensive formality."

So far as the Conservative and Liberal Parties are concerned, in the United Kingdom the answer is reassuring. They neither select ministers nor take decisions binding on members. So far as the Labour Party is concerned, the answer is satisfactory on the former point. The Parliamentary Labour Party has never claimed the right to nominate ministers. As regards the second point, there is one noteworthy difference. In New Zealand and Australia the principle of collective ministerial responsibility does not prevail in the caucus, and ministers may there be ranged on opposite sides. In the Labour Party however, ministers are expected to preserve a united front at all times.

The organization of a parliamentary party is not elaborate. Its members elect a chairman, and perhaps other officers and a committee from their own numbers. A back-bencher held in general respect is almost invariably selected as chairman and he presides over the party meeting. It is part of the old parliamentary conception that members and ex-members of the Cabinet hold themselves rather aloof from their parties and that the organization of a parliamentary party, and especially its party meeting, is mainly an affair of the back-benchers for the purpose of conveying collective opinion to the party chiefs; and although the Labour Party differs somewhat in its

[1] *Sunday Times,* 27th March, 1949.

views it conforms in this matter of the back-bencher chairman. A number of committees with their own officers are appointed for the different classes of business handled in Parliament, e.g. foreign affairs, imperial affairs, finance, trade and industry. It is normally possible for all members to attend committees in which they are interested, though the Labour Party has had to impose a limit on those wishing their views heard on foreign affairs. There are also committees composed of members from the various geographical areas to consider their attitude to matters of local interest. Such committees, whether functional or geographical, may report to the party meeting or direct to the minister or front-bencher concerned.

There are now only three fully articulated parties in Parliament—Conservative, Liberal and Labour. The National Liberals call themselves in Parliament the Liberal Unionist Group; they have their own group organization and hold their own group meetings, but policy is concerted with the Conservatives. The Co-operative members also hold their own private meetings, but they are an integral part of the parliamentary Labour Party, whose meetings they attend on the same basis as other members; and these Co-operative meetings should therefore be regarded as having the same status as meetings of trade unionists or Scottish members rather than as meetings of a separate party. The secretarial work for parliamentary parties is done by the head offices.

The members of a parliamentary party are those who are given and accept its whip. The term whip is used in Parliament to denote both one of the party officials charged with the oversight of parliamentary business, and the paper which they issue to party members every week-end, and on other occasions as required, to inform them about approaching business, and especially when their attendance is required for divisions. The Chief Whip must be in constant attendance upon the Leader of the party, and before we proceed further these terms must be explained.

The party organization so far described is essentially a back-benchers' organization, but when the whole body of members is concerned, front-benchers as well as back-benchers, there is another organization in which the Leader and the whips are the chief elements. The party Leader is an old and honoured title which has not been sullied by the misuse of the word in other lands and to some extent in our own. Originally the party Leader was simply the Leader of the parliamentary party in the House of Commons or House of Lords elected by the party members in that House. Such a post is absolutely essential in each House, as decisions have frequently to be taken on the spur of the moment and can be taken only by someone who has the confidence of those sitting alongside and behind him. As party organization developed throughout the country, the Leader of the parliamentary party in the House of Commons or House of Lords was accepted also as the Leader of the party throughout the country, though there was at first no formal post. It would have been incompatible with the place of Parliament in the Constitution that a party should have had any other Leader than the Leader of the party in either the House of Commons or the House of Lords. As between the two in the nineteenth century, one of them generally had an obvious claim to be regarded as the party Leader, especially if the Sovereign's choice had fallen on him as Prime Minister. In the present century it has come to be recognized that the Prime Minister, and therefore the Leader of the party, must be a Member of the House of Commons; and since this question was finally settled in 1923 we may say that the party Leader is the Leader of the parliamentary party in the House of Commons. At first he was chosen exclusively by his Party colleagues in the House of Commons, and this is still the position in the Liberal Party. But in view of his wider responsibilities the Conservative Party has gradually admitted other electors. In 1922 Conservative peers and prospective parliamentary candidates were invited to attend, along with Conservative Members of Parliament, the meeting which confirmed Mr. Bonar Law as Leader. (He was already Prime Minister, and it has several times happened in the present century that a Conservative has been elected Leader after being invited by the King to be Prime Minister.) In 1937 the number of electors was further increased by the addition of the Executive Committee of the

National Union. In the Labour Party the Leader of the parliamentary party is chosen by a joint meeting of Labour M.P.s and peers. Until recently there were few Labour peers, and it was virtually election by the Labour M.P.s, but the 'thin red line' in the upper house has now increased to the not inconsiderable total of sixty-four.

The Leader of the party appoints the whips, and when the party is in office they are ministers, the Chief Whip being known as the Parliamentary Secretary to the Treasury or Patronage Secretary. In office or in opposition, the Chief Whip has the main responsibility for the efficient discharge of the party's business in Parliament. In the early development of party organization outside Parliament, he had also the responsibility for that work; and this survives to some extent in the Liberal Party and in the Scottish Unionist Association.[1] In the Conservative Party the Chief Whip had charge of the Central Office until 1911, when the creation of the post of Chairman of the Party Organization enabled him to give his whole time to the parliamentary business. In the Labour Party also the Chief Whip is solely concerned with the work inside the House.

If we may revert now to the other sense of the word whip, the paper giving information about coming business, in the Conservative Party the Leader decides which members are entitled to receive it, and he may withdraw the whip if occasion so requires. Normally the whip is given without question to members who were officially approved Conservative candidates, but odd cases occasionally justify the withholding or withdrawal of the whip. In the Labour Party the whip is automatically given to members whose candidature was endorsed by the National Executive Committee and its withdrawal needs a vote by the party meeting. Such a withdrawal is then to be 'reported' to the National Executive Committee, which will proceed to action against the member in his constituency. In any party a member may decline to receive the whip or ask for it to be

[1]In the Liberal Party, as already noticed, the Central Association is commonly known as the Whip's Office. It was as recently as November 1950 that responsibility for Unionist organization in Scotland was devolved by the Scottish Whip; the Scottish Whip now reserves his attention for Scottish parliamentary business and has handed the oversight of the Edinburgh Office to another Scottish Member.

no longer sent to him, which is tantamount to resignation from the party. In either case it is only the member's relationship with his party and not his position in the House which is affected. He continues to remain, if he so chooses, the member for his constituency with all its rights and duties; and this right of a member to withdraw from his party and to 'cross the floor' if he thinks fit is one of the most vital safeguards of the constitution in a period when party organization has grown so powerful.

To sum up, the British parties are a typical product of the British empirical character. Their organization is the result of a hundred years of growth in which several conceptions are intermingled. They show features which may be called democratic, such as the ultimate authority of the members, either in their local associations or in the party conference; oligarchic, as in the powers of the party's national executive committee; and autocratic, as in the place of the Leader and his unquestioned right to choose his own colleagues. Two main systems of organization, one spreading from the constituency associations upwards and the other from the central headquarters downwards, are fused with each other. The relation between parliamentary parties and the organization of the same parties in the country is left undefined. History and common sense, rather than *a priori* considerations, have made the British parties what they are, and their justification is that on the whole the system works very well and fulfils the needs of a democratic people better than any other method that has been proposed. The steady growth of party organization has come to a point where some observers see a danger of the machine suppressing the individual, especially in the Labour Party; but the jealousy with which local associations preserve their rights against direction from London, the respect paid throughout the country generally to the position of Members of Parliament, and the determination of Members of Parliament of all parties to uphold their privileges have so far worked together to prevent these dangers from becoming an actuality; and we need not doubt that the British genius for compromise will guide the political parties over any new dangers that may arise in the future.

CHAPTER IX

A SECOND CHAMBER

By F. W. Lascelles

MAY I say at the outset that I propose to treat this question from the point of view of whether the constitution can be improved by a reform of our second chamber and not from the point of view of party politics? I shall have to touch on controversial matters but where I do so I shall merely state what the issues are. It is indeed from this point of view that the question should be studied. Our ancestors devoted much thought to the improvement of the constitution of which they were extremely proud and it is a mistake to suppose that it only developed by accident—often it was the result of conscious direction.

Our generation has seen the most alarming constitutional developments in Europe—nations carried away in a frenzy of enthusiasm for leaders whose whims they found themselves unable to control and whose rule left them without the power of protest or dissent—the reins of government seized by minorities whose weapon was the suppression of the freedom of the ballot—and, while one would certainly agree with any-one who might say we are too level headed for such things to happen here, we have to remember that something of the sort did happen here 300 years ago when, with monarchy and second chamber abolished, rule by the House of Commons led Cromwell to say, "By the proceeding of this Parliament you see they stand in need of some checking or balancing power; I tell you that unless you have some such things as a balance we cannot be safe."

Of course no second chamber can stop a revolution but it can check the abuse of power by constitutional means or the use of it in an oppressive manner, and our history does not appear to be free from this either: Macaulay writes of the early years of the eighteenth century:

"No portion of our parliamentary history is less pleasing or more instructive. It will be seen that the House of Commons became altogether ungovernable, abused its gigantic power with unjust and insolent caprice, browbeat King and Lords, the Courts of Common Law and the constituent bodies, violated rights guaranteed by the Great Charter and at length made itself so odious that the people were glad to take shelter under the protection of the Throne and the hereditary aristocracy from the tyranny of the Assembly which had been chosen by themselves."

I am not going to spend any time on the general question of one chamber or two. Single chamber Government was tried here in abnormal times, but it has been tried in the United States and twice in France. Both these countries found it a failure. Nor is there anything undemocratic or reactionary in a second chamber—on the contrary, bicameral government has been adopted in the newest republics, such as Eire and India.

But in our constitution there are special features—or rather perhaps a lack of them—which are considered to make it specially necessary. I will only recapitulate them very briefly as they have been developed in other chapters in a slightly different context.

Our constitution, being mainly unwritten, is protected by no special provisions against alteration such as exist in the United States and in most of the Dominions. Parliament which is all powerful—for no legislature in the world has so much power—can pass a bill altering the constitution as easily as any other bill. The implications of this are limitless. Further, as has been explained, party discipline is now far stricter than it used to be, so that this immense power which is theoretically delegated to Parliament is in fact to some degree delegated to the Cabinet, and if there is a risk in delegating such power to a body of 625 persons, there is infinitely more risk when it is exercised by a body of twenty. Our electoral system too may result in the return of a minority government or of a government returned under the influence of some occurrence which temporarily so dominates all other issues that it may not represent the general wishes of the people. Finally there remains the undoubted fact that the Commons are overburdened with work; in modern times when the scope of legislation covers all the nation's activities, the work can only be got through by curtailing private members' time, by adopting expedients for limiting discussion, by sitting far into the night or by rushing bills through without adequate consideration.

We are still proud of our constitution, but we are conscious of certain imperfections in it. The question we have to consider is whether these could, *or should*, be remedied by a second chamber. The difficulty begins when one gets down to details. Lord Morley, in his *Life of Cromwell*, wrote:

> "There is no branch of political industry that men approach with hearts so light and yet that leaves them in the end so dubious and melancholy, as the concoction of a Second Chamber. Cromwell and his Parliament set foot on this *pons asinorum* of democracy without a suspicion of its dangers. To call out of empty space an artificial House, without the hold upon men's minds of history and ancient association, without defined powers, without marked distinction of persons or interests and then to try to make it an effective screen against an elected House to whose assent it owed its being was not to promote union but to provoke dissension and intensify it. Like smaller reformers since, Cromwell had never decided whether to make his Lords strong or weak; strong enough to curb the Commons yet weak enough for the Commons to curb them. The riddle seems unanswered to this day."

The riddle is unanswered, but the problem is to some extent simplified by changes in the conception of the role of a second chamber which have taken place over the course of time, for some doctrines which were tenaciously clung to in the past are now no longer material.

In the old days when it was a body small in size, containing the principal ministers of the day, its membership more or less equally divided between the political schools of thought of the time, and respected because of, rather than in spite of, its hereditary composition, the House of Lords could exercise equal powers with the House of Commons, except in finance, without serious challenge, that is to say it expressed its own views and used its powers to support them. There were frequent clashes between the two Houses and the only way to end deadlocks was for Parliament to be prorogued or dissolved.

But in Queen Anne's reign twelve peers were created in order to provide a Tory majority in the House of Lords for the purpose of passing the Treaty of Utrecht. This seemingly innocent expedient created a great political disturbance. It was apparent that if this became the practice the will of the House of Commons could always be made to prevail, and an attempt was made, and fortunately defeated, to prevent this solution being applied in future by imposing a statutory limit to the numbers of the House of Lords. This solution was applied again in 1832—though in this case the threat of it was sufficient —to secure the passing of the Reform Bill; but by then the House had acquired a large Conservative majority, and the Lords recognized that, composed as they were, it was not their own views that should dictate the exercise of their powers but the views of the people. They claimed, however, the right to use their veto till the verdict of the people had been definitely expressed. This attitude brought them into conflict with Mr. Gladstone and later with Mr. Asquith. The question of the limitation of their powers came to the front and resulted in the passing of the Parliament Act of 1911, which, while leaving their composition unchanged, removed their veto and left them with a two-year suspending power.

Since then there has been a development of the 'mandate' theory and the policy of the Lords today appears to be that no measure included in the programme of the party victorious at the polls should be rejected by them, but they hold that it is the duty of a second chamber to use its suspending power in relation to any measure on which the attitude of the country is in doubt and in particular if it affects the constitution.

This conception of the role of a second chamber is in exact harmony with the functions which the Bryce Conference advocated in 1918. After declaring that a second chamber should not have equal powers with the Commons, nor the power of making and unmaking ministries nor any marked permanent one-sided political bias, the Conference laid down four functions as appropriate for a second chamber. These have been generally approved.

The first was the revision of bills, particularly in view of the fact that the Commons sometimes resort to procedure curtailing discussion; the second, the initiation and examination of comparatively non-controversial bills; the third, the interposition of so much delay (and no more) in the passing of a bill as may be needed to enable the opinion of the nation to be adequately expressed upon it; the fourth, full and free discussion of matters of public policy.

About the first, second and fourth there is no dispute. These may be described as the 'useful' functions of a second chamber; but there is controversy over how the third should be interpreted. There is no doubt what the Bryce Conference intended, for in another part of their report they say:

> "The Second Chamber should aim at ascertaining the mind and views of the nation as a whole, and should recognize its full responsibility to the people, not setting itself to oppose the people's will, but only to comprehend and give effect to that will when adequately expressed."

This, however, was written thirty-three years ago and it has been contended that since then, with higher educational standards, wider press publicity, the radio and gallup polls, public opinion can assert itself without the intervention of a second chamber. This was in part a reason for the passing of the recent Parliament Act, by which the period of delay is reduced to one year, for underlying that measure was the contention that it is not in accordance with true democratic government that a second chamber should act as interpreter of public opinion.

The importance of this lies in the bearing it has on the type of second chamber you require—for if there is any value in the experience of second chambers elsewhere, this function can be exercised satisfactorily only by a chamber which is in some way elected and so can claim the confidence of the country. We are back at Cromwell's riddle, the need to decide on how much power the second chamber should have.

I shall discuss this issue later when I deal with proposals for reform, but first I propose to look at our present second chamber and see how it fulfils these functions, and I shall have to explain briefly how it came to be what it is.

The House of Lords is the descendant of the Magnum Concilium of the Norman Kings; its history therefore goes back far beyond the days when its meetings came to be styled Parliaments and far beyond the days when it was reinforced by an elected element which became the House of Commons. Its history has been the gradual transfer of the power, which it then enjoyed alone, to the House of Commons.

The Magnum Concilium consisted of Earls, Barons, Bishops, Abbots, the King's Ministers and the Judges. None sat solely by hereditary right. Basically its composition has not changed. New degrees of peerage have been created—the Abbots lost their seats when the monasteries were dissolved—representatives were added from Scotland and Ireland and a new category of judicial life peers has been established to carry out the appellate work of the House. None of these changes was fundamental. Two great changes, however, have taken place which have in succession completely altered its character. The first, its development into an hereditary body, took place early in its history—the second, the immense expansion of its numbers, is a comparatively recent development.

How did it become hereditary? The Earls were originally territorial officials and the Barons men who for some service to the King had been rewarded with an extent of land which carried with it the obligation to attend the King's Council if summoned. The King could issue or withhold the summons at his pleasure and in fact the numbers summoned to successive Parliaments differed very widely. In this way he could exercise some control over the composition of his Council. Since, however, land descended from father to eldest son, the writ of summons came to be looked on as a privilege and later as a right which the King found it impossible to refuse. By the reign of Richard II the House was well on the way to becoming hereditary. By Tudor times the hereditary right to a writ of summons was established.

The establishment of the hereditary right made the House in the eighteenth century an exclusive and aristocratic body. But this feature of it has disappeared in consequence of the second great change to which I have alluded, the immense increase in its numbers. At the beginning of George III's reign, 1760, there were 174 peers—at the end of it there were 562 and the numbers have gone on increasing. There have been 652 creations since 1900, and now the peerage is recruited from all sections of the community and represents nearly all the interests in the life of the nation. The exclusive and aristocratic atmosphere has gone and the result of the increase in its numbers has been to restore it to a basis of service. This conception cannot be carried too far—it has validity if applied to the House as it is in practice but, of course, it has less validity if applied to the House as it might be if all its members attended.

Today there are 849 Members of the House; 788 hereditary peers, two archbishops, twenty-four bishops, sixteen representative peers for Scotland, five for Ireland (the number has dwindled, for since 1922 there have been no elections to fill vacancies), nine Lords of Appeal, and five retired Lords of Appeal. Four hundred and six are creations of the present century, 170 are first creations. In the 1945 Parliament there were 217 who did not attend. The biggest attendance numbered 288.

Two questions are often asked about the composition of the House of Lords. Why, it is asked, since women are admitted as Members of the House of Commons, are they excluded from the Lords? There are at the moment twenty-four peeresses in their own right. They fall into two categories—the first and by far the biggest category consists of those who are descendants and heirs of the old baronies by writ, which descend to heirs general—the second category consists of those who are peeresses by virtue of special remainders under which a peerage may descend to the daughter of the first holder and, on her death, to her male heirs. The letters patent granting such a peerage have always drawn a distinction between her (the daughter) and her male heirs, giving the latter only a 'seat, place and voice' in Parliament. By the common law of England, women were not able to sit in either House of Parliament till 1918 when an act was passed enabling them to sit in the House of Commons. In the following year the Sex Disqualification (Removal) Act was passed prescribing that no person was to be disqualified by reason of sex from the exercise of any public function, and under this Act Viscountess Rhondda, who had succeeded to her father's peerage by virtue of a special re- mainder, petitioned for a writ of summons. The petition was refused on two grounds, firstly that by the terms of her Letters Patent she was not entitled to a writ and the 1919 Act was passed not for the purpose of creating new rights but for removing disabilities and, secondly, on the ground that the composition of Parliament is not altered in such a manner. A special act had been passed for the House of Commons and if it had been intended that peeresses should be admitted, the Act would have said so specifically.

Various attempts have since been made to correct what is generally regarded as an anomaly, but they have failed to come to fruition, partly because it was supposed that a general reform of the composition of the House was impending and that it would be better to wait for this and partly because the admission of these peeresses would be a further extension of the hereditary principle which was out of harmony with modern ideas.

So they have been obliged to wait, but as recently as 27th July, 1949 the House of Lords carried a resolution that, without pre- judice to any subsequent change in the composition of the House, steps should be taken to confer upon women peers the same rights, duties and privileges as are enjoyed by male peers.

The second question sometimes asked is: "Why cannot life peers be created?" so enabling a peerage to be conferred on an individual for his distinguished services without the eventual succession to his heirs who may be unfitted for it. This question again involves abstruse matters of peerage law, but when in 1856 a life peerage was conferred on Sir James Parke, who was a judge, with a view to enabling him to assist in the judicial work of the House, it was decided that although life peerages could be created they did not carry with them a seat in Parliament. This decision has had a restrictive effect on the recruitment of the House.

There have been many proposals for the creation of life peers by statute but, as with the peeresses, the matter has had to await the general reform of the House.

Such is the present composition of the House; I will now turn to the question of how it carries out the four functions of the Bryce Report. It had been frequently predicted in past years that in the event of a left wing Government assuming office, the House of Lords with its overwhelmingly conservative outlook would inevitably come into violent conflict with it. The realization by the House of the role which it is now expected to play has falsified this prediction and so far as relates to the first of the functions, the revision of bills, the House has received high praise from all parties for its work. In the ten major bills of the sessions of 1946 and 1947, several of which had been subjected to the guillotine procedure in the House of Commons, the Lords made 1,222 amendments, a high proportion of them proposed by the Government themselves. Only fifty-seven were rejected by the Commons and of these fifty-seven, forty-two were amendments to the Transport Bill and related to ten subjects.

These figures speak for themselves, for while the large number of Government amendments is evidence of the need for a revising Chamber, the small number of Lords amendments rejected, less than five per cent over the whole of the ten bills, is evidence that the efforts of the House were directed to improving, and not to destroying, the bills.

The second function was the initiation of bills of a comparatively non-controversial character. Examples of the work of the House under this heading in recent years are the Companies Bill, the Crown Proceedings Bill and the Justices of the Peace Bill. These were all introduced in the Lords and examined in great detail, 360 amendments being made to the Companies Bill. As a result, these bills had a quick and easy passage through the House of Commons, where time could not have been found for the detailed examination that was necessary before they could pass into law. It cannot be doubted that, in view of the congestion of business in the Commons, the work of the Lords in this respect is most valuable and it is an old complaint of the Lords that the Parliamentary time-table is not eased by the introduction of more bills in their House.

The third function was the interposition of delay. This period is now statutorily reduced to one year, which runs from the date of the first occasion on which a bill receives a Second Reading in the House of Commons to the date on which it receives its Third Reading in that House in the following session, I shall deal with the controversial issues arising under this heading when I come to deal with the most recent proposals for the reform of the House. At this point I will note that only three bills have become law under the Parliament Act of 1911, two of them, the Government of Ireland Bill and the Welsh Church Disestablishment Bill in 1914, and the third, the Parliament Bill, in 1949.

The fourth function was the discussion of important questions of policy. With the limitations imposed on the opportunities of Members of the House of Commons for raising debates, the ventilation of questions of public policy in the Lords serves a most useful purpose and it is a function which they are well equipped to carry out. Containing as the House does a wealth of expert and mature opinion on almost every subject, its debates are generally admitted to reach a high level and opinions are the more freely expressed in that they are not widely publicized and adverse resolutions of the House do not occasion the fall of an administration.

Besides these functions, there is other work which the House performs. Private bill legislation is shared equally between the two Houses and much time is spent by peers in committees on these bills. In the important sphere of delegated legislation too, the Lords have equal powers with the Commons, an order being annullable by resolution of either House. Although the Lords were the first to insist that the more important of these orders—those requiring a positive resolution by both Houses before becoming effective—should be scrutinized by a select committee, they have been extremely sparing of their powers and rarely press objection to departmental orders.

Finally, the House of Lords is supreme Court of Appeal. Theoretically any peer is constitutionally entitled to take part in this work, but in practice the Court is confined to the Lords of Appeal and such peers as are qualified under the Appellate Jurisdiction Acts.

If then the House of Lords is able to carry out effectively the duties of a Second Chamber, why not, as has often been suggested, leave it alone? It has many merits; its members are independent, they retain their seats for life, they are not obliged to pay attention to party pressures or to electoral considerations. In practice the chamber is not attended by peers who have no qualification other than birth—those who attend and do the work are in the main persons of experience, distinction and ability; their procedure is extremely business-like; there is no obstruction and few rules of order. What other assembly could conduct its business with no Chairman possessed of powers of ruling on points of order? Yet the Lord Chancellor who presides has no authority beyond that of any other peer. Matters of order are decided by the sense of the House which is speedily and effectively conveyed to an offender, the functions of the Lord Chancellor as Speaker being limited to putting the question. Nor does he call on the next speaker to address the House; these matters are usually arranged unofficially behind the scenes, but if two peers rise to speak together and neither gives way, the House calls for the one whom they prefer to hear. These things are the fruits of tradition. The House takes pride in the elasticity of its procedure. It gets through its business in its own way. It does not rely on divisions nor on the exercise of its constitutional powers; for its influence depends on the weight attaching to the opinions of its individual members expressed in debate.

The objections to it as a second chamber are, however, too well known to require explanation in detail. Its size; the possibility, however unlikely, of the invasion of its lobbies by large numbers of unqualified 'backswoodsmen'; its hereditary composition and its overwhelmingly one-sided political outlook are serious defects. As a corporate body it has little authority. However efficiently it performs the functions of revision and deliberation, it cannot pull the full weight of a second chamber in the constitution. A sentence of Lord Samuel's well sums up the position when he said: "It is a grave weakness that it rests on a basis which no one can seriously defend and is only kept efficient by the permanent absenteeism of the great majority of its members."

The need for reform is universally admitted, by none more than the Lords themselves. So far back as 1910 they passed these resolutions:

"1. That a strong and efficient Second Chamber is not merely an integral part of the British Constitution, but is necessary to the well-being of the State and to the balance of Parliament.

2. That such a Chamber can best be obtained by the reform and reconstitution of the House of Lords.

3. That a necessary preliminary of such reform and reconstruction is the acceptance of the principle that the possession of a peerage should no longer of itself give the right to sit and vote in the House of Lords."

These resolutions show that it is not from the Lords that obstacles have been placed in the way of reform; in fact most of the reform schemes have been initiated by them.

Before looking at these it would be reasonable to look round at some other second chambers. No one, of course, would dream of importing a ready-made second chamber here just because it worked well in its native country, but it is possible to get an idea, especially from the Dominions, as to the results which different types of second chambers have produced.

Generally speaking, second chambers in the Dominions are either nominated bodies or on an elective basis. The broad conclusions as to their working are that the system of nomination leads to appointments being made on party lines, the Senate becoming a tool of the party machine; elected Senates on the other hand tend to claim greater powers than is agreeable to their Lower Houses and so to cause friction between them; but there is less friction between an elected and a nominated House than between two elected Houses. In Canada, for instance, Senators are nominated for life—the Senate was intended to be an independent forum, composed of men of substance and distinction who would not be swayed by party pressures. But it has turned out quite differently—nominations are made on a party basis. The Senate is therefore a somewhat spineless body—subservient to the Lower House.

Moreover, the system has this drawback—when the government changes, the incoming administration finds the Senate packed with nominees of the previous government and then relations become strained until the balance can be restored by filling vacancies with supporters of the new government. Even where, as in Italy under the monarchy, nomination was restricted to categories of different qualifications the same tendency occurred.

In Australia, a more modern and democratic constitution, the Senate is directly elected—so many from each State as a single constituency. This has not resulted in smooth working. Such large constituencies make personal candidature impossible and elections have been carried out on the party basis, which means that all the Senators returned by a State will probably be of the same party. In fact in 1920 only one opposition Senator was returned although the total of votes cast on each side was nearly equal. The Senate being directly elected has at times threatened to disturb the balance of the constitution by claiming financial power. These chambers all do useful work, but in the main they count either for too little or too much.

Differences between the two Houses in the Dominions are

usually settled by a period of delay—(in Australia by a dissolution also)—followed by a joint sitting of the two at which a majority vote prevails, thus favouring the Lower House in consequence of its larger size.

In the Dominions, too, there is usually some special machinery for amendments to the constitution—in Australia a referendum, in South Africa a two-thirds majority at a Joint Sitting. It is interesting to note that the referendum in Australia has almost always produced a negative vote.

The foreign second chambers were closely examined by the Bryce Conference and clearly influenced them in their conclusions. They rejected nomination and direct election for the reasons I have mentioned; they considered it inadvisable to bring local authorities into the political arena by imposing on them the duty of electing the second chamber, rather as is done in France, and they came to the conclusion that the method open to least objection was election by Members of the House of Commons, not acting as one body but distributed in geographical groups. It was thought that by this method a chamber would be produced different in composition from the House of Commons and, since the election would be influenced by local considerations, independent of it. In addition a small number of hereditary peers was to be selected by a Joint Committee of the two Houses for the purpose of preserving the historic continuity of the House and to ensure the continuance of the services of some of its members.

The reconstituted House was to have concurrent powers with the House of Commons except in finance, and an intricate scheme of free conferences was devised for the solution of deadlocks.

This would have resulted in a strong—perhaps a too strong—chamber. In the stress of events in 1918 when the Conference finished its work it had little chance of real consideration.

There have been many schemes since then; some confined to eliminating from the House those of its members who have no qualifications for service; some proposing a combination of a reduced number of hereditary peers and a proportion of nominated life peers; some facing a break with history and proposing an elected Senate; and some more imaginatively envisaging devolution to local or industrial chambers.

Why have they all failed and nothing been done? Partly because at no time has it been essential to achieve success. Reform has been recognized as desirable and proposals have been made, but when it was seen that they aroused controversy they were allowed to drop. Sleeping dogs could lie a little longer.

Some have been viewed with suspicion by the House of Commons. Professor Pollard has said that, in the series of struggles of which our constitutional history is made up, the Party which emerged victorious was always content to enjoy the fruits of victory but never to share them. The House of Commons, having achieved supremacy, has shown no disposition to admit a second chamber to any greater share of the power which they themselves have gained over the centuries.

It seems doubtful now whether the retention of any hereditary element would meet with approval. It is held that such an element would always be considered a weakness and that its removal would only be a matter of time. From the point of view of continuity, it is not essential—we have seen that the House only gradually became hereditary and the substitution of another form of composition need not constitute a break in its history. Greater changes took place in the composition of the House of Commons after the Reform Bills.

There are many Members of the House whose services would have to be retained, but this could be done by a system of basing the composition of the House on qualification by service. This indeed would be an adaptation to modern conditions of the original composition of the House. The features of the House which are inherent in its history and which I think everyone would wish to preserve are its independence, its indifference to unpopularity, its capacity for transacting business and the prestige derived from the experience and authority of its Members.

In 1948, during the discussions on the Parliament Bill, the

proceedings were adjourned while the Party Leaders met to see whether they could arrive at an agreed conclusion of the matter. They nearly achieved success. A statement was published (Cmd. 7380) embodying the points on which they agreed and those on which they differed. They were agreed on composition—appointment on grounds of personal distinction or public service. They were agreed that women should be included, and, in order that no one should be excluded by lack of means, that some remuneration should be paid. They were agreed that the second chamber should be complementary to, and not a rival to, the House of Commons, and that it should not be so constituted as to give a permanent majority to any political party.

They differed, however, on the old question of powers— 'the so long (and no longer)'—the period of delay. On the one hand it was contended that a period of time which was sufficient to enable the second chamber adequately to examine a bill was also sufficient to enable the country to make up its mind about it, and that a government should have the same freedom for implementing its programme in the fourth year of its term as it had in the first three. Therefore it was urged that a delay of one year was enough.

On the other side it was contended that much of that year would be occupied in parliamentary discussion, and the country required some period after the issues had been crystallized in Parliament to consider them. This was an essential constitutional safeguard. There was no danger of a second chamber using its powers frivolously since its very existence depended on its behaving in a responsible manner.

So matters stand today. Are we back where we started, at Cromwell's riddle? Not quite, for the issue is narrowed down to a very fine point, though a fundamental one. It is not simply a question of the length of the delaying period measured in years or months; the question now is—do the principles of democratic government require that the second house should be merely a 'useful' chamber, performing the very necessary functions of revision and discussion, or should it be a Chamber which could have enough power and authority, if circumstances ever made it necessary, to assert itself as a balancing factor in the constitution and give the country an opportunity for second thoughts?

The time seems suitable for coming to a decision; relations between the two Houses are not strained; the peers are no longer 'Public Enemy No. 1'. If the matter could be approached from the point of view of discovering what adjustment our constitution requires, it should not be impossible to find a solution which would be of benefit to all parties alike as well as to the nation.

CHAPTER X

THE COURTS AND THE CONSTITUTION

By E. C. S. Wade

THE chapters already included in this survey of Parliament by men prominent in public life have dealt with the nature of parliamentary government and the place of the Executive in such a system. They have rightly been concerned with political relationships. Why, then, is there included in the series a lecture on the courts? Some explanation is required why a lawyer who has no connection with Parliament or public life writes about the courts in a series which has Parliament for its title. So far as the enacted law of the constitution is concerned, Parliament is supreme and it has been seen that the Executive for the time being, if reasonably sure of a majority in the House of Commons, can put through all the legislation which it wishes to enact. Such a combination can compel in whatever direction is desired. There is no direct role of interpreting the constitution, as with a written constitution, but there is a part to be played by an independent judiciary concerned with ensuring that administration is conducted according to law and that arbitrary conduct by the rulers shall not be substituted for law—at all events as long as the law does not expressly sanction arbitrary conduct. We start then with the requisite that the judges must be independent. If judges were in subjection to the Government of the day, their task would be to interpret the wishes of that Government in any dispute between citizen and the State, or even between citizen and fellow-citizen if the State wanted to intervene. Every schoolboy knows that the Act of Settlement, 1701, secured to the higher members of the judiciary independence from control and fixed salaries guaranteed by Parliament.

Even before our judges attained independence they were principally concerned with administering the common law of England which they had themselves evolved largely by following precedents and expanding the law by analogy from existing decisions of the higher courts. The common law was not made by the King nor yet by Parliament. It was concerned with the protection of rights of the individual as well as the maintenance of public order. We can see this in the old decisions on which are still based the protection which the law gives to freedom from arbitrary arrest and search on mere suspicion; or again in relation to the right to speak freely in criticism of Governments. Free action so long as no threat of violence is the theme. Nothing would be more convenient for those in authority than to stifle criticism by arresting its suspected authors and keeping them in safe custody without bringing them to trial. Even modern Governments sometimes resent press criticism. An independent judiciary saved us from that device of totalitarian rulers, the so-called people's courts. I refer particularly to the General Warrant Cases of the second half of the eighteenth century. Nowadays so strong is the tradition of the fundamental political freedoms of the person, of speech, including the Press, of public meetings that Governments accept them as axiomatic. Yet they were gained for us through the courts and are still enforced through the courts. They have never been embodied in those parts of the constitution which have been enacted. Nor must we overlook the part played by the common jury in securing these fundamental freedoms for the individual. The development of the law of seditious libel in the eighteenth century shows that without a jury to return the general verdict judges of those days were apt to find criticism of the Government seditious. But 1792 saw, at the climax of the French Revolution, the enactment of Fox's Libel Act. Prior to that Act the task of the jury in a criminal libel case was limited to findings as to the fact of publication and as to the truth of innuendoes. Juries could not give a general verdict on the issue, libel or no libel. That was for the judge alone. Fox's Libel Act entrusted the general verdict to the jury and so made them, the representatives of the common man of that day, the organ to determine the limits of fair criticism of Government by applying objective standards. At first such was the reaction to events across the Channel that juries were wont to find against defendants in cases of seditious libel as readily as the judges had done before the Act. But all that has changed and only where violence is threatened will a jury find seditious conduct today.

One consequence of the supremacy of Parliament is that any law can be changed and no court can deny validity to that change. How then can there be any assurance that the law as made by the judges in favour of liberty will not be changed? It is true that all that a court of law can do with an Act of Parliament is to apply it, i.e. to interpret it literally, or when that is impossible, to decide what Parliament intended by applying certain rigid rules of construction. (With the merits or demerits of the policy to which an Act gives effect judges are not concerned.) If they were, they would quickly become tools of the Government or alternatively its opponents. That would be the end of their independence and of their function of administering justice according to law. But no such assurance can be given. The law has changed and continues to be changed by Act of Parliament. Freedom of contract in particular has been narrowed. Yet no serious inroad has been made on the fundamental freedoms of a political character except temporarily and reluctantly during war; the climate of political opinion safeguards us against this sort of change.

All, or nearly all, current public law is contained in statutes or instruments made under the authority of statutes which the courts can only apply and not change. Certainly this is true in the constitutional sphere where Parliament has evolved new rules of law and new machinery of administration for giving effect to the conception of the welfare State. This process has involved considerable modification of the rules of common law; particularly the common law rights of owners of property of all kinds have been restricted and considerable limitations have been put by Parliament on that freedom of contract which the common law has evolved. At the same time Parliament has imposed new duties upon private citizens in the

form of heavy taxation, their use of land, their freedom to trade, and even on the purposes for which they can spend their money. It has created big monopoly corporations which on behalf of the State get and sell coal, produce and distribute gas and electricity, provide rail and road transport and other means of communication. It has also given citizens certain benefits in the form of insurance, medical benefits and pensions for war service or war injuries. What then is the role of the courts in those matters where they are concerned only with the interpretation of novel provisions in statutes and not in applying by reference to previous decisions the rules of the common law with all their emphasis upon the rights of individuals and the corresponding duty of men and women to their neighbours? Briefly it is to see that, when Parliament has given a right to any individual citizen, it shall be respected by an official; where the public interest has led to a duty being imposed upon the citizen, he must observe that duty as laid down by statute.

There are two separate matters to consider. Firstly, the rights and duties of the citizen in his relationship to the modern State. The rights are mainly those arising out of the modern social services; the duties result from the economic controls which, in addition to the financial consequences to the tax-payer of the social services, are imposed to maintain our position in international trade so vital to our very existence. But, of course, social services also involve duties on the individual, such as payment of contributions, just as economic controls confer rights and benefits in which all share, such as protection for industry and food subsidies. We must examine the role of the courts in deciding disputes which arise over these rights and duties. For this is a strictly judicial function.

Secondly, the modern State needs wide discretionary powers over the exercise of which a court has no direct control; for they do not raise justiciable issues, but questions of policy. A court is only concerned to prevent an excess or misuse of governmental power, not to question its due exercise. It is not for a court to enforce a political duty, such as the provision of efficient free education or health services or the building of houses to let or the integration of all forms of transport or the planned use of land. These matters are nevertheless duties placed upon particular Government departments or other public authorities to the exclusion of all other agencies and means must exist in a free society to prevent abuse of power or neglect to exercise it. These means are mainly political. There are virtually no legal ways of redress to compel the performance of public duties. But there is redress if the power is exercised illegally.

Where there is a justiciable issue to be determined in a dispute with a public authority, how is justice to be done between the citizen and the State? It is to be noted that in those matters which still fall to be decided by the principles of common law; namely, breaches of contracts for the supply of materials or services rendered (other than service by civil servants or members of the armed forces) or for injury caused by negligence or wilful intent, as in a road accident, the State and its servants are subject to the ordinary measure of liability for money damages. The action is tried in the courts by the ordinary procedure. This is a recent development. Until the Crown Proceedings Act, 1947, it was seldom possible to assess accurately the liability of the State at common law; and for injuries other than breach of contract the State (but not the official who committed the wrongful act) was generally protected from liability to pay damages to the injured citizen. The courts then have a role to perform in ensuring that justice according to law shall be done when the defendant is a powerful Government department whose employee has inflicted wrongful injury upon an individual citizen.

It must not be forgotten that all criminal law involves a contest between the Crown and the citizen. The primary function of all States is the maintenance of order. But every disorder which is alleged to be a breach of the criminal law can only be punished after its commission has been proved in open court, in most cases summarily in a magistrates' court, but in serious cases after trial by judge and jury. The impartial enforcement of the criminal law in itself is sufficient grounds for retaining an independent judiciary whose task is to see that no alleged offence is punished except on conviction and by sentence imposed by the court before whom the commission of the offence has been proved. It must be remembered that nearly all the controls which war and its aftermath have made necessary are enforced by the ordinary process of the criminal law.

So far there is really no controversy. The necessity for independent courts is generally accepted. But the advent of the social services has brought with it many experiments in the form of other tribunals, which some people regard as encroaching upon the sphere of the ordinary courts, particularly the civil courts. Thus there can be seen a preference for a local tribunal of three to determine, on appeal from the refusal of the Minister of National Insurance, acting through his local official, a claim to insurance benefit whether for sickness, unemployment, industrial injury or old age or widow's pension. A similar tribunal hears appeals from the refusal of a claim to a war pension by the Minister of Pensions. A Lands Tribunal— one of the latest additions to the lengthening list—will determine compensation to be paid for land acquired compulsorily by public authorities. In a sphere where contractual rights between landlord and tenant may be overridden Furnished Rent Tribunals have been given power to determine rents all over the country. Here is an example where the State is not a party and yet access to the ordinary courts is not allowed. Although there are still some who think that much of this work could be done by the magistrates' courts or the county court, most people have come to accept these specialized tribunals as necessary under modern conditions. Nor indeed do they compare unfavourably with courts of summary jurisdiction. Like them, there is usually no provision for a chairman with legal qualifications for the various local tribunals, but e.g. War Pensions Appeal Tribunals are given a chairman with legal qualifications appointed by the Lord Chancellor. In many cases the other two members are drawn from panels representative of employers and employed persons and sit by rotation under an independent chairman appointed by a Minister for a fixed term. This form of tribunal was first used in connection with appeals against a refusal of unemployment benefit. It now extends to all insurance claims. Sometimes representation of an applicant by a lawyer is forbidden, though not usually when the tribunal has a lawyer as chairman. In this respect anybody who has had experience of magistrates' courts will probably feel that the applicant may be at a serious disadvantage. Even in the simplest case it is an ordeal for anyone who is without previous experience of judicial process to appear before a tribunal, however informal the proceedings may be. The ban on representation does not, however, extend to officials of trade unions or to a friend of the applicant.

The surest safeguard against errors and injustices undoubtedly lies in a right of appeal to a court or to a judge appointed to exercise a specialized jurisdiction. If an independent judge has power to determine disputed questions of law or to regulate proceedings in an administrative tribunal to prevent such important errors as the failure to hear evidence from both sides or the inability to decide what proof is required, then there is impartial guidance which all tribunals must follow. Moreover, in this way there is a safeguard to protect them from improper pressure from outside. The local War Pensions Tribunals have often received rulings from the High Court judge to whom lies an appeal on a point of law from the awards of the tribunals. For example, the High Court has laid down what burden of proof lies on the Pensions Ministry and has refused to allow that department to disregard a certificate of disability given by one of the Service Departments.

Again, Commissioners, who have the same powers as High Court judges so far as the law of National Insurance is concerned, sit to hear and determine points of law which may arise under this great scheme. Their rulings are a safeguard that the numerous local tribunals shall not go wrong in their law. Taken as a whole, recent legislation relating to the administration of the social services has made adequate provision for appeals to a higher tribunal on questions of law. Sometimes the tribunal is a judge of the High Court to whom the task of taking this class of case is specially allotted; sometimes Parliament has preferred a commissioner who enjoys the independence and security of tenure like a High Court judge, but his jurisdiction is limited to a particular field. Either safeguard secures to the

P

local tribunals independence from departmental pressure and goes a long way towards securing a uniform administration of a national service. No doubt rulings could be given by a Minister in much the same way, but there would always be the feeling that the Minister and his confidential advisers in London were less likely to be unbiased than a judge who decides after hearing arguments on both sides. For although as a general rule legal representation is not allowed before social service tribunals at the lower level, there is a right of audience at the final appellate level, whether before a High Court judge designated for the work or the insurance commissioners.

There are, however, cases where there is no appeal to a court nor any review by a local tribunal from a decision of a Minister or his agent which is adverse to the claimant. The most obvious instance of this is the civil servant who, on dismissal, can appeal to the Minister in charge of his department, but never to the courts. The decisions of the Furnished Rent Tribunals are subject to no appeal nor even ministerial review. There are several score of these tribunals operating over the whole country to give effect to a general policy of fair rents. Each tribunal consists of three members who are appointed by the Minister; they enjoy no security of tenure and require to have no special qualifications for appointment. The tribunal operates under rules made by the Minister. There is no provision for formulating standards of fair rent, but the parties may be represented by counsel or solicitor. Where a tribunal acts outside its jurisdiction, it can nevertheless be restrained by the courts by processes, which lie to prevent an excess of jurisdiction whenever a body is adjudicating upon an issue in dispute between two parties which may affect their respective rights. This is not an appeal against a decision by the agency which Parliament has appointed to determine the issue. Any decision of a rent tribunal, though patently wrong and unjust, must stand unless the court is satisfied that the tribunal has exceeded its jurisdiction in deciding the matter at all or has arrived at a decision without hearing relevant evidence on both sides. By this means administrative tribunals can at least be kept from determining cases which Parliament never intended them to hear.

There are thus two ways where the Courts are able to adjudicate in administrative disputes. The first is as an appeal court on any point of law. If this is not allowed, there is normally the procedure to restrain an excess of jurisdiction, i.e. going outside limits which Parliament has prescribed. In the latter case there can never be a review simply on the merits of a dispute. Some lawyers advocate the establishment of a central administrative tribunal whose jurisdiction presumably would cover all the cases which have been discussed; they have in mind the central administrative tribunal of France; the *Conseil d'État*. They would not presumably advocate that in every case there should be a rehearing on the merits before this tribunal; for that would clearly be impracticable if only on account of the volume of work. I confess that I can see little advantage in such a tribunal except such as may be derived from tidiness and uniformity. It is not an inevitable feature of administrative law that jurisdiction should be removed from the courts, though there were historical reasons for this having been done in France. The great advantage of entrusting the ultimate jurisdiction to the High Court lies in the integrity of the English judiciary. No one would suggest that the members of the *Conseil d'État* are not men of integrity as well as competence; they are both, but it would be hard to persuade the English public to respect the decisions of a body of officials, even if they were trained in the ways of the judiciary, in quite the same way as they accept the rulings of His Majesty's judges.

The last and most difficult subject is: how to control the exercise of a power which Parliament has entrusted to a government agency to use at its discretion; for example, the choice of a site for a new town or strengthening of the coast against encroachment by the sea. These are not matters which can be directly enforced by the courts, even though Parliament may have formulated the power in terms of a duty entrusted to a particular Minister or a particular local authority. Why should the judges be asked to decide what places round London are suitable for new towns? Or whether a sea-wall should be built in a low-lying area on the East Coast? Nevertheless, as a result of such activity—or for that matter inactivity—much can hap-

pen to inflict loss or injury on private citizens. A river board
may be so dilatory in repairing a bank at the river mouth where
the sea has broken through that a farmer's marshland grazings
may be put out of action. Similarly untold loss may be inflicted
upon the owners of a certain class of residential property by a
decision which puts the industrial element of a new town close
to the private houses. The power of deciding these matters is
given by Parliament to a public authority and generally they
are determined as matters of policy. It is only very occasionally
that the courts can intervene and then usually it is to enforce a
statutory duty under a penalty, such as a fine levelled summarily on a waterworks company for failure to keep up the
pressure in its mains. There will be agreement that a public
authority would find it very difficult to carry out its administration—and all powers of public authorities are conferred by
Parliament—if its decisions could be appealed against to the
courts. This is equally the case if instead of taking action a public
authority decides to remain inactive. Generally speaking, the
remedy must be a political one and the courts cannot help to
resolve what is really a conflict between public and private
interest. Even in the illustration of the flooded land, although
the farmer may have suffered grievous loss as a private individual, there are difficulties in allowing him to recover that
loss at the expense of the general taxpayer whose contributions
maintain the authority.

In discussing challenge to the exercise of discretionary power
it is necessary to distinguish two cases: Parliament may have
placed upon an administrator the duty of deciding whether or
not to initiate action, as when it requires the Minister of Local
Government and Planning to select sites for new towns at his
discretion. On the other hand, Parliament may have appointed
a higher public authority, say a Minister of the Crown, to
decide whether an act done by another administrative agency
at its discretion is right or wrong, i.e. an appeal may lie from
the decision of the initiating agency to a higher administrative
official. This occurs when the Minister is required by the Housing Act, 1936, to decide whether or not to confirm a clearance
order which a district council has submitted in face of local

opposition from property owners. In either case the decision taken may vitally affect the rights of private citizens, particularly where the acquisition or control of property is required to give effect to the decision. In practice this is usually the real ground upon which appeals are made to the courts. There has been, and perhaps still is, a good deal of confusion on the function of the courts in this type of case. A few years ago the courts were disposed to find that they had power to review administrative decisions whenever there was contained in the function which the administrator was exercising an obligation to act judicially (i.e. to listen to two or more opposing parties) at any stage in the administrative process. The review could only take place if the administrator had failed to carry out that part of the procedure which required him to act impartially, e.g. as between a local authority and a ratepayer, if as Minister he was asked to confirm a proposal of the local authority which hit the ratepayer hard. In recent years there has been a tendency in the other direction. Parliament has deliberately limited both in scope and duration the opportunities for review by the courts. The courts have inclined to regard more strictly the definition of what is a dispute between parties and accordingly the field of judicial control has narrowed. It is not simply a dispute between a landowner and a local authority that is in issue; the public are also interested; and it is for the Minister to weigh up their interest as well as that of the contending party. Nor is there any room for judicial review if Parliament authorizes action in the public interest at the expense of private rights and lays down that it is for the administrator to decide when to take action. The latter acts, or refrains from action, in accordance with the general policy to which the statute directs him to give effect. No matter how hard hit the private citizen may be as a result of the decision, he is not normally given a right of appeal to the courts to review that decision. On the other hand, even if Parliament has not expressly so provided, the courts can still entertain a challenge to the validity of the administrative act if the administrator does something which the statute does not allow him to do; or if he fails to carry out the proper procedure laid down; or if he can be shown to have acted out of malice or spite. The last ground is not easy to establish. But if a public authority has power to acquire land for a given purpose, it must not use the land for another, if equally meritorious, object. If a town council decides to build a sub-way, it cannot acquire the land under an Act which only authorizes the acquisition of land for bridging a river. Usually an administrator before taking a final decision is required to hear objections from interested parties. The procedure laid down for this by Parliament must be followed. Generally this takes the form of requiring a public inquiry to be held in the locality. This must be done, or else the objector on showing substantial injury to himself (the statute usually requires this nowadays) can get the final decision set aside by the courts. This is not to say that, if the inquiry is held properly, the courts will intervene, if asked, to ensure that proper consideration has been given to the result of the inquiry. But if the administrator has gone through all the steps which the law requires before he acts finally, the courts cannot review his decision. Administration according to law does not mean that a court acts as an appeal tribunal, but it does mean that the procedure prescribed by Parliament must be followed. If that procedure is unfavourable to private interests, then only Parliament can change the balance. Often there is provision for review by higher administrative authority, but that is another matter, which raises the interesting question of how far departmental bias prejudices a fair decision being reached. It is not always easy to decide whether a particular act by a public authority can be challenged or not by the courts. One thing is, however, clear, simply to challenge on the grounds of unreasonableness is never sufficient, if it is impossible to show any departure from what Parliament has laid down as the regular process.

Because of border-line cases lawyers have been driven to use the term, quasi-judicial. They have used it in more senses than one. When a procedure like that of arriving at the facts in a court is laid down, the term is easy to understand. The process is judicial at that stage, irrespective of whether the final stage is determined by reference to a rule of law or simply by considerations of policy. When quasi-judicial is applied, as it sometimes is, to the whole process, there is some confusion. On the whole it is perhaps safer to say that, when an administrator is given power to decide a dispute by applying the law to the facts as found by him, he is exercising a judicial function just like a court. If he goes wrong on the law, his decision should be reviewable by further judicial process, as it is with national insurance claims. If the law gives him so wide a discretion, that he cannot exceed his lawful powers in deciding a conflict between private interests and public rights, and there is no dispute as to the facts, but only on the merits, there is no advantage in describing the process as quasi-judicial.

Finally can any conclusions be drawn from present tendencies? For the lawyer it is essential to analyse the nature of the power which has been exercised to his client's hurt or annoyance. The problem is one of the interpretation of statutes and that does not mean simply looking at a particular section of the relevant Act. The background of the legislation must be considered and by reading the whole Act an endeavour made to understand what it seeks to achieve. The long title and the opening sections sometimes, but not always, help. The student of our political institutions should recall that the constitution has so far stood the stress of the evolutions of a changing society. If we want to continue government within the law as a sure guarantee of freedom, we must somehow contrive to balance the increasing power of the Executive (with the latent dangers of abuse) by external control. Within a limited but all-important field the courts can supply the answer; outside that field the only sure safeguard is vigilant and enlightened criticism. When legal control is weak or absent, political control is the more valuable.

CHAPTER XI

DELEGATED LEGISLATION

By Cecil Carr

I F Walter Bagehot were alive today, would he still speak of the 'inbred insubordination' of the English people and their 'natural impulse' to resist authority? The English, he explained, had won their freedom during centuries of resistance, more or less legal or illegal, more or less audacious or timid, to the Executive Government; "we have accordingly inherited the traditions of conflict and preserve them in the fullness of victory; we look on State action not as our own action but as alien action, as an enforced imposed tyranny from without, not as the consummated result of our own organized wishes." When the First World War, with its proliferation of executive law-making, had temporarily tilted the imaginary axis of our constitution, Lord Hewart's *The New Despotism* revived the old notion that government is an extrinsic agency and indeed a potential enemy. The book accused the departments of usurping the legislative functions which belong to Parliament and the judicial functions which belong to the law-courts; it charged civil servants with conspiring to undermine the independence of the judges. An occasional critic might murmur that Sir Gordon Hewart, as Attorney General from 1919 to 1921, had advised and defended the departments during a period when exceptional powers were being exercised. The indictment, nevertheless, framed by a Lord Chief Justice, was formidable; there was clearly a case to go to a jury. The Lord Chancellor chose the jury conscientiously. He set up a strong committee, whereof Lord Donoughmore was the first and Sir Leslie Scott the final chairman, to consider the powers exercised by departments by way of delegated legislation or of judicial decision and to report what safeguards were desirable or necessary to secure the constitutional principles of the sovereignty of Parliament and the supremacy of the law.

"The sovereignty of Parliament"—Yes, but what if Parliament is content to play second fiddle? Whose fault is it if the Government majority in the House of Commons, more intent upon political results than anxious about traditional methods, divests itself, without care for limits or controls, of its legislative powers? How do we, if this be what we really want, recall Members of Parliament to greater prudence and less prodigality? Revolutionaries in a hurry, launching totalitarian plans both from the Right and the Left, have proposed to turn our traditional structure upside down by Orders in Council to be made under unlimited statutory powers. If that be our destiny, is it not our trouble that Parliament is all too sovereign?

The jury's verdict was comforting. The conspiracy charge was easily dismissed, and the country was told that delegated legislation was valuable and indeed inevitable. Having classified certain apparently transient types of executive law-making as 'abnormal', the committee suggested that, with reasonable vigilance and proper precautions, we had nothing to fear. In that soporific state of reassurance we might perhaps still have been living happily enough, had not World War Two involved recourse to abnormal types which began again where those of World War One had left off.

A century before Lord Hewart published his book the enemy was centralization rather than delegation. Centralization, declared the Bishop of Exeter in 1836, was 'a word no more strange to our language than the practice is foreign to our ancient habits and feelings'. Fifteen years later Joshua Toulmin Smith uncompromisingly attacked this undesirable alien. Centralization, he said, necessarily engendered 'servility, sycophancy, selfishness and apathy'. His book, *Local Self-Government and Centralisation*, definitely linked delegation with centralization. One chapter, headed 'Delegated Legislation', had the following sentences:

"It is the natural object of every government having

despotic ends, and seeking to narrow the liberties of the people, to encourage the disposition to delegate legislative authority. By this means the ends of centralization are more effectively accomplished than by any other that ingenuity can devise. While the outward show of representative institutions is preserved, an arbitrary and wholly irresponsible power is, in reality, lodged in the hands of a few."

Toulmin Smith followed up his writings by forming the Anti-Centralization Union in 1854. It endured for only three years; his protests came too late. Centralization was on the march. Its chief officers and their staffs were elaborating its organization and developing its lines of communication. Some significant stages were the Highway Act of 1835, the great rush of Railway Acts culminating in the boom or mania of from 1845 to 1847, the coming of the electric telegraph in 1837 and the penny post in 1840.

The arch-centralizer was Edwin Chadwick, disciple and literary secretary of Jeremy Bentham. Mr. G. M. Young has summed him up in a sentence: "Born in a Lancashire farmhouse in 1800, where the children were washed all over every day, he made it his life's business to wash everyone in England all over every day by Executive Order." In the famous report of 1834 on the poor law, which he claimed to have largely written himself, Chadwick condemned as 'unskilful and irresponsible' the 1500 local authorities dealing with poor law throughout the country. His report advocated a Central Board to control them. He had no doubt of the relation between central administration and the delegation of legislative power by Parliament. The Board was to be empowered and directed to frame and enforce regulations, uniform throughout England, for the government of workhouses and as to the nature and amount of relief to be given and the work to be expected in them. The regulations would inevitably be numerous, and they would have to be varied periodically because they were experimental. Obviously this meant delegation.

"Suppose a general regulation were prescribed by Act of Parliament and it was found to want alteration; you must

wait a whole year or more for an Act of Parliament to amend
it, or else the law must be broken. A central authority might
make the alteration or supply unforeseen omissions in a day
or two.''

Then followed the often-quoted comment that grave legislators
in Parliament could hardly be asked to devote their attention
to the amount of the pauper's butter ration or the length,
width and material of the old women's under-petticoats, and yet
on such details the successful management of the whole scheme
would depend. At the age of seventy Chadwick was still ex-
tolling the virtue of subordinate legislation. 'An extension of the
power of sub-legislation by departmental rules and orders'
would be 'the means of a relief to the occupation of the superior
legislature with details for which it is unfitted.' He undertook
to prove that 'the worst ordinary sub-legislation by rule and
order is equal in benefit to the people to the best ordinary
legislation of the superior legislature in its present condition'.

Chadwick, we see, was justifying recourse to delegation on
just the same grounds as those which the Donoughmore-Scott
Committee specified in 1932. It could be quickly made and
altered; it could save parliamentary time; it could deal with
technical matters with which Parliament was inadequately
equipped to deal; and there was hope that it would state the
law in terms more intelligible than those employed in statutes.

Meanwhile, what did the lawyers and the constitutional
pundits make of the Chadwick doctrine? One conspicuous
development of delegation in the 1830s was its application
to judicial procedure. Of various statutes which seek at
this period to improve and unify the arrangements of the
courts some are self-contained codes, covering every detail.
Others, especially an Act of 1830 which served as a precedent,
delegated to the judges the task of prescribing rules of procedure,
much as today a Rule Committee fixes the procedure of the
High Court and the county courts. In 1833 the Commissioners
on the Courts of Common Law reported in favour of extending
the method of the Act of 1830. Parliamentary sanction, they
said, would be needed, because 'the extent to which the courts

are competent to introduce by their own authority alterations in matters of process, pleading and general practice, is occasionally a subject of considerable doubt and difficulty'. When in the 1870s the Judicature Acts revolutionized forensic practice by fusing common law and equity, the value of delegation and the propriety of conferring rule-making power upon the judges were recognized and exploited. In this context, incidentally, the older and slower machinery of parliamentary control, whereby rules and orders were required to be laid in draft before the two Houses and to be approved in both by affirmative resolution, was replaced by the speedier and nowadays more usual pattern which allows departmental legislation to take effect on making but exposes it to annulment within a time limit on an adverse address in either House. Conservative minds are not unknown among lawyers and there were some who, not enthusiastically welcoming the principle of the Judicature Acts, raised obstacles to the method. In an open letter to Lord Chancellor Hatherley Chief Justice Cockburn, while not actually attacking fusion, asked suspiciously if the new rules of court would be allowed to abolish trial by jury or to substitute for the oral examination of witnesses the Equity Courts' practice of admitting affidavits. "It will be said indeed that the rules so made are to be laid before Parliament. But this is but a poor protection if a Government has the good fortune to have a commanding majority at its call. Moreover, in the interval the rules will have had the effect of law." Cockburn went on to cite Lord Westbury as having used the happy term 'skeleton Bills'—"namely, Bills in which Parliament, instead of itself legislating, is asked to give subordinate powers to somebody else by which vital and organic changes may be made in our law and procedure such as Parliament, in passing the Bills, may never for a moment have contemplated". One of the Judicature Bills had proposed to give the rule-making power to the Privy Council. This was too much for the *Saturday Review*.

"That Lord Hatherley should have thought it possible that Parliament would ever consent to pass blank Bills to be filled up at pleasure by a committee to be selected by the

Government is only to be explained by the fact that his career has removed him for a very long interval from the atmosphere of political life. There are some practical conveniences, no doubt, in giving to the Crown the power of legislation, subject only to a possible veto of the Legislature after a project of law has been laid complete upon the tables of the two Houses of Parliament. But such advantages are wholly inconsistent with constitutional government and must be reserved for countries whose highest ideal of liberty is absolutism tempered by a plebiscite. No modern innovation . . . needs to be watched with more jealousy than the practice of delegating the authority of Parliament—even in small and local matters—with no better check than the chance that some unusually vigilant legislator may move an address to reject the scheme of law before it had time to mature into an indefeasible enactment.''

Among the pre-Dicey writers on constitutional law Alpheus Todd is instructive for our purpose. The first edition of his *Parliamentary Government in England*, published in 1867, has a chapter on 'The Royal Prerogative in connection with Parliament'. It discusses Orders in Council and royal proclamations, Minutes of Committees of Council and other departmental regulations. Experience has proved, he says, that subordinate law-making powers must be entrusted to almost every leading department of State, but they must be exercised by responsible ministers with the knowledge of Parliament and in direct subjection to its control. His emphasis on the prerogative is explained by his illustrations. He had in mind the anomalous position of the education codes wherein were prescribed the conditions on which a school could qualify for grant. What we know now as the Ministry of Education began in 1839 when an Order in Council set up a committee of the Privy Council 'to superintend the application of any sums voted by Parliament for the purpose of promoting public education'. Until the great Act of 1870 these grants and the codes under which they were awarded had no more specific statutory authority than a vote in Supply and the annual Appropriation Act. In August, 1861, on the very day of prorogation, the Government laid before Parliament without any explanation a new code making extensive changes. Complaints were vigorously voiced during the recess. A fresh code was laid, but the complaints were redoubled, not only against the substance but also against the procedure. Motions for the annulment of the contents of the codes, forerunners of the modern 'prayers' against Statutory Instruments, were repeatedly moved. The Committee of Council was, like the Poor Law Commissioners, accused of being a despotic and irresponsible Board. Critics naturally said that the matters prescribed in the codes ought to be directly enacted in the form of a statute or at least should be justified by statutory authority. At length in 1870 Parliament gave that authority to the Minutes of the Education Department, though not allowing them to take effect till they had been laid before both Houses for at least a month.

A second edition of Todd's two volumes appeared in 1887, edited by his son. By this time there was a separate chapter on 'Legislation by Public Departments'. The arrangements for laying before Parliament are explained and there is reference to the formula, now so familiar, that rescission shall be without prejudice to proceedings already taken. The illustrations by this time included the Inclosure Commissioners' provisional orders (not a true type of delegated legislation), the Privy Council's orders and regulations about the diseases of animals under an Act of 1848, and the schemes and ordinances made under Acts relating to Oxford and Cambridge and the public schools. There is mention of a local scheme which required the head master of Harrow to be a clergyman. A humble address has been successfully moved against the scheme and Her Majesty has answered that she will signify Her disapproval thereto.

Pausing at this point, we note that Todd the father and Todd the son have recorded the recognized arrival of delegated legislation, the essential responsibility of ministers therefor and the technique of parliamentary motions for its rejection. Dicey himself, in the most attractive of textbooks, advocated the recourse to delegation. The substance no less than the form of the law, he said, would probably be improved 'if the Executive

Government of England could, like that of France, by means of
decrees, ordinances or proclamations having the force of law,
work out the detailed application of the general principles
embodied in the Acts of the Legislature'. Considerations of
legislative form alone, through the deliberate practice of the
official draftsmen and the general desire to curtail the length of
Bills, have been persuasive enough to make delegation a
commonplace. We can roughly date this development. When
Arthur Symonds published his monograph on drafting in 1835,
he recommended lightening the body of a statute by relegating
to schedules such matters as procedure, lists of repealed enact-
ments, lists of penalties and anything else which was merely
incidental. Twenty years later the recently established Statute
Law Commission drew up some 'Instructions for Draftsmen'.
These, after discussing how far it is worth while to insert in
statutes any model forms of documents likely to be required,
state that it is better to empower some competent person or
court to prepare them.

"The same remark," they continue, "applies to the
insertion of detailed rules directing the mode in which the
principle of an enactment is to be carried out. Where no
considerations of practical convenience interfere, it is better
to leave these also to be settled by the authority entrusted
with the working of the Act. This course both greatly shortens
Acts of Parliament and makes it easier to alter the rules
from time to time after they have been tested by experience."

Thring, appointed to the new office of Parliamentary Counsel
to the Treasury in 1868, gave identical advice in his classic
manual *Practical Legislation*. To take two other dates, Lord
Brougham's statute of 1850 'for shortening the language used
in Acts of Parliament' makes no reference to subordinate law-
making, whereas its more elaborate successor, the Interpretation
Act of 1889, has five sections which refer to it. Thring's official
successors followed his advice whole-heartedly. One of them,
Sir William Graham-Harrison, summing up to the Donoughmore-Scott Committee his nearly thirty years' experience as

Government draftsman, said it would be 'impossible to produce the amount and the kind of legislation which Parliament desires to pass, and which the people of this country are supposed to want, if it became necessary to insert in the Acts of Parliament themselves any considerable portion of what is now left to delegated legislation'. In 1901 Sir Courtenay Ilbert had written, in his *Legislative Methods and Forms,* that the delegation of legislative power 'should not extend to matters of principle on which a decision of Parliament ought to be taken'. Recent statutes, however, have frankly delegated the power to prescribe 'principles'. Some delegations—for example in 1931 the power of 'removing anomalies' by regulations under an Unemployment Insurance Act and of cutting down salaries and social benefits by Orders in Council under the National Economy Act, seem designed to remove acute political controversy from the floor of the House of Commons; others seem useful for postponing decision on awkward points arising during the progress of a Bill when 'the blue prints are not ready'.

As for the rate of increase in subordinate legislation, the annual statistics give a rough idea. What were then called 'Statutory Rules and Orders' were required by the Rules Publication Act of 1893 to be sent, as soon as made, to the King's Printer of Acts of Parliament (i.e. the Controller of His Majesty's Stationery Office) to be by him registered and, with certain exceptions, printed and put on sale. The Statutory Instruments Act of 1946 gave them the more comprehensive label of 'Statutory Instruments' as from the end of 1947; it repealed the Act of 1893 but reproduced the requirement of registration and printing. We thus have the annual totals from 1894 onwards. The gross annual totals do not provide a perfect guide; they are better broken down into the separate classes of 'general' and 'local' under which they have always been entered in the official register. If subordinate legislation does in fact contain any potential threat to personal liberty, it is in the 'general' class that the danger will probably be found. The locals, being mainly the administrative application of some adoptive or discretionary enactment to a particular class or area, may be ignored. In peace-time, by the way, the local class is at least twice as big as the general; in war-time the generals far outnumber the locals.

Taking then the general class alone, one finds that from 1894 to 1913 the average annual total was about 210. During the First World War the figure soared. In 1918 it was over 1,200. When that war ended, there was a fairly swift recovery from emergency to normal conditions. From 1922 to 1931 the average remained fairly steady around 400—twice as large as in pre-war years, but a smart drop from the high record of 1918. From 1932 it climbed again and straddled 600. In 1938, the year of Munich, it rose (for the first time since 1920) over 800. The seven years of the Second World War produced further increases. The total just topped 1,900 in 1942, sank again by nearly a half to just over 1,000 in 1944, went up steadily to over 1,500 in 1948, dropped below 1,400 in 1949 and fell again to 1,211 in 1950.

It did not need those tedious figures to convince us of the influence of emergencies upon legislative method. The historic preamble to the Statute of Proclamations made the point on behalf of Henry VIII in 1539.

"Considering that sudden causes and occasions fortune many times which do require speedy remedies and that, by abiding for a Parliament, in the meantime might happen great prejudice to ensue to the Realm. . . . It is therefore thought in manner more than necessary that the King's Highness of this Realm for the time being, with the advice of His Honourable Council, should make and set forth proclamations for the good and politic order and governance of this His Realm . . . for the defence of His Regal Dignity and the advancement of His Commonwealth and good quiet of His People as the cases of necessity shall require."

The Act of 1539 was repealed in the next reign, but sudden causes have continued to require speedy remedies in the form of delegated legislation. When there was plague in the Baltic in 1710, Queen Anne imposed quarantine arrangements by Orders in Council and a proclamation. There was difficulty in

Q

enforcing them without statutory backing; a statute was therefore passed to give the force of law to 'such orders, rules and
directions touching quarantine as hath been or shall be made
by Her Majesty and noted by proclamation'. An Act of 1745
recites that a contagious distemper is raging among the cattle
of the country and 'remedies for preventing the spread of this
dreadful calamity cannot so effectually be provided as by
enabling His Majesty to make rules, orders and regulations
concerning the same from time to time as occasion may
require'. Later Acts of 1832, 1846 and 1848 refer to the threat
of other epidemics and the need of rules and regulations to
combat them, 'but it may be impossible to establish such rules
and regulations by the authority of Parliament with sufficient
promptitude to meet the exigency of any such case as it may
occur'. In 1877, though by this time preambles are no longer
fashionable and delegation no longer needs justification, an Act
authorizes the Lords of the Council to 'make such orders as
they think expedient for preventing the introduction into Great
Britain of the insect designated as doryphera decemlineata and
commonly called the Colorado beetle'. Thus delegation plays
its part in the battle against the enemies of human, animal and
vegetable welfare.

If, in all this range of sudden causes requiring speedy
remedies, Parliament had not armed the Executive with such
powers, would the country have been left helpless? Well, the
Crown (i.e. the Executive) might have made rules or orders
by virtue of the prerogative, which was memorably described
by Locke as 'the power to act according to discretion for the
public good, without the prescription of the law and sometimes
even against it'. But this course would have involved the
subsequent passing of an Indemnity Act to cure retrospectively
any illegal action, as was done, for instance, after Chatham's
Order in Council of 1766 stopping the export of corn or the
younger Pitt's in 1797 forbidding the Bank to pay in cash till
Parliament could be consulted. There may be crises when the
Government, in Locke's phrase, must for the public good act
even contrary to the law. The Order in Council is then a sort
of *senatus consultum ultimum*, bidding the consuls do their best to

see that the State takes no harm. But the technique of taking drastic action in emergency subject to subsequent validation by Parliament is very different from the technique whereby Parliament is persuaded to delegate in advance a power so wide in range and terms that judicial control is in effect excluded and no subsequent Act of Indemnity seems needed.

We are speaking now of events within living memory. On 4th August, 1914, Britain found herself at war with Germany. The following proclamation was published a few hours later:

> "Whereas by the law of our Realm it is Our undoubted prerogative and the duty of all Our loyal subjects acting on Our behalf in times of imminent national danger to take all such measures as may be necessary for securing the public safety and the defence of Our Realm:
>
> "And whereas the present State of public affairs in Europe is such as to constitute an imminent national danger:
>
> "Now therefore We strictly command and enjoin Our subjects to obey and conform to all instructions and regulations which may be issued by Us or Our Admiralty or Army Council . . . and not to hinder or obstruct. . . ."

His Majesty's advisers considered that the prerogative in time of war was absolute and that any officer would be justified in taking whatever steps he reasonably deemed necessary for public safety, relying on being indemnified by Act of Parliament at the end of hostilities. Soon, however, the military authorities were representing that an intolerable and invidious burden was being placed upon the officer and were pressing for specific powers. So on 8th August the Defence of the Realm Act, familiarly called 'DORA' for short, was hastily passed. Its phrasing was declaratory.

> "His Majesty has power during the continuance of the present war to issue regulations as to the powers and duties of the Admiralty and the Army Council for securing the public safety and the defence of the Realm."

Some brief additional clauses dealt with courts martial and the offence of sabotage. The regulation-making power, at first entirely military, was presently extended by amending Acts into every field of governmental activity; people found themselves forbidden to hold dog shows or to whistle for a taxicab in London. Occasionally, but not often until the guns had stopped firing, somebody asked the courts to rule that a particular exercise of the power was outside even these wide and vague limits. Occasionally, but rarely, the courts did so decide. But this exceptional power was temporary and, by the end of 1920, the war-time regulations had substantially lapsed or been terminated; a few which had filled conspicuous gaps in our peace-time law (controlling, for example, the possession of firearms and dangerous drugs) were replaced by permanent statutes. Moreover, perhaps because the statutory grant of regulation-making power had not been enacted at the outset of hostilities, the precaution was taken of passing an Act of Indemnity.

Unhappily a fresh chapter in the convenient delegation of blank-cheque powers was already opening. In Ireland there was civil war; courthouses were being burnt down and prosecutions and imprisonment became difficult. In August 1920, an Act was passed for the restoration of order in Ireland; it authorized the application to Ireland by Order in Council of the war-time regulations made under 'DORA'. If they were, as Lord Justice Scrutton remarked in the Art O'Brien case, clumsily applied, the method was attractively simple. Fortunately order was presently restored. Meanwhile, in October 1920, in the middle of a fortnight of coal strike, with the railwaymen talking of coming out in sympathy, an Emergency Powers Act was passed, which employed something like the blank-cheque technique of the Defence of the Realm Act then about to expire. The new Act said that, if it appeared to His Majesty that the life of the community, its food, water, fuel, light or means of transport were threatened, a proclamation might declare a state of emergency. The proclamation would last a month; during that month regulations might be made, but they would last only seven days unless both Houses of Parliament approved their continuance for the full month;

proclamations could be renewed month by month. The Act was operated in the coal strike of 1921, in the long General Strike of 1926 (when proclamations were renewed monthly from April to December), again briefly in 1949, and for a few days in the dock strike of 1950. There is some constitutional safeguard in the requirement that Parliament must be summoned or kept sitting in order to debate and confirm the regulations monthly; but the Act necessarily perpetuates what had been improvised as a temporary expedient by a liberty-loving nation when faced with the aggression of the 1914 war.

If any weak places had revealed themselves in the Executive armour forged for the purposes of the First World War, the prudent framers of the 1939 legislation managed to make them good. War was declared on 3rd September, 1939, but, previous experience having been turned to account, an Emergency Powers (Defence) Act was ready to be hurriedly passed on 24th August in the twilight period. Each blank-cheque precedent was remembered. The Act authorized His Majesty to make by Order in Council such Defence Regulations 'as appear to Him to be necessary or expedient' for the following generously wide purposes:

"securing the public safety and the defence of the Realm" (an echo of the 1914 Act);

"the maintenance of public order" (a hint from the 1920 Act for the restoration of order in Ireland);

"the efficient prosecution of any war in which His Majesty may be engaged" (another echo of the First World War); and

"maintaining supplies and services essential to the life of the community" (a reminiscence of the Emergency Powers Act of 1920).

In the 1914 war the regulations brought forth a teeming progeny of subsidiary orders, so that the Act had not only children but also grandchildren. If the maxim that a delegate cannot himself delegate is applicable, the legitimacy of these grandchildren was dubious, but it does not seem to have been

challenged in the courts. In the 1939 Act (as in a very few intermediate precedents) express authority is given for a limited
sub-delegation; Defence Regulations could empower any
specified authorities or persons to make 'orders, rules or bye-
laws' for any of the purposes for which the regulations could
themselves be made. The philoprogenitive Defence Regulation 55 (for the general control of industry) has headed a
family tree of wide-spread ramifications; the thousands of orders
made thereunder have, amongst other things, instituted and
facilitated drastic schemes of food rationing, clothing coupons,
petrol allowances and the control of raw materials. As the
recognized grandchildren of the 1939 Act, the orders are
unquestionably legitimate; some of them, however, instead of
being self-contained, begat yet other generations; the orders
authorized the issue of 'directions', and the 'directions' in turn
authorized the issue of 'licences', framed in general terms legislative in character and prescribing 'conditions'. The statute
had not mentioned 'directions' or 'licences' or 'conditions';
Parliament had apparently not intended that there should be
more than three tiers of this legislation. If the orders were not
framed as self-contained documents, the contemplation of
further generations could be an excuse for postponing decision
on material points or for taking wider powers than would
ultimately be found necessary. In a few cases the courts were
invited to consider the effect of these great-great-grandchildren
of the statute, but the argument that this sub-sub-delegation was
not authorized by the Act of 1939 was either not pressed upon
the judges' attention or was unsuccessful. The Executive, as
Lord Sumner once observed, does many things purporting to
be for the public good in times of crisis which Englishmen have
been too patriotic to contest. In any case the subordinate law-
making which flowed from the 1939 Act proved to be invulner-
able; such was the virtue of the master-words which protected
His Majesty's Defence Regulations if they 'appeared to Him to
be necessary or expedient'. An amending Act, passed at a
grim moment in May 1940, had stretched the regulation-
making power to include power to 'require persons to place
themselves, their services and their property at the disposal of

His Majesty'. Those words seem to remove all limitations upon Executive law-making; yet, perhaps because they were regarded as a mere symbol of the country's resolution or because fresh Acts of Parliament are passed in order to teach us that there is a fresh crisis, further embroidery and expansion of the original statutory purposes was presently enacted.

The war was won in 1945. Some of the exceptional war-time restrictions (such as the power to detain under Defence Regulation 18 B without trial) were promptly dropped, but the emergency technique of Defence Regulations and orders was summarily continued for another five years. The most powerful of all Prime Ministers had been obliged to ask Parliament for the renewal of these unaccustomed aids to government every twelve months in the gravest years of the war. This five-year continuance was enacted by the Supplies and Services (Transitional Powers) Act which, in terms still of generous width, switched the war-time apparatus of subordinate law-making over to the peace-time purposes of 'so maintaining, controlling and regulating supplies and services as—

"to secure a sufficiency of those essential to the well-being of the community or their equitable distribution or their availability at fair prices, or . . .
"to facilitate the readjustment of industry and commerce to the requirements of the community in times of peace. . . ."

Even these elastic powers were in 1947 expanded to include 'additional purposes', than which, Lord Samuel has said, it would be impossible to imagine a wider range—

"for promoting the productivity of industry, commerce and agriculture . . . and
"generally for ensuring that the whole resources of the community are available for use, and are used, in a manner best calculated to serve the interests of the community."

During 1950 these blank-cheque post-war powers, otherwise expiring towards the end of the year, were extended for a further twelve months and proposals were made for making them permanent.

The Donoughmore-Scott Committee recognized that a modern State may encounter a sudden need of legislative action, and that 'it may be not only prudent but vital for Parliament to arm the Executive Government in advance with almost plenary powers to meet occasions of emergency'. The committee did not attempt to lay down rules about such delegation in time of crisis beyond stating that 'it is of the essence of constitutional government that the normal control of Parliament should not be suspended either to a greater degree, or for a longer time, than the exigency demands'. When the committee described as exceptional and abnormal the type of delegation which confers 'so wide a discretion on a Minister that it is almost impossible to know what limit Parliament did intend to impose', it was thinking of contemporary conditions in 1932. Many pages of its report are of merely historical and academic significance today. The great safeguard of judicial control has been nullified; if unlimited statutory power is delegated, judges can no longer be invited to declare that a particular departmental exercise of the power is *ultra vires*—outside the scope of the parent statute. And, with the intensification of party politics, parliamentary control has also, in effect, disappeared; when, with the aid of a substantial majority, the Government side has secured the enactment of the parent statute, the Opposition side has little hope of success in moving a motion for the annulment of the resultant Statutory Instrument. These are issues of political partizanship, not of political theory. Only the Opposition will be challenging the Executive, and the Executive has the means and the will to crush the challenge.

Mr. G. M. Young has spoken of delegated legislation as Legislation without a Legislature. Well, the Modernists may say, why drag in the Legislature? Does not the law, in this age of prefabrication, come down, ready made, from above? Wars teach us new inventions and speedier processes; are we not to take advantage of time-saving gadgets in law-making? The Methusalehs (a little inarticulate perhaps, since they may feel these to be matters of instinct rather than of argument) may be expected to answer that speed is not everything, and indeed that many legislative proposals will be, or would have been, the better for delay and deliberation. They may recite for our amusement the 'setting test' in the Food Standards (Table Jellies) Order, 1949, and ask whether that legislative journey was really necessary. They may suggest that, if delegation expedites law-making, it may go too fast for the public and even for the police, as the unhappy episode of the Lincolnshire Church Bells prosecution indicated. Moreover, they may add, it may be set to do too much; the effort to fix the minimum prices of milk, cattle and eggs in some future year produced arithmetical headaches over the 'appropriate coefficients' in a batch of orders in March 1950. Finally they are likely to hint that members of Parliament, a fair cross-section of the community, possess a certain waywise experience, gumption, sense of the ridiculous and readiness to compromise which not every tidy-minded administrator can bring to bear upon departmental regulations. Would Parliament have tolerated in a Bill the element of unfairness which appeared in the Seizure of Food Order, 1948? Would a Bill have been allowed to create the muddle of the Electric Lighting (Restriction) Order, 1949, which, in spite of its title, had the unobtrusive effect of allowing gardeners to heat their greenhouses once more? And, as we have mentioned short titles, would a Bill have been christened at the same categorical length as the Control of Bolts, Nuts, Screws, Screw Studs, Washers and Rivets (No. 1) Order, 1943? These may be petty points but they are symptomatic.

There then is our problem. Are the Modernists right who are content or even anxious to see the delegation of permanent blank-cheque powers of law-making without limit of scope or time? Or are the Methusalehs justified in hoping that in some post-crisis period (if any) the Legislature will return to the old ideal of deciding itself upon principles and essentials while delegating the power to deal with details and mere trimmings? The old ideal is in line with the Germanic convention observed by Tacitus—*de minoribus principes consultant, de maioribus omnes*. But it must have been the *principes* who drew the line between matters major and minor. Who, if the Methusalehs' wishes are ever fulfilled, will decide where the line is drawn between matters of principle and matters of detail? The parliamentary draftsmen and the legal advisers of government departments must have guided the decision fifty years ago; anyone who knows their combination of professional integrity and official responsibility would trust them to try again. But the House would hesitate to hand over such jurisdiction to any external authority; an independent judgment could not prevail against political pressures and the Whips' ever growing distaste for lengthy Bills. The House of Commons would have to assert its own independence as, in a modest degree, it did when considering the Police Pensions Bill in 1948. It then insisted on putting squarely into the Bill the policeman's right to his pension (which otherwise might have been left to delegation) and on tightening the parliamentary control of the Minister's regulations. To improve the application of such control in general and to make sure that Parliament realizes what is going on, the Donoughmore-Scott Committee recommended the setting-up of two Standing Committees in each House, one to examine every Bill for the purpose of drawing attention to any unusual or novel proposal to delegate legislative authority, the other to scrutinize the rules, regulations and orders resulting from the exercise of that authority, when the Bill has become an Act, in order to draw attention to any special feature. Ever since 1924 the House of Lords has had its Special Orders Committee for looking at all instruments which require an affirmative resolution; it reports whether they raise important questions of policy or principle and whether there should be further inquiry before the resolution is moved. Since 1943 the House of Commons has had a sessional Scrutinizing Committee for looking at every instrument laid before the House which either requires an affirmative, or is exposed to annulment on a negative, resolution. This latter body studies something like a thousand instruments in the year, but too much must not be expected of its patient labours. Its routine reports convey little; they may state the opinion that an instrument requires elucidation or appears to make some unusual or unexpected use of the power conferred by the parent statute, but they do not specify the grounds for their opinion. Usually once in each session the Scrutinizing Committee makes a general report, largely on technical aspects of delegation. The committee's virtue is that it acts with independence and without partisanship; it can do so because it is debarred from reporting on matters of policy or merits; it is entirely uninfluenced by the Executive, and it has established the interesting convention that its chairman must be a member of the Opposition. But its work is imperfectly geared in with the machinery of parliamentary control. Members of the House usually table their motions for annulment long before the committee has reported on, or perhaps even seen, the challenged instrument; and the reasons for their challenge will probably be reasons which the committee was debarred from considering. Neither House has set up the potentially more valuable committee to examine Bills which contain proposals of delegation and thus to give Parliament the chance to lock the stable doors before the horses are stolen.

Foreign observers have been praising the British constitution for its resilience in meeting the strains and stresses of two World Wars. But they remark that the sovereignty of Parliament is now a legal fiction and they warn us that, in the face of an omnipotent Executive, our unwritten constitution lacks the bulwark of fundamental laws which the Judiciary can enforce. They note the evolution of blank-cheque delegation into which they saw us stumble almost accidentally in the war of 1914. They fancy they detect a reluctance to abandon it and they recall that the precedent-loving Englishman will tolerate anything if told that the same thing has been happening to him for a year or two. Montesquieu, in a well-known chapter on the effect of climate upon a country's attitude to its laws, opines that the English climate breeds a spirit of impatience which, when allied with courage, can be very proper for disconcerting any projects of tyranny. Foreign observers today sometimes seem to wonder if perhaps our climate is on the change.

CHAPTER XII

PARLIAMENTARY CONTROL OVER THE NATIONALIZED UNDERTAKINGS

By A. L. Goodhart

WHEN we speak of nationalized undertakings we mean undertakings which are publicly owned and are national in character. Although most of them are industrial in nature, some of them, such as the British Broadcasting Corporation for example, cannot be properly described as industries. These undertakings can be divided into two classes. The first consists of those undertakings which are directly under the control of the Crown and are staffed by civil servants. The Post Office and the Woolwich Arsenal are examples of such Crown-administered undertakings. The second class consists of undertakings which are organized and administered as independent Public Corporations, and are only indirectly subject to governmental control. This is the modern technique which has been applied in the cases of the Port of London Authority, the London Passenger Transport Board (now replaced by the British Transport Commission), the B.B.C., the Bank of England, Civil Aviation, Coal, Electricity, Gas, Transport, Raw Cotton, and Steel.[1] It is essential to keep the distinction between these two classes clearly in mind because, although they resemble each other superficially, nevertheless there is a radical constitutional and legal distinction between them. The comparison is impor-

[1]The pre-1939 Corporations were the Central Electricity Board (now replaced by the British Electricity Authority), The London Passenger Transport Board (now replaced by the British Transport Commission-London Transport Executive), the Port of London Authority, and the British Broadcasting Corporation (first Charter granted in 1926). For an interesting comparison of pre-1939 and post-1945 Corporations see D. N. Chester, *The Nationalized Industries, A Statutory Analysis*, (Allen & Unwin for Institute of Public Administration, 1951).

tant because it will help us in analysing the nature and function of a Public Corporation.

From the standpoint of parliamentary control there is not much that need be said about the undertakings, such as the Post Office, which are administered directly by the Crown, because in their case Parliamentary control is, in theory, complete, although in practice this control is put into effect only occasionally. The Minister is directly responsible to Parliament for the proper functioning of the undertaking, although he may, and, of course, does, delegate authority to the officials who actually manage it. Nevertheless, he must shoulder the blame if anything goes wrong, and in Parliament he must answer all questions which the Members may ask concerning day-to-day administration. If a postman behaves in an illegal manner in his official capacity, it is the Postmaster-General who must reply for his act. The finances of the undertaking are under the direct supervision of the Treasury, and are subject to Parliamentary examination as are all other public accounts.

The great advantage of this system is that responsibility is always clear and definite. If something goes wrong it is not possible for those in charge to shift the blame to others. There is a single line of responsibility from Parliament, through the Minister, to the most junior official. Anyone who compares this centralized system with the division of authority which exists under the American Constitution, with its resultant confusion and uncertainty, cannot fail to realize that the centralization of authority under the British procedure has been a major factor in the establishment of the honesty and fairness which characterize all British governmental activities.

If, as I believe, this centralization of responsibility has in the past been the essential feature of the British method of government, why has it been discarded in the case of the recently nationalized industries? Why are the coal mines not directly managed by the Minister of Fuel and Power, the railways by the Minister of Transport, and the steel industry by the Minister of Supply? What reasons have induced Parliament to surrender the direct control of these industries, when it guards this control so jealously elsewhere? We must try to answer these questions before we discuss the position of the new Corporations, because we cannot understand why a comparatively novel and revolutionary system has been adopted until we realize what were the disadvantages to be found in such complete governmental control as exists, for example, in the case of the Post Office.

The first, and the most serious, criticism that is brought against all government departments is the criticism of 'red tape.' Public administration, when compared with private enterprise, is said to be slow, complex, and incapable of rapid adjustment to changing conditions. This criticism is advanced against public authorities in every country so that it must be based on something inherent in the system itself, and not on a superficial fault which can be easily eradicated. The existence of 'red tape' is sometimes blamed on the 'bureaucratic mind' which is said to be over-cautious and unwilling to accept responsibility, but this conflicts with the other view expressed by the late Lord Hewart in his book *The New Despotism* in which he attributed to the civil service a secret desire for autocratic power. Whether there is any truth in either of these divergent opinions it is not necessary to consider here because, even if all civil servants were ideal administrators, nevertheless public business would still have to be conducted in a slow and formal manner. This is a price which must be paid if public officials are not to be autocrats. In a recent article entitled *Red Tape*[1] Sir Henry Clay, then Warden of Nuffield College, pointed out that every Government department, however efficient its administration may be, must have red tape if it is not to function in an arbitrary manner. A private business to be efficient must, of course, keep records, but these can be limited to the accounts and the correspondence files. There is no need to keep a record of the grounds on which action was based nor a complete history of the various steps taken. But this is not possible in the case of a public file. As Sir Henry Clay said:[2]

[1] 1949. 65 *Law Quarterly Review,* 172.
[2] At p. 176.

"The file is primarily a record, a record of relevant facts and arguments, but a record also of the part every person concerned played in the making of the decisions or public statements in which the discussion issued. The record is necessary in order to allocate responsibility; the Minister acts through the higher officials in immediate touch with him, and they through subordinate officials; and the practice of recording every intervention in the making of the decision reminds the participants of their responsibility and makes it possible to bring it home."

Without a complete file the Minister would not be able to explain why his officials had acted as they did when, perhaps months later, their acts were challenged in Parliament. Such a detailed history is a necessary guard against arbitrary action by the Crown, but its inevitable corollary is red tape.[1] Perhaps the difference between private and public records can be summarized by saying that the private ones must show what was done, while the public ones must show, not only what was done, but also the grounds on which action was taken or refused. The private ones speak of 'what' while the public ones speak of 'why'. Only an autocrat, who is not responsible to a Parliament, can administer a government department without red tape, but even he will in time have to reintroduce some comparable system if he is to retain adequate control of his officials.

The second objection to direct governmental administration of an industry is that it places an undue burden on the Minister and on his senior officials. As he is responsible to Parliament for everything that is done by his ministry, it follows that each new activity must add to his work. The Minister can, of course, delegate most of this work to the permanent officials, but in the last resort he must decide all questions of major policy and he must also see that the executive machinery is running smoothly. He cannot share this responsibility with any one else for he alone

---

[1]Sir Henry Clay at p. 174: "Because we accept the principle that government may use force, we seek to circumscribe and attach conditions to Government action which are not necessary where action by other forms of social organization is concerned. The peculiarities of Government administration spring from this distinctive power; they explain and are illustrated by the Red Tape we are examining."

is answerable. If too much of the Minister's time is occupied by executive activities, then he will tend to become an administrator rather than a statesman which is his true function.

The third objection to governmental administration is that it is difficult, if not impossible, for a government department to decentralize. Here again the reason is that the Minister must retain ultimate responsibility, even when he delegates his authority to subordinate bodies or officials. Large-scale industrial undertakings can, when they threaten to become top-heavy, create self-managing subsidiaries which are run as independent units. Under such an arrangement the officers of the parent or holding company are not responsible for the day-to-day management of the subsidiary organization. If the latter makes a loss owing to inefficiency on the part of its managing directors, then these can be replaced by others, but until this is done they remain solely responsible. Such decentralization is never possible in the case of a government department because the Minister, even though he has delegated some of his functions to others, must remain responsible himself for what they are doing. On this point Sir Henry Clay has said:[1] "Devolution must be carried as far as possible; but this is not far, if any Minister is liable to be challenged on any act of his Department, and the Government as a whole to be involved in the outcome of the challenge."

The fourth objection to governmental administration is that it may introduce political considerations in the conduct of undertakings which ought to be administered on non-political lines. It was in part for this reason that the B.B.C., with its tremendous propaganda potentiality, was established as an independent body with an independently appointed board of governors, subject only to the minimum of control by the Post-master-General. The force of this objection seems to be less compelling in the case of other undertakings, for they are less capable of being used for political purposes. Thus no suggestion has ever been made that the Post Office has at any time been conducted with any political bias. The experience of other countries has, however, shown that public undertakings can be

[1] At p. 186.

used for political purposes unless the most careful controls are exercised.

It was the recognition that direct government management of the nationalized undertakings might lead to red tape, to placing an undue burden on the Minister, to over-centralization of the industry, and to possible political bias in management which led to the creation of the modern Public Corporations in the hope that they could avoid these handicaps. The purpose was to devise a system under which these new bodies could function efficiently and without red tape, while still remaining subject to the necessary Parliamentary control. As Mr. Herbert Morrison, the Lord President of the Council, said:[1] "When we set up a public corporation what are we trying to do? We are trying to get the best of both worlds." Whether this attempt has succeeded or not will depend on the answers to two questions. The first is, 'Has Parliament maintained an adequate control of the Corporations?' The second is, 'Has Parliament devised a method which, while allowing for adequate control, has provided some guarantee for the efficient management of these industries?' In the literature on this subject most attention has been directed to the first question, but it is the second one which is the more important.

To get rid of red tape it would have been possible for Parliament to create completely independent Corporations, making no provision for control of their activities either by itself or by the Ministers. This would have meant that these Corporations, although owned by the Crown, would in practice have been completely autocratic. Such uncontrolled power is conceivable in a totalitarian State, but it is hardly consonant with a democratic form of government. Even though we were convinced that the board of management would act only from the highest motives and with unexampled energy, it would still be necessary to devise some method by which its activities could be judged and controlled. Nor would a financial check of its accounts be sufficient, because by its nature the Public Corporation is not intended to be primarily a profit-making organization. This is obvious, because these Corporations have been created on the

[1] *Parliamentary Debates* (Hansard), 1950, Vol. 478, c. 2807.

R

ground that private industries may be inclined to ignore the public interest in their pursuit of financial success. As a Public Corporation is usually a monopoly, with all the power of the State behind it, it is clear that the final decision as to what is in the public interest cannot in all cases be left in the hands of a small body of men, who are almost unknown to the general public, and whose outlook, owing to the position they hold, may tend to become bureaucratic.[1] The only body which can adequately express this public interest is Parliament, and it is only through parliamentary control that the public, which must otherwise be helpless when faced by a complete monopoly, can be assured that its interests will be properly recognized. It is not surprising therefore to find that so much of the literature relating to Public Corporations is concerned with this point, with the result that the more important and more difficult problem concerning efficiency has not been sufficiently stressed.

Although the various Public Corporations follow no single pattern, nevertheless, the post-1945 Corporations bear a strong resemblance to each other.[2] This is true in particular of parliamentary control which is exercised in substantially the same manner in all instances.

It is essential to realize that parliamentary control can always be divided into two classes. In the first, the control is indirect because it is exercised by a Minister, but it can nevertheless be described as Parliamentary control, as he is Parliament's agent and is responsible to it for the exercise of all his powers. The second class consists of those powers which are exercised directly either by the House itself or by one of its committees. It is the first class which is the more important, although most of the emphasis in the debates has been placed

---

[1]Cf. editorial note in *The Political Quarterly: Special Number—Nationalized Industries* (1950, Vol. XXI, p. 113): "Administrators of nationalized industries, our contributors believe, are particularly liable to the diseases of security, conservatism and procrastination. To combat these diseases they must be required to show that their undertakings satisfy appropriate tests of efficiency applied to such criteria as productivity, economy in staff, industrial morale and goodwill, public satisfaction, and lowered prices." Unfortunately the various contributors seem to have been unable to agree on what constituted appropriate tests of efficiency or how these could be applied in practice. This number of *The Political Quarterly* is of outstanding interest.

[2]For a detailed analysis see D. N. Chester, *op. cit.*, n. 1.

on the second one. It is necessary therefore to consider in some detail what powers of control have been given to the Ministers in the various statutes.

With the exception of the B.B.C. and the Bank of England,[1] all the Acts provide that the Minister of the appropriate Department is to appoint the Chairman and the other members of the governing body of the Corporation. Most of the Acts contain certain provisions relating to the experience and other qualifications of the members, but these are of minor importance. The choice of the members must always remain a personal choice, and whether it is well or badly exercised will depend on the judgment of the Minister, whatever exhortation the statute may contain. The Minister is also empowered to make regulations concerning 'the tenure and vacation of office by the members of the Board'. In most instances the term has been fixed at five years. Having appointed the chairman and the other members, the Minister's powers of dismissal are strictly limited. Thus in the case of the Coal Board a member can only be dismissed (apart from such obvious grounds as conviction for crime or bankruptcy, etc.) if in the opinion of the Minister he becomes 'unfit to continue in office or incapable of performing his duties'. As the decision concerning fitness is left to the unfettered opinion of the Minister, it follows that he could arbitrarily dismiss any member, but such a dismissal could be questioned in Parliament. It is clear that the Minister is not intended to use this power to dismiss a member merely because there is a difference of opinion concerning policy between them. The members of the Board are in no sense the agents of the Minister, and he must respect their independence. The power of dismissal must therefore not be regarded as a means of control.

The fact that the Minister has the power to reappoint members at the end of their term of office is of much greater importance. A member who is too independent or too critical may have reason to fear that he will not be chosen again. This fear, whether justified or not, is of particular effect in the case

[1]The Chairman and other members of the B.B.C. are appointed by the King in Council. The Governors and Directors of the Bank of England are appointed by His Majesty.

of a nationalized industry, which is a complete monopoly, because if a member, or other officer, loses his position, he cannot hope to obtain a comparable post in the same industry. Thus if an expert in coal mining ceases to serve the Coal Board, either voluntarily or involuntarily, he will not be able to find any other scope for his talents in this country. It is unlikely therefore that he will take such an appalling risk if he can avoid it by acquiescing with the Minister. It is not suggested, of course, that a Minister would ever use this power for any improper purposes, but it is inevitable that the existence of this power will to some degree affect the independence of the various Boards.

A more direct and obvious power of control is found in the provisions contained in all the post-1945 Acts whereby the Minister may issue certain directions to the governing Boards. Thus Section 3 of the Coal Industry Nationalisation Act provides that:

"(1) The Minister may, after consultation with the Board, give to the Board directions of a general character as to the exercise and performance by the Board of their functions in relation to matters appearing to the Minister to affect the national interest, and the Board shall give effect to any such directions."

This clause may in practice turn out to mean much or little depending on whether the Minister does or does not wish to interfere in the management of the industry. It is for him to decide whether the matter appears to affect the national interest, and no one can question his decision on this point. This is fortunate for it would seem to be impossible to draw a line between a national and a local interest. He can only give 'directions of a general character', but there is hardly any direction which cannot with some ingenuity be framed in general terms. Would a direction that the railways should not run special trains to race meetings be a direction of a general character? In the case of a strike for increased wages, would a direction to pay such an increase be of a general character because it applied to employees generally, or would it be particular because it related to an individual dispute? It is not clear whether a Board could refuse to carry out such a direction because it was of the opinion that it lacked generality, and whether in such a case it would be necessary to ask the Courts in an appropriate proceeding to settle the dispute between the Minister and the Board.

The existence of this power to issue directions of a general character gives rise to two considerations. The first is that although the Minister may hesitate to exercise it with any frequency, for every time it is used there is an implication that there has been a difference of opinion between the Minister and the Board, nevertheless, its mere existence will induce the Board to acquiesce in any recommendations made by the Minister because it is always unpleasant to be overruled.[1] The second consideration is of more importance for it illustrates how great is the gulf between the Public Corporations and the classic English constitutional doctrine of unified responsibility. As the Minister may issue directions it follows that responsibility for the proper conduct of the industry is divided between him and the Board so that in certain cases it will be difficult to allocate the blame. It will always be possible for a Board to say that on a matter affecting the national interest the Minister ought to have given it the necessary directions, while the Minister may claim that he was relying on the initiative of the Board. There is the obvious danger that at a time of emergency each may wait for the other to take the first step. Division of responsibility always runs the risk of leading to a clash when both parties are strong-willed or of leading to inaction when both are anxious to avoid unnecessary exertion; it is the second danger which is the more acute where public affairs are concerned.

[1]Mr. Ernest Davies, M.P., in his article 'Ministerial Control and Parliamentary Responsibility of Nationalized Industries' (*The Political Quarterly, op. cit.,* n. 7, p. 150) said: "There is no question but that ministerial influence over the public corporations is considerable, but it is exercised largely behind closed doors. The national interest is thereby safeguarded in practice, but the ministerial responsibility which this entails, is not always answered for. In other words, Ministers, in preference to making use of the statutory powers conferred upon them, take advantage of the existence of these powers to influence the public boards."

If the Minister is to be in a position to issue directions of a general character it is essential that he should have the necessary information on which to base his decision. Section 3, sub.-s. 4 of the Coal Industry Nationalisation Act, 1946, therefore provides:

"The Board shall afford to the Minister facilities for obtaining information with respect to the property and activities of the Board, and shall furnish him with returns, accounts and other information with respect thereto and afford to him facilities for the verification of information furnished, in such manner and at such times as he may require."

As the Minister cannot be expected personally to study the returns, accounts and other information in any detail, it is highly probable that this duty will be assigned to officials within the Ministry. Being trained civil servants it is not unlikely that the information they will require will be detailed and complete because they must protect the Minister against any accusation that he has not performed his supervisory functions with thoroughness. This will be a guarantee that the industry is not being administered in a lax or wasteful manner, but the obvious danger is the return of the red tape which the Public Corporation was designed to avoid. It may lead to unnecessary duplication of work between the officials who administer the industry and the civil servants who question what the officials have done.

On the financial side important powers of control are given to the Minister. Thus Section 3, sub.-s. 2 of the Coal Industry Nationalisation Act, 1946, provides that:

"In framing programmes of reorganization or development involving substantial outlay on capital account, the Board shall act on lines settled from time to time with the approval of the Minister."

Under s. 26 the Minister may make advances to the Board of sums not exceeding £150,000,000 within five years from the commencement of the Act, and thereafter of such sums as Parliament may determine. S. 27 provides that the Board may, with the consent of the Minister, borrow temporarily sums not exceeding £10,000,000. S. 28 provides that the Minister may, with the approval of the Treasury, direct the Board to pay certain sums by way of recouping the Crown. Under s. 29 the Minister may give directions to the Board concerning a reserve fund, and s. 30 enables him to give specific directions to the Board concerning the application of any surplus revenues. The Transport Act, 1947, provides that the Minister must give his consent before the commission may borrow money by the issue of British transport stock. The other Nationalisation Acts contain similar provisions concerning the relevant Minister's financial powers.

The relation between the Minister and the Public Corporation can therefore be summarized by saying that the Minister can issue general directions in relation to matters affecting the national interest which are binding on the Corporation, that he may require the Corporation to furnish him with such information as he may consider necessary, and that he has important financial control. Only the future can tell whether these powers will be exercised in a wide or in a narrow manner by the Minister. In exercising or in failing to exercise them the Minister is responsible to Parliament and can be held to account. It is true, therefore, to say that Parliament has important indirect powers of control over these undertakings through its agent, the Minister.

When we turn to the problem of the direct control exercised by Parliament we find that it has given rise to far more discussion than has the question of indirect control, although in fact it is less important. Even in the case of an undertaking directly administered by the Crown, such as the Post Office, Parliamentary control is at best sporadic and uncertain. A large assembly, organized primarily for the purposes of debate, cannot deal successfully with technical problems. It is more in the threat of what it may do than in what it actually does, that the force of Parliamentary control lies.

It has frequently been said that asking questions is the most important function that a Member of Parliament can perform. It is during the question hour that the Minister must justify all actions taken by the officers of his ministry. This is the most potent guard against arbitrary action that exists in any country, because every official, from the highest to the lowest, knows that he may be called to account through the Minister. This system presupposes, however, that the Minister is himself responsible, and therefore it has proved difficult to apply it to the Public Corporations. A debate of outstanding interest on this point was held in the House of Commons on 3rd March 1948.[1] It became clear that there were really two issues: (1) What questions are admissible, this being for the Speaker to determine as guided by the Standing Orders of the House, and (2) How far can the Minister legitimately go in declining to answer questions which appear on the paper?

It was the first issue which was the difficult one. The two opposing views were stated by Sir John Anderson who said:[2] "I would submit therefore that all questions relating to the activities of these boards of socialized industries are *prima facie* admissible"; and by Mr. Herbert Morrison, who said:[3] "Has the Minister responsibility; has he done anything, and can he do anything about it? If the answer to these questions is 'No', then a question is not admissible." The latter view, which may be described as the narrow one, finds support in the statement in *Erskine May*[4] on this point: "Questions addressed to Ministers should relate to the public affairs with which they are officially connected, to proceedings pending in Parliament, or to matters of administration for which they are responsible." As a Minister is not responsible for matters of administration in a Public Corporation, this provision, if strictly construed, would exclude most questions concerning the socialized industries. This would be undesirable under modern conditions, and therefore a compromise, which is not very precise but may thus prove the more workable, was reached when Mr. Speaker said:[5] "If the

[1] *Parliamentary Debates* (Hansard), 1948, Vol. 448, c. 391–455.
[2] At c. 443. [3] At c. 447.
[4] Thomas Erskine May, *Treatise on the Law, Privileges, Proceedings and Usages of Parliament,* 14th ed., p. 334.
[5] *Parliamentary Debates* (Hansard), 1948, Vol. 451, c. 1641.

subject appears to me to be of sufficient public importance, then I allow a question; I authorize the Table to pass a question to ask for a statement, whether it has been asked before or whether it has not.[1] The decision, therefore, is mine. As regards the decision from the Minister, of course, he may choose to answer or not to answer—that is his affair." A Minister who refused to answer a question, except on the ground that it would be against the public interest for him to do so, might find himself in difficulty with the House.[2]

On the 25th October 1950[3] the House of Commons held the first full-dress debate, apart from the 1948 one which related primarily to Parliamentary Questions, in which the accountability of Public Corporations was considered. The motion was 'That this House notes the steps which have been taken to give effect to the responsibility to the community (including consumers and workpeople) of the socialized industries, and will welcome any further measures to increase their public accountability, consistently with the duty of the Boards to manage the industries with maximum efficiency in the public interest". Mr. Herbert Morrison,[4] the Lord President of the Council, explained that 'socialized industries' and 'nationalized industries' were synonymous, and that both referred to publicly owned industries. In discussing the question of Parliamentary control he said that there were six occasions on which this could be exercised: (1) Members could ask Questions provided they fell within the statement made by the Speaker in 1948. It was necessary to limit these Questions, because otherwise the officials of these Corporations would become as cautious as civil servants, who look over their shoulders in case they may be pulled up by a Parliamentary Question. (2) Debates on the Adjournment could be held on questions arising out of the work of these industries. It was pointed out that such debates would be of a limited character. (3) Special days were agreed to

[1]Erskine May states at p. 338 that questions will not be accepted by the Speaker if they are "repeating in substance questions already answered or to which an answer has been refused".
[2]Erskine May, p. 334: "The refusal of a Minister to answer a question on this ground (public interest) cannot be raised as a matter of privilege."
[3]*Parliamentary Debates* (Hansard), Vol. 478, cc. 2082—927.
[4]cc. 2803—22.

by the Government on which a full-dress debate concerning the work of a particular industry could be held. Thus the Reports of the Coal Board and of the Transport Commission had been recently discussed. (4) The Opposition might contribute a Supply Day or Supply Days if they wished to criticize the conduct of an industry. (5) Debates on the Address, being unlimited as to subject matter, would give an opportunity for debating the affairs of these Corporations. (6) Private Bills have to be promoted by the Corporations from time to time, and on the Second Reading wide debates can be held.

This list is more formidable in length than in content, for it was generally agreed in the discussion that followed that the House was not so organized as to enable it to exercise any efficient control. Mr. Molson pointed out that debates tended to be discursive:[1] "In the case of the Transport Debate last week, one hon. Member referred to coal prices, another to restaurant cars, someone else to 'C' Licences on the road, and then steamers to Ulster came up, and, finally, interest rates and the Hotels Executive were mentioned." It is clear that such a debate, however interesting the individual speeches may be, can hardly be regarded as a practical instrument for managing an industry. Unless some other machinery is adopted, Parliament can itself play only an intermittent and uncertain role in controlling these new bodies which it has created.

To put order and vitality into Parliamentary control it was suggested that a Select Committee, served by an appropriate staff, should be established to inquire into and to report on the functioning of the nationalized industries. This Committee would be analogous to the Estimates Committee and the Public Accounts Committee. At first sight this idea is an attractive one, but it is open to serious objections. The work of such a committee would tend to be negative rather than positive. It could criticize any extravagance on the part of the Corporation, and it might investigate any mistakes made by the officers, but it could hardly recommend any active steps to be taken by the Board because it would have neither the responsibility nor the expert knowledge on which to base such a recommendation.

[1] c. 2849.

The examples furnished by similar committees in other countries are hardly encouraging. In 1933 in his Message to Congress President Roosevelt in recommending the formation of the Tennessee Valley Authority described it as: "Clothed with the power of Government but possessed of the flexibility and initiative of a private enterprise." Unfortunately the Authority, which began its work under the most favourable circumstances, has been frequently hindered in its work by the interference of Congressional committees. The same is true of the United States Atomic Energy Commission. When the chairmanship was recently vacant, it was suggested that a candidate for the post should be warned: "Ability to defend yourself before Congress is essential." Although a Select Committee would probably not act in such a partizan spirit, it is unlikely that it would not be influenced by political considerations as long as nationalisation remains a political question. It is not surprising therefore that Mr. Morrison rejected the idea, emphasizing that such a Committee would take up a good deal of the time of the officers of the Board, and would tend to make them nervous.[1] In a previous debate he said:[2] "As Members of Parliament, we have every right to boast about our virtues, and to assert our abilities, but we had better remember our limitations as well, and, that being so, I am not quite sure that a committee of the House of Commons would be the right body to conduct an efficiency audit." In attempting to supervise the work of the Public Corporations Parliament might be acting as a brake on their progress, and it might thus cause the very evil which it was intending to prevent.

In answer to the first question whether Parliament has adequate control of the Public Corporations it may therefore be said that from the negative standpoint it probably has all the power that is necessary. By means of questions any serious derelictions of duty can be called to public attention, and by the debates on the annual accounts and reports emphasis can

---

[1] c. 2813: "It would take up a good deal of the time of the chairman and the other Members of the board and their principal officers. It would take them away from their business, and it would tend to make them nervous throughout the year about appearing before the Select Committee."

[2] *Parliamentary Debates* (Hansard), 1948, Vol. 448, c. 450.

be placed on errors of policy which have led to financial loss or to failures in production.

It is when we turn to the second question which concerns the efficiency of the Public Corporations that the answer seems much less certain. If Parliament cannot itself conduct "an efficiency audit' can it provide some other method by which it can be guaranteed that these industries will be managed, not only honestly, but also efficiently? By efficiency is meant not only the proper running of existing machinery, but the ready acceptance of new discoveries and the adoption of novel methods and ideas. A sailing ship may be brought to the highest state of efficiency, but if it is cheaper to substitute steam for sail, then the continued use of sailing ships is inefficient. In this connection it may be noted that steam was used in commercial ships before it was introduced in the Navy, and that the iron steamer preceded the iron warship. Private enterprise was more prepared to take a risk than was a government department. Can Parliament, having created industrial monopolies belonging to the Crown, devise some method which will prevent these industries from becoming static?

It is sometimes said that there is no difference in this respect between public and private monopolies, and that therefore there is as much, if not more, risk that a private monopoly will fail to improve its methods of production or adjust itself in other ways to the needs of the public than will a public corporation. The answer in most instances is that the profit motive, whether we like it or not, will induce the private monopoly to expand its business as much as possible even if there is no danger of competition. It is best to take a foreign monopoly, such as the American Telephone and Telegraph Company, as an illustration. As the rates it can charge are controlled by law, it can only increase its profits by increasing the number of its customers. There is, therefore, a strong inducement to efficiency which works automatically. It is interesting to compare the development of the telephone system in the United States with that in this country. This does not mean that the officers of a private corporation are abler or more progressive by nature than are those of a public one, but it does mean that the atmosphere in which they work is different. The public official is not concerned with creating a new demand, for every new demand may give rise to new complaints, and the avoidance of complaints must always be his primary aim. If people are content to ride in horse-drawn vehicles, there is no reason, from this standpoint, to encourage them to ask for motor-cars. On the other hand the officer of the private company, even if it is a quasi-monopoly, must be concerned in most instances with the expansion of its activities, and is therefore prepared to take a risk. He is always faced with the danger of competitive alternatives, for no private monopoly can be complete. As Sir Ian Fraser pointed out in the debate, the profit motive when combined with the customer's choice is the most effective efficiency audit that can be devised.[1]

It is important to remember that the need for an efficiency test varies in the different industries. In such an undertaking as railway transport it is at a minimum because it is unlikely that novel ideas can be introduced to any serious degree. It is the sound administrator rather than the original thinker who is needed here. But in industries which are dynamic rather than static the problem is a different one. If, to take an unlikely example, the motor industry were to be nationalized it would be necessary to place great emphasis on the opportunity for experiment and change. The industrial adventurer is required if new territories are to be explored, especially if adventurers from other countries are anxious to occupy the land. It is doubtful, however, whether the officers of a public corporation would be prepared to take the risks which experimentation implies, when there is every inducement for them to play safe.

To what extent Parliament can introduce machinery which will guarantee dynamic, and not merely administrative, efficiency in the management of Public Corporations remains an unanswered question. Mr. Morrison[2] proposed that periodical

[1]*Parliamentary Debates* (Hansard), 1950, Vol. 478, c. 2865: "The normal checks on efficiency in industry are those occasioned by the existence of shareholders who desire profits and customers who desire services. . . . When the customer was able to choose which of two or more sources of supply to go to for the thing he wanted, and was able to choose whether this alternative or that suited him best, he was an automatic and effective check. That check has now gone."

[2]*Parliamentary Debates* (Hansard), Vol. 478, c. 2814.

reviews of the Public Corporations should be held every seven years so as to make recommendations on policy and structure. The examining body, while including a limited number of Members of Parliament, would in large part be unofficial in character, and its report would be available to Parliament and the public. Such a periodic examination would undoubtedly be of value, but there is little in past experience to justify the hope that such an inquest would by itself encourage that day-by-day initiative which is so essential if an industry is to prosper. It is even possible that the prospect of such a Day of Judgment might encourage some Boards to play safe because inaction is less vulnerable to criticism than action which has gone wrong.

Finally, a rather half-hearted proposal was made that outside consultants should be called in from time to time, but it was not made clear whether or not their recommendations should be made binding on the Boards. Valuable as the advice of an outsider may be, it can never be an adequate substitute for the dynamic efficiency of those who are responsible for the management of an undertaking.

It would be unfair to suggest that this problem of economic efficiency is limited to the Public Corporations. Owing to various causes, which cannot be discussed in this paper, economic efficiency declined in certain industries in this country in recent years. Thus Mr. Geoffrey Crowther, the editor of the *Economist*, said in a talk on "The Way Back to Solvency":[1]

"We have concentrated on stability and security, which are indeed good things to concentrate on, but we have done so to the exclusion of the efficiency of our economic mechanism, with the result that today there is hardly another country in the world where less emphasis is placed on economic efficiency than here. ... In the longer run, for this country at any rate, there is no antagonism at all between efficiency and security. Quite the contrary. If we do not look to our efficiency, we shall soon lose our social security and our full employment."

[1] *The Listener* (1950), p. 184

There are some who believe that this essential economic efficiency can best be secured by the competition of private industry, freed from some of the handicaps of the past. There are others who believe that this economic efficiency can only be developed through public corporations, freed from the profit motive. It is this problem which Sir Arthur Salter has called "The Crux of Nationalization".[1]

After analysing the present situation, he said: "It cannot be denied that in nationalized industries there is in practice nothing which encourages and compels efficiency, adaptability, initiative—and the rapid scrapping of the obsolete—which can compare with the ever-present consciousness of possible gain and ruin." He reached the pessimistic conclusion that 'a combination of bureaucratic traditions and a highly centralized structural organization will have fatal results. It may be that correctives will be found; but they have not yet been found'. Unfortunately the debate in Parliament of 1950 does not suggest that we are on the road to finding any solution other than the vague hope that the various boards and their officers will be of such a high quality that no test is really necessary. This view was expressed by the Minister of Fuel and Power (Mr. Noel-Baker) when he said:[2] "We have to get the best men we can to run the Corporations and then let them do the job." It is a sobering thought to realize that a major part of the economic life of this country will soon be placed in the hands of a few men, who, although comparatively unknown, will be solely responsible for the efficient development of the fundamental industries. Whether it will be possible to find men capable of solving the vast problems which must arise when so much power is concentrated in a few bodies is a question of tremendous importance for the future welfare of this nation. It is not surprising therefore to find that Parliament is showing increasing concern when it has to consider control of the nationalized industries, because up to the present time no answer to this major problem has been discovered.

[1] *The Political Quarterly* (1950), pp. 209–17.
[2] *Parliamentary Debates* (Hansard), Vol. 478, c. 2920.

CHAPTER XIII

THE FUTURE OF BRITISH PARLIAMENTARY GOVERNMENT

By G. M. Young

THE English Constitution, historians tell us, is one of a large family, the other members of which succumbed to the necessities of the new dynastic States, Hapsburg and Valois and Bourbon, to gunpowder and standing armies. Historians have also explained to us how the ancient prerogatives of the Crown and the more recent privileges of Parliament were reconciled in the device of Cabinet Government, by which process the conception of Fundamental Law was lost in the doctrine of Parliamentary Omnipotence. Finally, by the extension of the franchise, the democratic element in our mixed constitution became a sovereign plebs, operating politically by means of two organized and disciplined parliamentary parties, membership of which in our days tends to become more and more a professional avocation. And there, having brought us to the general election of 1945, the historians leave us to find our own way down the corridors of speculation. I do not apologize for that word. I even emphasize it. I am not providing a blueprint for a new parliamentary constitution. But historians of the next age will, I think, agree in regarding that year 1945 as closing a period which opened with another election, that of 1784. So perhaps I may repeat here what I said seven years ago.

"When the counties and boroughs rose in 1784 and ground the Coalition into the dust, they transferred 'the real monarchal power' from the King to the Cabinet, and so fixed the seat of that sovereignty which had hitherto floated vaguely between the two. Indeed I have sometimes thought that the reason why American notions of our constitution in general, and of the monarchy in particular, so often strike us as antediluvian is that they are antediluvian, derived from the lost landscape and submerged configuration of the world before the flood.

"There cannot in a well-ordered State be two centres of ultimate authority, but where was the centre to be fixed? That was the problem. It is one that must constantly recur in a moving and developing State, because in such a State there will always be acknowledged powers which time is antiquating, and latent powers which time is calling into action. It was so in England between King and Cabinet. Some day," I said, "it might be between Cabinet and Parliament."

Since I wrote those words in 1943, the two processes have gone on apace and there is very little I can add to Sir Arthur Salter's analysis of a situation in which, beyond all question, the Executive is far stronger in relation to Parliament, and Parliament far weaker in relation to the Executive, than either has been since cabinets were invented. At the same time, the control of the Executive over individual behaviour grows more intimate and searching as the years go by. And that is beyond doubt a very dangerous situation. But at this point in our reflections, I ought to insert a parenthesis. We have been there before: and not very long ago. From 1918 to 1922 we did pass through a period of what might be called Personal Government, following on what Baldwin used to call the Infamous Election of 1918. And I thought at the time, and have thought so ever since, that the Tory revolt in 1922 which overthrew Lloyd George pulled us back from the edge of a precipice.

I remember one summer evening in '21, sitting with Maynard Keynes and talking of these things. I said "Has it ever occurred to you that Lloyd George has designs on the Constitution?" "Oh," he said, "so that has passed through your mind too, has it?" It certainly had. I had watched English affairs from the continent, listening to continental comments, and I did not think that the Constitution could stand another *Quinquennium Neronis*. But in the very first days of the new Parliament, Bonar Law used words which made it clear that, in future, things were to be done in a ministerial and constitutional way. With that the episode of government by a Camarilla and a nominated

S

Parliament came to an end, and I only mention it now to make the point that all this had, I think, no effect whatever on subsequent events. The disturbance of equipoise between Parliament and Executive is not the result of any one man's designs or of any Party's activity but has come about, one might say, by the irresistible operation of natural forces; by the emergence of new conceptions; not least among them being the conception of the Welfare State.

Now I have suggested that from 1784 to 1945 is politically a rounded period of history with a beginning, a middle and an end; the middle being, I suppose, that phase of constitutional government between, say, 1840 and 1870 when Parliament and the Executive seem to have achieved a proper balance, resting largely on the presence in Parliament of a substantial body of experienced, knowledgeable, independent, members. At that time (perhaps this is open to controversy) I should say, the proportion of trained men, capable of forming a judgment on matters of policy and finance, was larger than it had ever been before or has been since. So you had a union not only of Parliament and Executive, but of both with public opinion. It was a golden age and, like most golden ages, perhaps it never really existed.

But that period, 1784 to 1945, happens very nearly to coincide with another which I always date from Burke's *Thoughts on Scarcity*, 1795, where we find not only the most eloquent (that we should expect from Burke) but the most exact statement of the doctrine popularly known as 'laissez-faire' or more correctly, State Abstention. Here is the passage to which I refer:

"The State ought to confine itself to what regards the State, or the creatures of the State; namely, the exterior establishment of its religion; its magistracy; its revenue; its military force by sea and land; the corporations that owe their existence to its fiat; in a word, to everything that is truly and properly public, to the public peace, to the public safety, to the public order, to the public prosperity. In its preventive police it ought to be sparing of its efforts, and to employ means, rather few, unfrequent, and strong, than many, and frequent, and, of course, as they multiply their puny politic race and dwindle, small 'and feeble. Statesmen who know themselves will, with the dignity which belongs to wisdom, proceed only in this, the superior orb and first mover of their duty, steadily, vigilantly, severely, courage-ously: whatever remains will, in a manner, provide for itself. But as they descend from the state to a province, from a province to a parish, and from a parish to a private house, they go on accelerated in their fall. They cannot do the lower duty; and, in proportion as they try it, they will certainly fail in the higher."

Now this doctrine was undoubtedly backed and supported through the nineteenth century by a great body of opinion, of experience, of principle, of sentiment, and no doubt of self-interest, all which had to be shifted before public opinion could cross the line drawn by Burke. But in the 1830s it was becoming evident to a generation perhaps more humane, certainly better informed, and living under the constant fear of what might happen if cholera broke out, or the underworld broke loose, that the line had been drawn in the wrong place; that there were things, public health, for example, which would not, as Burke supposed, 'provide for themselves', and yet had a very direct bearing on public prosperity. There we might have stayed, wondering what to do next, if that same generation had not discovered the efficacy of statistics and of administrative research and experiment, conducted by a trained and specia-lized service. As these forces, humanitarian, scientific, admini-strative, come into play and gather strength, we see Burke's lines sinking lower and lower and the range of State inter-vention growing larger and larger. It was no longer possible to say that statesmen 'could not do the lower duties', because Chadwick and the Assistant Poor Law commissioners, the factory inspectors, and mine inspectors, were actually doing them. And so the period of which I have spoken as beginning with Burke, rounds itself off, one might say, with the Beveridge Report of 1943.

But, there are always anticipations of everything, and two

wars have upset the symmetry of our historic patterns; otherwise we might have taken for our curtain a measure which
from one side may be viewed as the last of the great Victorian
statutes, and from another the first essay in the Welfare
State. I mean the Insurance Act of 1911. From that year
onwards the process of social legislation has brought more
and more clearly into view the truth latent, one may say, in the
Poor Law of 1834 that to apply general legislation to the multi-
farious circumstances of millions of individuals (fourteen
millions to be got into insurance and only six months to do
it) necessarily requires a large and therefore costly administration with wide powers of special legislation. And, latent
again in 1911 but warmed to vigorous (unless you prefer to call
it 'venomous') life by war taxation, was the widespread conviction that, just as in war there is no assignable limit to the
wealth that may be extracted from all, and expended on the
defence of all; so in peace there is no assignable limit to the
wealth that may be extracted from some and spent on the welfare of the rest. In other words, the course of history created an
executive which is immensely powerful and is widely believed
at least to be immensely rich. Powerful, because it has in effect
all the authority of Parliament behind it, rich because (I am
using Mr. Aneurin Bevan's own words) it has at its disposal all
the resources of the State, and are they not unlimited?

Once, when he was still in the House of Commons, Sir
William Jowett ventured to doubt it. "We must remember,"
he said, "that our resources are limited." The remark, I
noticed, was greeted with cries of 'Nonsense!' And you will
remember the reception of the Beveridge Report, when all
doubts were silenced, all questions answered, with one benign
phrase. "Can we afford to do it?" someone might ask, and pat
came the rejoinder, "But can we afford *not* to do it?" Next to
'collective security', I think that was the most disastrous phrase
ever coined in a generation more fertile in phrases than in
ideas. But, as Sir Arthur Salter tells us, much may be learned in
Hyde Park, and a friend of mine once picked up there an
oracle, not without its bearing on what we are now considering. "When I hear a man," the speaker said, "talking of

sound finance, I know him for an enemy of the people." But the same lesson may be learned in a more august arena. In the last Parliament one Member asked if the accounting arrangements of U.N.E.S.C.O. were efficient, and as the chief finance officer had just disappeared with a million francs in his pocket, there was some reason to suppose they were not. A Member rose on the other side. "True to the policy of his Party," he said, "the Hon. Member is trying to obstruct the enlightenment of the people."

Do not lay too much stress on these things. I have dwelt on them because it seems to me to be of the first consequence that we should realize how completely the political climate has changed in the last few years, how misleading and therefore how dangerous it is to apply the categories and co-ordinates of the past to our present circumstances. For example, those who remember the First War know what indignation the very words 'industrial conscription' excited. In 1945 a friend of mine thought that he could stir an equal emotion by denouncing the direction of labour. He was shouted down, and it was explained to his young innocence that direction of labour now means regular employment.

Let me give you one final example from a different field, an example I own which fairly startled me when I read it in the paper one morning. Last year four men, admitted by the court to be of good character and repute, were prosecuted by the Treasury for an offence against the Exchange Control Act and Regulations, 1942. From the proceedings, it appeared that the Treasury may address inquiries to any person whom it suspects. If he fails to reply, he may be prosecuted, and if he does reply, he may still be prosecuted on the evidence furnished by himself. In explaining this to the Bench Counsel for the Treasury used these words: "These," he said, "are revolutionary powers." They are indeed, because this procedure is nothing else than a revival of the ex-officio oath, devised by the Inquisition for the detection of heresy; employed, to the intense indignation of William Cecil, by Archbishop Whitgift for the extirpation of the puritan clergy; abolished, we had supposed, once and for all by a unanimous vote in the first session of the Long

Parliament; and restored by another Parliament in 1942.

But does any one *mind*? And if no one minds, is it worth talking about? I will confess that at times I feel that the discipline of the First War, followed and prolonged in the far more intense discipline under which we have been living since 1940, has, as the psychologists might say, conditioned us into a habit of passive obedience and acceptance of authority; and when I am in that mood the discussion of these subjects often calls up to my memory one of those Homeric similes with which Sir Walter Scott adorned his Life of Napoleon. It runs somehow thus: As when children playing together make a little hut of boughs and branches, hoping that their elder kinsfolk will take refuge in it, but they pass by unnoticing or tread it under their foot, even so did the Girondins think that they had made a constitution. Perhaps you remember another fancy fabric sketched by certain persons of eminence nearly twenty years ago. Parliament was to assemble, pass one Enabling Act giving the Government unlimited powers of regulation and then adjourn, the supporters of the Government being appointed local commissioners to see that the regulations were enforced. All of which could be done with strict legality. Now we are told every day that the advance of the physical sciences bids fair to destroy everything, physical sciences included, and everybody is looking for a way to avert such a deplorable consummation. Equally the omni-competence of Parliament might be used to destroy Parliament. Now we, I take it, do not want to see Parliament destroyed. We should like to see it in its relations with the Executive more independent, more vigilant, more critical. But in face of that omnipotence exercised by a strictly disciplined Party, are the various devices, which we, here and elsewhere, so diligently canvass for the improvement of Parliament: the revival of the powers of the Courts, Second Chambers, alternative votes; are they anything better than the children's hut of boughs and branches?

To put it another way, for centuries our parliamentary habits were closely woven into our social habits, our parliamentary structure was exactly, one might almost say beautifully, integrated with our social structure. But, when that structure has

collapsed and those habits are almost forgotten, is it possible
that Parliament should carry forward into the new age functions and powers created by, and designed for, wholly different
conditions? On the other hand, who can foresee what powers
and functions will be needed when the new structure has
revealed itself and new habits have been created?

Five years ago I wrote, "By the convergence of processes
internal and external, a situation has been created for which
neither precedent nor parallel is to be discerned. Since the
Norman conquest there has been no such solution of continuity
in our history." I repeat those words today because I think they
are true, and would, I believe, be no less true even if there
had been no Socialist Government in 1945 and no nationalization of industry. (If you consider that the first General Railway
Act providing for the ultimate acquisition of the railways by
the State was a Conservative Act, and that another Conservative Act nationalized the Telegraph Service, that observation
may be thought to be less paradoxical than at first hearing it
seems.) Never mind that: but for proof, I would say, look at the
electoral manifestoes of 1950 on both sides. On one side you will
find it argued that nationalization would increase the public
wealth, on the other that it would diminish the public wealth.
But in either case what the disputants have in mind is, will it
diminish or increase what I may call the welfare fund available
for redistribution? and whether that redistribution is effected
by increase of wages, by subsidies, by gratuitous or assisted
services, does not seem to me to alter the essential quality of the
revolution through which we are passing. If I were asked to sum
up in a phrase the difference between Liberal-Conservative and
Tory-Socialist England, I should say: "Property is no longer to
be taken for granted. All tenure is now a precarious tenure."

Now in that light consider the conception, or the phrase:
"Parliament is the guardian of our liberties." There are, as I
read history, three main types of political freedom. There is
the aristocratic type based on extensive, inherited, property,
with the watchword 'let no one govern too much. *Magna
Charta est lex: deinde caveat Rex*.' Then there is the type based on
moderate property, the yeoman in the country, the burgess in

the town—let no one break my hedges: let no one interfere with my trade. And there is the peasant type; not very well represented in Westminster: let no one ride over my corn. But what history, so far as my reading goes, fails to reveal is a conception of liberty not founded on property—property enough to furnish the man with some area, however small, of choice and self-determination, an area in which he can really be himself. That area is contracting. But can we expect a Parliament chosen by the suffrages of the unpropertied to be very forward in arresting, much less in reversing, that contraction?

This redistribution involves two processes, taking and giving, and the line of division between the parties in Parliament will, I should judge, be drawn between those who want to take more and give more, and those who want to take less and give less; between those who would like to leave the individual taxpayer with a substantial surplus for private experiment, enterprise and adventure, and those who think that experiments, when they affect the welfare of multitudes, ought to be directed by public authority, that is, by a powerful executive enjoying, incidentally, immense powers of patronage. But there can be little doubt that to the political sovereign of these realms, the Sovereign Plebs, and especially to the urban plebs, private experiment, pursued over generations, is inextricably associated with misery, and the directed experiments of the last few years with well-being. Now that association may, perhaps sooner than we all realize, be violently disrupted by forces over which we shall have no control. And what happens then, it is beyond me to say. But so long as that association does persist, though Parliament may oscillate and the electors may oscillate in the future as they have in the past, there will be no such swing as could in any serious degree be called reactionary. There may be a slowing-down balanced by a speeding-up, rather more legislation here and rather less there, but the arc of oscillation will not be very wide, and therefore I cannot foresee any substantial reduction in the range or power of our new executive. We may regret it, we might prefer to live under the constitution described, or as Professor Wade might say, invented by Dicey, but that is not the constitution we have to live under and we must lay our account accordingly. Perhaps we would rather live in Athens than in Sparta. But *Spartam nanctus es, hanc exorna.*

This Executive is, as I have said, always thought of as being immensely powerful and supposed to be immensely rich. There-fore it is from those two characteristics that I should deduce the main functions of our future Parliament, if Parliament is to survive as a true and faithful representative of public opinion. Its business will be, not as the Pelagians do vainly talk, to stop planning and abolish control, but to see that in the exercise of its powers, the Executive is intelligent, in the application of its resources frugal. By frugality I do not mean the crude economies of 1931, but wise expenditure; that is, expenditure controlled by a careful setting of immediate loss against ultimate gain and immediate gain against ultimate loss. Now I agree with those who doubt whether the House of Commons is capable of taking and maintaining such a view of our national resources as that control requires. If I had any doubt it would have been dis-pelled by the recent debate on the supplementary estimates. But what can Parliament do to ensure an intelligent executive? We know the existing devices; supply days, question time, the adjournment, letters to the Member, the letter to the Minister, the deputation. But these are fitful and, one might say, acci-dental. They derive rather from that conception of Parliament as the redressing place of grievances than as the controller of the executive. What we are looking for is some mode of regular pressure which would keep the executive more constantly in touch with public opinion and with life as it is really lived. And how completely detached from that life it may become, we who lived in reception areas at the time of the evacuation will never forget.

Now to begin with what is easiest to bring about, I agree with those who think that one of the best ways of achieving this purpose is by regular, but informal, conferences between the Minister and his chief officials, and interested groups in Parlia-ment. It would be very good for both sides. In the nature of things, Members of Parliament before they attain to office themselves, can know very little of the day to day problems of administration, while officials necessarily, and indeed rightly, are bound to be thinking at least as much of what *ought* to be done as what at any moment *can* be done: in Cromwell's phrase, what is good for people rather than what they want. A certain tension between Westminster and Whitehall is inevitable and, I think, healthy; the tension between the man who has no constituents to conciliate, and the man who has no precedents to observe; and in such conferences the tension would be discharged, and the two sides would go away with a clearer view of each other's attitude to the problems with which both are concerned. Such meetings, too, would add greatly to the information available to the House of Commons, and on the other side would check the tendency inherent in every administration, to enlarge its sphere of action, to cover the whole ground, to round off awkward corners, to be symmetrical. I have said nothing of blind adherence to precedent and other common charges against our administration because they are very rarely made by those who really understand the conditions under which our administration works—conditions of publicity for example, such as no business has to face—and those who do make them will go on making them long after they have been disproved. But let me give you two instances from my own experience of how I think these conferences would work and, if you like, what I should say if I was there.

Some few years ago the head master of a large grammar school decided to take his sixth form to a performance of the London Philharmonic Orchestra; the proposal was vetoed by the Ministry on the ground that it would interfere with the curriculum. Now I should very much like to have that official before me and ask in the friendliest way: "Why did you do that? Did it not occur to you that in a school life of ten years, two hours abstracted from trigonometry and French and devoted to music could not seriously interfere with those boys' progress? Did it not even occur to you that a man qualified to be head of a large school was probably in a better position than you to say how the afternoon could best be spent? Or were you, perhaps, following a precedent; or, on the other hand, afraid of creating one? Anyhow, let us know, because you may have been quite right." But that is the sort of incident that does

make the public question the intelligence of our administrators, and that is one of the things I should hope to avoid.
Passengers on the nine-twenty to London ten years hence will
still be telling the story of the official who thought that Bristol
Cream came from cows.

Another example, and I am sure you will understand that it
is cited in no spirit of ill-will; no one can have a warmer regard
for the service than I have, but there are such things as diseases
of occupation. Early in 1944, an Advisory Council, all experts
in the matter, strongly recommended a certain change of
organization in the Scottish Record Office. The Minister,
desiring a second opinion, referred their report to a judge of
the High Court and two others. We concurred with the report
in every detail and so advised the Treasury. 'Forty-four came to
an end, '45 passed, so did '46. Only in '47 did we learn that our
proposal had been pronounced to be 'contrary to common
sense'. Now I should have thought that a wise official in those
circumstances would have said "I shall never get a stronger
opinion than this; there is no reason for further investigation,
and, incidentally, I know nothing at all about the subject
matter. So I shall advise the Minister to send the necessary
instructions to the draftsman and ask the Whips to find parliamentary time for an unopposed Bill six lines long." And I
should very much like to ask that official, whose industry in the
matter I am bound to respect, why he thought it necessary to
investigate the whole matter *de novo*.

I should like to go further than this informal questioning,
and here, I know, I am entering on controversial ground; but
among the elements we have to reckon with in the new constitution, is the enhanced position of the Prime Minister, as chief
of the Executive. Of course, the personal equation must always
be allowed for, and individual Prime Ministers in this respect
vary from Peel, who knew everything that his colleagues were
doing, to another whose final profession of faith I heard myself
in the House of Commons. Asked to take certain Board of
Trade matters into his own hands, he said: "His Majesty's
Ministers are co-equal," and then as he sank back on the
Treasury bench, "luckily they are not co-eternal." But the

office does or should carry with it the control or supervision o
the whole administration; and how this control can best be
exercised is a question to which I have never found a completely satisfying answer. But on the whole, I favour the appointment of a Minister of State as general visitor of the Civil Service,
acting as the representative, and carrying the authority of, the
First Lord of the Treasury, acting both on his own initiative and
also in response to complaints or recommendations, and assisted
by a rotating team of experienced Civil Servants, reinforced, if
necessary, from outside. The team is the essential thing.

By these contrivances the Civil Service and, when we talk
of the Executive, it is really the Civil Service that we mean,
would be brought under the view of an authority, in one case
extra-departmental, in the other super-departmental; and this
latter body should, I think, have control of a very important
thing, the recruitment and training of the Civil Service with its
fine old tradition that is not yet quite broken. That tradition was
(I don't think there is a better one) given ability and character,
you want a man of liberal education, with some knowledge
of the world, a proper regard for all existing rights, and above
all a man who gets no kick out of ordering others about because
he takes himself for granted. That was the spirit of the old Civil
Service and I should like to see it constantly reaffirmed.

A third suggestion. My contemporaries in the Civil Service
would agree with me that when we were young the seat and
centre of Dicey's doctrine of the Rule of Law was Whitehall.
Respect for its own limitations was a sentiment inbred in the
English administration and I should be very glad to think there
still existed the fear of Mandamus, as a grave and living
presence. Now the official handling public money knows that
the eye of the Public Accounts Committee is on him. Whose eye
is on the official exercising public power? Is the regulation
intra vires? Has the department in exercising quasi-judicial
functions informed and addressed its departmental mind
judicially? The courts who used to ask these questions have
been ousted, and, much as I should like to see it, I doubt
whether their powers will ever be restored because no Party
taking office is likely to begin by weakening its own executive

authority. And on the principles we are employing, is it necessary that they should be restored? The Courts can restrain the executive in its dealings with persons and property, but can they make it more intelligent or more frugal? Here I should expect much better results from the Select Committee on Statutory Instruments, especially if, besides the invaluable assistance of the Speaker's Counsel, it was provided with an advisory or reporting staff on the analogy of the department of the Controller and Auditor General.

Now here then are three devices, the informal conference, the visitation, and the select committee, all moving in the same direction, a running audit, one might say, of our administration, not an occasional tempest or an intermittent flurry but a steady wind of mutual intelligence and understanding to keep the atmosphere clean and lively.

But might we not go one step further or, more exactly, one step back and tackle our problem at an earlier stage? Sir Cecil Carr, I noticed, quoted a phrase I once used when I said that delegated legislation is legislation without a legislature. Let us consider for a few minutes how this omission can best be supplied. The structure of the Executive, that is of the Government in the common use of the term, and the various related issues of departmental and non-departmental Cabinets have been actively discussed for thirty years or more, so that by now we ought to have accumulated a sufficient body of experience with which to make up our minds on that matter. I will only say that in the abstract I favour the system of grouped departments under suzerain ministers—the suzerains and certain others forming the Cabinet. I say 'in the abstract', because I am well aware of the difficulties in that or any other system which may be projected, but perhaps you will allow me for my particular purpose to assume that something of that sort is in existence. My suggestion, then, is that there should be an advisory council not of the departments severally but of the groups—a council representing the various interests coming within the purview of the group. Such a council would naturally work through committees, one of which should be a committee on regulations and so would furnish the legislature which we are looking for.

Suppose now such a committee brought into being. In practice, as we all know, the work of every committee is performed chiefly by the chairman and the secretary. And so it would be here. What I have in mind is that all draft orders would go to the secretary for submission to the committee—which, in practice, would probably mean that the chairman would discuss them with the departmental officers concerned and would use his own discretion whether to approve them and report or refer them to the committee for consideration.

I should like these councils to be taken seriously and to take themselves seriously. If the members chose to add the letters MAC to their names, so much the better, but I want to see them attracting impartial men as members. And as regards their composition, while they should in the first instance be nominated with regard to the diverse interests which they serve, I should hope that in course of time they would come to be filled by what I should call confidential co-optation: each committee putting forward names, and everybody understanding the object, namely, to secure an Advisory Council of all interests.

One step further: suppose a joint meeting of two advisory councils or delegations from both—and if of two, why not of three or four? We should then be on our way towards that subsidiary or collateral assembly which has been advocated in various quarters as a means of relaxing the pressure and reducing the burden on Parliament.

Now in this matter I have tried to get some light from our Oldest Ally, because, as I understand it, under the new Portuguese constitution such a collateral parliament is in effective existence. I must admit that the light was rather dim, none the less the main conception was fairly clear. The National Assembly is, or was to be, elected on a basis of geographical constituencies like ours, while its collateral, the Chamber of Corporations was to represent the natural or functional groupings of the people: the Universities, the Church, the Guilds of employers and workpeople and so forth. Bills went as far as second reading in the Assembly, the committee stage was taken in the Chamber of Corporations, for which purpose the Chamber was divided into committees or panels corresponding with the different types of Bill. The Bill was then reported to the House and so the sovereignty of Parliament was preserved. I own that this attracted me very much. One can see many points at which such an arrangement might go wrong, but if it succeeded you would have a regular and well-informed review of our primary legislation, just as the Committee on Statutory Instruments serves to review our secondary legislation. I think that the strongest reason I felt for disliking the abolition of University seats was that they furnished a model for group representation on a natural basis, as contrasted with the very casual aggregation of individuals which makes up a good many of the geographical constituencies. Now I do not see the slightest prospect of any change in the fundamental constitution of the House of Commons. It is convenient, we are used to it and it works well, but I certainly feel that it needs to be supplemented by some representation of those major interests which, simply because of their natural power and influence, ought to have a collective voice in the discussion of national affairs. In particular I have often thought that the Local Government areas in their five orders of Counties, County Boroughs, Municipal Boroughs, Urban Districts and Rural Districts, ought to have direct representation in Parliament, but I see no likelihood that that will ever come about, whereas in the formation of a collateral Chamber they would naturally be accorded a substantial representation of their own. And it seems to me that along these lines we might find the solution of one of the most difficult problems of our time, i.e. the relations between the National Boards, Parliament, the Trade Unions and others. It struck me as being of good omen when I had woven this fancy of mine, that I was simply recapitulating what I believe to be the history of the House of Commons itself. If the King wanted money, it was no use asking Fitzwalter or Neville where a tax on fleeces would come to rest, or how to raise a loan in Ghent. They simply would not know. So you called in the merchants and asked them to work it out and tell the Exchequer what to do. And being assembled, they took the opportunity to remark on certain malpractices which needed attention, certain improvements which might be taken in hand, and their remarks in due course became Bills and the Bills became law and so the House of Commons came into existence.

In conclusion there is an idea which I think deserves fuller consideration. You remember I said how misleading it is to apply the categories of one age to the political circumstances of another. One of these categories was entire national independence and the other the absence from our political thinking of the conception of fundamental law. But it is observable how this conception seems to be finding its way back hand in hand with the conception of the Welfare State. Thus the Constitution of Eire lays down certain social directives with which all legislation must accord. The newest of all constitutions, that of India, first assures the rights of man by specifying certain things which the Sovereign may not do, and goes on to specify others, all of the kind called social service, which the Sovereign must do. And, of course, we have the United Nations Declaration of Human Rights.

That the Atlantic nations are moving towards some sort of perpetual association, a term I much prefer to either union or federation, seems to me historically certain. But each step in that direction involves a limitation of national sovereignty and the acceptance, over a range of activity larger or smaller, of some fundamental law. And this is what I propose, because it would be an experiment of very great interest and would throw much light on the way, and the difficulties of the way, we have to tread. Take any one of these directives that you like and see how far the legislation of one session of the English Parliament would be allowed or disallowed by a Supreme Court applying that directive as a fundamental law.

What after all is the sum of the matter which has been under discussion in this series of Papers? Surely it is the conciliation of authority and freedom. And I do not believe that we shall arrive at that end by any abstract debating, by any juristic de-limitations, but only as I have said, by mutual intelligence, and I hope that some of the suggestions I have made may help others in thinking out how that intelligence can be made to permeate, and ultimately to control, the relations between Government and People.

INDEX

T